The Which? Guide to Giving and Inheriting

About the author

Jonquil Lowe trained as an economist, worked for several years in the City as an investment analyst, and is a former head of the Money Group at Consumers' Association. She now works as a freelance researcher and journalist. She writes extensively on all areas of personal finance and is author of several other books, including *Be Your Own Financial Adviser*, *The Which? Guide to Planning Your Pension*, *The Which? Guide to Money in Retirement*, and, with Sara Williams, *The Lloyds-TSB Tax Guide*.

The Which? Guide to Giving and Inheriting

Jonquil Lowe

which

?

Which? Books are commi   ᵗⁱᵒⁿᵉᵈ ᵇʸ
Consumers' Association aı   ᵖᵘᵇˡⁱˢʰᵉᵈ ᵇʸ
Which? Ltd, 2 Marylebon
Email: books@which.co.ı

Distributed by Littlehamp
Faraday Close, Durringtoı

First edition October 199.
Eighth edition September

Copyright © 1992, 1994,

British Library Cataloguing
A catalogue record for thi

ISBN 1 84490 016 9

For a full list of Which? books, please call 01903 828557, access our website at www.which.co.uk, or write to Littlehampton Book Services, Faraday Close, Durrington, Worthing, West Sussex BN13 3R. For other enquiries call 0800 252100.

Editorial and production: Angela Newton and Ian Robinson
Original cover concept by Sarah Harmer
Cover photograph by Mark Stevenson, ace photoagency

Typeset by Saxon Graphics Ltd, Derby
Printed and bound by Creative Print and Design (Wales)

Contents

★An asterisk next to the name of an organisation in the text indicates that the address can be found in this section.

If you are writing your own will or sorting out someone else's will, setting up a trust or considering tax avoidance schemes please note that it is important to consult a legal adviser if substantial sums of money are involved and/or the situation is at all complex.

Introduction

When the Labour Party returned to power in 1997, it was widely thought that the new government would seek to tax wealth more heavily by tightening up the relatively lenient rules regulating inheritance tax. In the event, no changes of substance have been made to inheritance tax. But that does not mean the taxation of wealth has remained benign. Even if your means are relatively modest, you now need to keep a weather eye on wealth taxes. The two factors which have created this change in climate are: the general rise in house prices since 1995 and the introduction of the pre-owned assets tax (POAT) from April 2005.

In the UK, wealth is taxed mainly when it changes hands on death. The first slice of each person's wealth can be passed on tax-free. Although this tax-free slice is usually increased each year, the rise is only in line with general prices as measured by the Retail Prices Index. Over the last ten years, the inheritance tax threshold has risen from £154,000 to £275,000 – an increase of around 6 per cent a year. Over the same period house prices have risen by over 10 per cent a year on average. As a result, increasingly more homeowners – especially those in the expensive South-East – are at risk of leaving estates at death on which tax will be due. This passive drawing of more people into the tax net is an effect which economists call 'fiscal drag'.

The very wealthy have long bought into complex schemes (typically involving trusts, loans and life insurance policies) designed to minimise the amount of tax payable on their estates. With the rise in house prices, people of modest wealth have also become interested in schemes to save tax, particularly those which enable them to give away the family home tax-efficiently but continue to live there during their lifetime. Not surprisingly, the tax authorities view such

7

gifts as artificial and aim to eliminate the tax savings. In the past, this has generally meant challenging schemes in the courts and, where the courts have found in favour of the taxpayer, changing the law to stop the schemes being successful in future. But from the tax authorities' point of view this approach has the drawback of leaving a residue of people who set up their schemes before the law change still able to reap the tax savings. To counter this drawback, the government came up with an unusual solution: the pre-owned assets tax (POAT).

POAT is an unusual tax on two counts. Firstly, it aims to plug loopholes in inheritance tax but is itself a different type of tax altogether – an income tax. Secondly, this is a 'retroactive' tax because it imposes a tax charge now on the benefit from actions taken in the past (as well as from relevant actions you take now). For example, someone who gave away their home in the past but continues to live in it, using a tax-efficient scheme to save inheritance tax, may now find themselves having to pay POAT on the value of the benefit they are deemed to get from living in the home. (For details of how POAT works and who may be caught by it, see Chapter 5 of this guide.) The government has made clear that it is prepared to introduce further retroactive measures in future in order to stop tax avoidance.

The government is determined to tackle tax avoidance because it is seen to be unfair. The tax savings that some achieve through avoidance schemes increase the burden on other taxpayers who are not making use of such schemes. On the other hand, it is well established in law that taxpayers may arrange their affairs in such a way as to minimise the amount of tax they pay as long as they use legitimate means. Tax evasion – in other words, saving tax by breaking the law – is illegal, but tax avoidance is not. Some types of tax avoidance – such as using your tax allowances to the full – are specifically permitted; others are not spelt out in the legislation but rest on a legal – though sometimes strained – interpretation of the law. The government's increasing intolerance of tax avoidance is blurring the lines between what is acceptable and what is not.

In the meantime, other injustices are sometimes overlooked. With inheritance tax, there is no tax on death where a person's estate is left to their husband, wife or civil partner. (Under new legislation effective from 5 December 2005 onwards, same-sex couples can register as a civil partnership and are treated for tax and most other legal purposes in the same way as married couples.) This is a welcome exemption. It means, for example, that a widow does not find her home being sold in order to meet an inheritance bill on her late husband's estate. But other people sharing a home are not so fortunate. For example, there could be tax due on the estate of someone leaving their home to their unmarried partner, or to a sister, brother, child or carer who had lived with them. In the past, such problems were unlikely to arise as the majority of estates, even including a property, were well below the inheritance tax threshold. But since the rise in house prices, more households could potentially face this sort of issue and need to plan ahead to deal with it.

This guide aims to steer you through the various taxes that may affect the gifts you make both on death and during your lifetime. It will help you make the most of legitimate methods of giving tax efficiently and alert you to key areas where your planning could fall foul of the tax rules or be vulnerable to attack in future from HM Revenue & Customs (the new tax authority formed by the merger of the Inland Revenue and HM Customs & Excise from April 2005 onwards). The guide also explains how you can arrange your giving to achieve specific aims by, for example, by using trusts, and considers the special issues relating to gifts of your home, giving to children and donating to charity.

The text is up to date as at summer 2005, including measures passed in the 2005 Finance Acts.

Chapter 1

Gifts and taxes

The distribution of wealth

Left unchecked, inheritance within families would, sooner or later, lead to a concentration of wealth in the hands of relatively few people. Most advanced societies take the view that wealth should not be distributed too unevenly. The reasons for this are varied – political, economic and humane. For example, a wide gulf between the poorest people and the richest may encourage political unrest; the votes of relatively poorer people can perhaps be 'bought' by redistributing wealth to them. Economic activity may be improved if wealth is spread more evenly as a result of the different spending and saving patterns of the rich and poor.

But there are less pragmatic reasons too. The majority of people want to accumulate enough possessions and wealth to support an enjoyable and sustainable lifestyle but are not comfortable ignoring the relative, or absolute, poverty of others. Our sense of justice demands that others should also have the chance of a reasonable life.

Yet, even in a society as mature as that of the UK, the distribution of wealth across the population is uneven, as Table 1.1 (see page 12) shows. Just one-tenth of the adult population in the UK owns well over half of all the wealth, and a quarter of the population owns nearly three-quarters of all the wealth.

The distribution of wealth is now more even than it was in the early part of the last century (see Table 1.2, page 12) which reflects, in part, the deliberate redistribution policies of successive governments. However, the trend reversed in the early 1990s with the gap between rich and poor widening again.

The main tool which governments use directly to influence the distribution of wealth is the tax system. Taxes can be used to 'take from the rich' in several ways. One obvious way might be to tax

Table 1.1 Who owns what in the UK (2002)

Percentage of population[1]	Percentage of wealth owned[2]
1	23
5	43
10	56
25	74
50	94

Notes: [1] Percentage of the most wealthy of the UK adult population.
[2] Percentage of all UK wealth excluding pension rights.
Source: Inland Revenue, October 2004.

Table 1.2 Changing fortunes

Year	Percentage of wealth[1] owned by the wealthiest 1%[2]	Percentage of wealth[1] owned by the wealthiest 10%[2]
1911–13	69	92
1924–30	62	91
1936–8	56	88
1954	43	79
1960	38	77
1966	32	72
1972	30	72
1976	21	50
1980	19	50
1985	18	49
1990	18	47
1995	19	50
1998	23	56
2002	23	56

Notes: [1] Percentage of all UK wealth.
[2] Percentage of the most wealthy of the UK adult population.
Sources: *Diamond Commission Initial Report on the Distribution of Income and Wealth*, HMSO, 1975; *Inland Revenue Statistics 2000*, London, TSO; Inland Revenue, October 2004.

people regularly on the amount of wealth they have. Wealth taxes are used in some countries and have been proposed for the UK in the past.[1] At present in the UK, however, there is no tax on simply *owning* wealth. Instead, the emphasis is on taxing wealth as it changes hands.

Taxing wealth and gifts

Originally, taxing the transfer of wealth was confined to a tax at the time of death and can be traced back to the Anglo-Saxon 'heriot' – a feudal tax paid to the local lord on the death of a tenant. But the modern form of this type of taxation started with estate duty, introduced in 1894 with a swingeing top rate of 8 per cent!

Although estate duty was designed mainly to tax the passing on of wealth at the time of death, it also taxed gifts made in the few years before death to close an otherwise obvious loophole: that is, avoiding the tax through last-minute 'death-bed bequests'. Even so, with planning, it was possible to avoid the worst ravages of the estate duty, particularly by giving away wealth during one's lifetime.

In 1975, Harold Wilson's government scrapped estate duty in favour of capital transfer tax (CTT). This was a fully fledged gifts tax and estate duty rolled into one. The aim was to tax all transfers of wealth whether made in life or at death – with a few exceptions, such as gifts between husband and wife, small gifts to other people and up to £2,000 a year (in the 1975–6 tax year) of otherwise taxable transfers. And there were special reliefs to help farmers and businesses. Taxable gifts were added together and the first slice of this total was tax-free. Tax, at progressively higher rates, was levied on subsequent slices until it reached a top rate of 75 per cent. Although this appeared to be a serious tax that would affect even people of relatively modest means, in the event CTT lasted only 11 years.

The Conservative government came to power in 1979 determined to reduce the role of the state and encourage individual initiative. Reform of the tax system was an important part of its strategy and CTT was on the agenda. In 1986, CTT was replaced by inheritance tax (IHT). In many respects the two taxes are similar but a major difference is that under the IHT regime most lifetime gifts between people are free from tax, apart from gifts made in the last seven years before the death of the giver. This means that the majority of gifts

---

[1] *Wealth Tax*, Labour government green paper, London, HMSO, 1974.

you make in the course of your day-to-day affairs are not caught up in the IHT net. When the Labour party came to power in 1997, its manifesto included a commitment to *'fair taxation'* designed to *'benefit the many, not the few'*. It was widely thought that a tightening of IHT was on the cards, in particular the possibility that the taxation of most lifetime gifts might be reintroduced. But, at the time of writing, Labour is into its third term and no substantial reforms have so far been made though rising house prices have drawn many more people potentially into the IHT net (see below).

Falling into the tax net

The switch from CTT to IHT has not been so benign in other ways. Until 1987, IHT, like CTT and estate duty before it, was levied according to a scale at progressively higher rates. From 14 March 1988 onwards, a single, hefty rate of tax (40 per cent on death, 20 per cent during life) is charged whatever the scale of the giving. The threshold at which tax starts has been raised substantially but, with UK house prices more than doubling over the last seven years, many people who consider themselves to have relatively modest means worry that they may now find themselves within the inheritance tax net. And government statistics do show a steady upward creep in the number of estates caught by inheritance tax (see Table 1.3).

You may need to watch out for other taxes too. When you give away something (other than cash) during your lifetime, you have 'disposed' of it – just as if you had sold it. If the value of the thing has risen since you first acquired it, you will be judged to have made a

Table 1.3 More estates falling within the inheritance tax net

	1998	2005–6
Proportion of estates paying inheritance tax on death	3%	6%
Number of estates paying inheritance tax on death	19,000	37,000
Average house price	£72,196	£163,615
Inheritance tax threshold	£223,000	£275,000
Average house price as a proportion of inheritance tax threshold	32.4%	59.5%

Sources: Inland Revenue statistics, Budget 2005 announcement, HBOS house price index.

profit from owning it and there may be capital gains tax (CGT) to pay – even though you did not actually receive the profit yourself. Income which you give away can sometimes be like a boomerang which keeps coming back to haunt your tax assessments. And, from April 2005, a new pre-owned assets tax can impose an income tax bill on the benefit you are deemed to carry on getting from gifts (and sales) you have made even if you don't have enough income to pay the tax.

The first part of this book examines the various taxes you need to watch out for when making gifts in your lifetime and looks at how to arrange your gifts tax-efficiently. Chapter 9 pulls together key tips for planning your lifetime giving. In addition, Part 1 discusses using 'trusts' (special legal arrangements), which can be a way of giving something but retaining some control over how the gift is used. Contrary to popular opinion, trusts are not just for the very wealthy; they can be useful even if you have fairly small sums to give.

Many of the worst pitfalls of the taxes on gifts to family and friends can often be avoided if you plan ahead. Nowhere is this more crucial than in the area of inheritance planning. The first step is, of course, to make a will – though seven out of ten people do not even do this.[2] Yet, without a will, your possessions may not reach the people you want to leave them to and you lose a chance to plan away a possible tax bill.

Part 2 considers the problems of estates where no will is made, explains how gifts made at the time of death are taxed and shows some steps which can be taken to help you develop an effective inheritance plan. In the last resort, it may even be possible for your heirs to rearrange gifts made to them under your will (or in accordance with the law if you left no will) and Part 2 also takes a look at how these measures work.

Part 3 draws together some of the issues covered throughout the book which you should consider when contemplating special types of gift. First it looks at what is possibly your most valuable asset – your home. Although essentially your home is no different from any other asset, it is often the one which poses the most difficult questions over how best to balance your intention to give against the desire to avoid

---

[2]Survey by NOP, 1998.

unnecessary tax. Secondly, Part 3 gathers together the planning points to consider when making gifts to children and grandchildren. The final chapter considers the more benevolent face of the tax system which encourages giving to charity.

Part 1

Lifetime gifts

Chapter 2

Tax-free gifts

THE CHOICE OF GIFT MATTERS

'Sylvia,' Jeffrey turned solemnly to his wife, 'I think we should give Tom a helping hand to buy a home now that he's settling down.'

'I couldn't agree more. But to be fair to the girls, we ought to set aside some money to help them later on too,' replied Sylvia.

'It doesn't have to be money, of course – they might like to have one or two of those paintings my mother left me. I wonder if it makes a tax difference? I do believe that we could give Tom a bit of money as a wedding present without running into tax problems ...'

You need to be aware of two main taxes when making a gift to someone: capital gains tax (CGT) and inheritance tax (IHT). Some gifts can also affect your income tax position – an aspect which can be to your advantage as long as you arrange the gift in a suitable way (see Chapter 6). And, if you give away something but still use or benefit from it, you might have to pay the new pre-owned assets tax, a special type of income tax (see Chapter 5). This chapter looks at gifts you can make during your lifetime that are either free of CGT, free of IHT or completely free of both taxes. Subsequent chapters look at gifts which may be taxable.

Capital gains tax

When you give someone something that you own, you are treated for tax purposes as making a 'disposal' of an 'asset'. An asset is simply something you own. Disposal means ceasing to own the asset, however this comes about – the tax position when you give away an asset is essentially the same as if you had sold it.

If an asset's value at the time you give it away is greater than its value at the time you first started to own it, there *could* be a CGT bill. But do not panic! Often, you will not have to pay any CGT, because:

- some assets are outside the scope of CGT
- gains from some transactions are always tax-free.

The scope of capital gains tax

CGT is a tax on the disposal of *assets*. Assets cover virtually all types of possessions: land, buildings (including your home), stocks and shares, paintings, furniture, patents and copyrights, debts owed to you. Assets, for CGT purposes, do not include sterling currency – so a gift of money cannot result in a CGT bill. By an interesting quirk of the law, sovereigns minted after 1837 still count as sterling currency and are therefore outside the CGT net. (Sovereigns minted before then count as 'chattels' – see below.)

Certain other assets are specifically exempt from CGT. These are looked at in the following sections.

Chattels

These are tangible, movable property – basically your personal belongings, such as clothes, books, compact discs and your household goods, as well as things like jewellery, antiques, paintings and many other collectibles. An item in this category is exempt from CGT provided it has a predicted useful life of 50 years or less and you have not used it in a business.

For chattels with an expected life of more than 50 years, any gain is exempt if the value of the item at the time you dispose of it is no more than £6,000. If a chattel's value is more than £6,000, any gain can be worked out in a special way which may reduce the CGT bill (see Example 3.4 on page 39). There are rules to prevent you reducing the CGT payable by splitting up a set – for example, a set of chairs – and then giving all the parts of the set to the same person.

If you give away or sell a decoration awarded (e.g. to you or a relative) for valour or gallantry, there is no CGT on any gain, unless you had originally bought the decoration or exchanged something of value for it.

Your home

There is no CGT to pay when you dispose of part or all of your only, or main, home. This exemption automatically includes your garden where your whole plot (house plus garden) comes to no more than half a hectare (about 1.25 acres). It covers giving away part of the garden while you retain the house, but not if it has ceased to be garden. For example, if you built a house in the garden and gave the house to your children, the gift would not be covered by the exemption. But you could give the children part of the garden free of CGT and leave them to develop the plot.

If your plot is larger than half a hectare, there is no automatic exemption and the garden is exempt only if its size is warranted by the nature of the house and deemed necessary for the reasonable enjoyment of the home. This can be hard to prove if you are disposing of part of the garden while keeping the home, since the act of disposal suggests that for 'reasonable enjoyment' you don't really need such a large garden after all. However, HM Revenue & Customs (HMRC) might accept that a gift of part of the garden is tax-free if made to a relative whose presence would not detract from your enjoyment of the rest of the garden.

If you have more than one home, you should nominate one as your main home for CGT purposes. A husband and wife or civil partners who live together can have only one main home between them. This is so even if they each spend a lot of time in separate homes, for example, because they live apart during the week for work purposes. (Couples who are not married or not in a registered civil partnership can each have a separate main home even if they live mainly together in just one home.) You must make your nomination in writing to your tax office within two years of acquiring a second or further home and, once made, you can change the nomination if you want to. But, if you fail to make a nomination within the two-year time limit, your main home is determined on the facts – for example, where your post is sent, where you are registered to vote, and so on.

You may lose part of the exemption if part of your home was set aside exclusively for business. The same applies if you let out part or all of your home, though you might qualify for another CGT relief called 'lettings relief'. There may also be a CGT bill when you dispose of your home, if you have lived away for long periods.

EXAMPLE 2.1

Frank and Janette have retired and plan to move permanently to their second home in Devon where up to now they have just spent holidays and some weekends. They want to give the family home in Kent to their only daughter, Marie. The home is worth about £600,000 but there will be no capital gains tax on the gift because the house has been Frank and Janette's main home throughout the whole time they have owned it.

However, Frank and Janette will need to consider the inheritance tax position of this gift (see Chapter 4).

Motor vehicles

There is no CGT on gains from selling or giving away a private car (including vintage or classic cars), a motorbike or other private motor vehicle. This exemption can also apply to a vehicle used for business provided it was 'commonly used as a private vehicle'. However, the exemption does not stretch to vehicles that are not commonly used as private vehicles and are unsuitable for use in that way – so watch out if you are tempted by surplus Ministry of Defence tanks or similar exotica!

A vehicle you sell or give away might have a personalised or cherished number plate. The right to use the combination of letters and numbers shown on the plate is an 'intangible' asset that is not covered by the CGT exemption for motor vehicles. If the value of the vehicle you sell or give away includes an amount in respect of the personalised plate, you need to apportion the proceeds between the value of the vehicle and the value of the right to use the registration shown on the plate, and there could be CGT to pay on the latter.

Foreign currency

There is no CGT on gains from buying and selling foreign money which you have obtained for your own use – for a holiday abroad, say, for buying or running a holiday home abroad or for use during a business trip.

Some investments

Gains on some investments are completely free from CGT: for example, National Savings & Investments products including

Premium Bonds, gilts, many corporate bonds, and shares held through an Individual Savings Account (ISA) or a Personal Equity Plan (PEP). Provided certain conditions are met, gains on shares bought through an Enterprise Investment Scheme (EIS) or Venture Capital Trust (VCT) are also free of CGT.

Insurance policies

Payment from a life insurance policy, whether on maturity, early surrender or even through selling the policy to someone else, is usually exempt from CGT. The exemption does not apply, however, if you bought the policy from someone else, for example through an auction.

Your rights to certain payments

If you dispose of your right to receive an income under an annuity or a covenant, say, there is usually no CGT on any gain you make as a result. Similarly, if you give away your right to benefit under the terms of a trust or your right to repayment of money you have lent someone, there is usually no CGT – but there could be, if in the first place you had bought these rights.

Tax-free transactions

Some *transactions* are also exempt from CGT. This means that the following types of gift are free of CGT.

Gifts between husband and wife or between civil partners

Gifts between husband and wife are free of CGT provided the couple are living together. The gift is treated as being made on a 'no gain/no loss' basis – see Chapter 3 for an explanation of this.

From 5 December 2005 onwards, the same treatment applies to gifts between same-sex partners who have registered their relationship as a civil partnership.

Gifts to charities and certain other bodies

Donations and gifts to charity, and to various other institutions, including many museums and art galleries, local authorities, government departments and universities, and, since 6 April 2002, community amateur sports clubs are CGT-free.

Gifts of national heritage property

The sale or gift of certain property, such as works of art, to a museum, art gallery, the National Trust or similar body, university, local authority or government department, may be exempt from CGT. So, too, is the acceptance by the HMRC of such property in lieu of inheritance tax (see page 26). The sale price or valuation must take into account the tax you have saved.

Eligible property can include pictures, prints, books, manuscripts, works of art, scientific objects, provided they are 'pre-eminent' for their national, scientific, historic or artistic interest. Buildings and land of outstanding scenic, historic or scientific interest and items associated with them are also eligible.

A gift of eligible property to anyone else can be free of CGT if it also qualifies as conditionally exempt from inheritance tax (see page 26) or would do so if it did not count as a potentially exempt transfer (see page 69). To qualify, the person receiving the gift must agree certain conditions with the HMRC including that the gifted property will stay in the UK, it will be properly maintained and preserved, and the public will have reasonable access to it. The exemption from CGT is lost if the property is subsequently sold, unless this is to a museum, art gallery, the National Trust or similar body, university, local authority or government department.

If the gift is not exempt, you might instead be able to claim hold-over relief (see page 53).

Gifts if you move abroad

Since 17 March 1998, if you leave the UK to take up residence abroad, you can give away assets you acquired while still in the UK without paying any CGT but only if you are resident abroad for at least five tax years (see page 139).

Gifts on death

When you die, you are deemed to make a gift of all you then own to your heirs but, whatever, and however much, you leave, it is always free of CGT.

Your heirs are treated as acquiring the assets at their market value at the time of your death, so any previous capital gains that had built up while the assets were in your hands are wiped out.

EXAMPLE 2.2

Frank and Janette give the family home in Kent to their daughter, Marie, and retire to their second home in Devon. The Devon home has increased in value considerably since they bought it. If they sold it there would be a hefty capital gain most of which would be taxable. This is because, while they lived in Kent, they elected for the property there to be their main home and so the one which would be exempt from capital gains tax (see page 22).

However, when Frank dies, Janette stays on in the Devon home, living there for the rest of her life. On her death, the property passes free of capital gains tax to Marie (but inheritance tax may be due).

Inheritance tax

IHT is a tax on the 'transfer of value' from one person to another. This means a gift (or other transaction) which reduces the value of the possessions (the 'estate') owned by the person making the transfer. In theory, IHT could apply to any gift but, as with CGT, there are exemptions and adjustments. This means that on most lifetime gifts there is no IHT to pay, because:

- various types of gift are always free of IHT
- some gifts, called 'potentially exempt transfers' (PETs), are free of tax, provided the giver lives on for seven years after making the gift (see page 69).

Gifts which are always free of IHT

The scope of IHT is, on the face of it, wider than that of CGT because IHT covers all assets – including money, as well as houses, land, pictures and furniture. Gifts made in certain circumstances or between certain people or bodies are free of IHT. This applies to the following gifts, whether you make them during your lifetime or as bequests in your will (see Chapter 10).

Gifts between husband and wife or between civil partners

Gifts between husband and wife up to any amount are tax-free as long as the couple are not divorced. Even a husband and wife who are separated benefit from this exemption. If the husband or wife receiving the gift is not 'domiciled' (see box below) in the UK, the exemption is limited to a total of £55,000.

From 5 December 2005, the same treatment applies to same-sex partners who have registered their relationship as a civil partnership.

DOMICILE

Your place of domicile is broadly where you make your permanent home and intend to end your days. However, for the purposes of inheritance tax you are treated as still UK-domiciled during the first three years after you have acquired a domicile in another country, or if you have been a UK resident for 17 of the last 20 tax years.

Gifts to charities and certain other bodies

This exemption from IHT is similar to the equivalent one for CGT (see page 23). It covers outright donations and gifts of any amount to UK charities, national museums and art galleries, universities, local authorities, government departments and a number of other bodies, including, since 6 April 2002, community amateur sports clubs.

Gifts of national heritage property

The gift of certain property, such as works of art, to a museum, art gallery, the National Trust or similar body, university, local authority or government department may be exempt from IHT. The transfer of such property to the HMRC in lieu of paying IHT (see page 184) is also exempt.

Eligible property can include pictures, prints, books, manuscripts, works of art, scientific objects, provided they are 'pre-eminent' for their national, scientific, historic or artistic interest. Buildings and land of outstanding scenic, historic or scientific interest and items associated with them are also eligible.

A gift of eligible property to anyone else can be conditionally exempt from inheritance tax. To qualify, the person receiving the gift must agree certain conditions with the Inland Revenue, including that the gifted property will stay in the UK, it will be properly maintained and preserved, and the public will have reasonable access to it.

You can't claim conditional exemption for a gift that is a potentially exempt transfer (see page 69) but you can apply if the gift subsequently becomes chargeable because the giver died within seven years.

A claim for conditional exemption must be made within two years of the gift (or death in the case of a potentially exempt transfer). You (and/or your husband or wife) must have either owned the property for at least six years or inherited it on the death of the previous owner with a conditional exemption also applying to that transfer.

Gifts to political parties

A gift to a political party is exempt from IHT, provided the party has at least two MPs or polled at least 150,000 votes at the most recent general election.

Housing Associations

Gifts of land to a Registered Housing Association are exempt.

Lifetime gifts which are free of IHT

The following gifts are free of IHT only when they are made during your lifetime (i.e. not in your will).

Normal expenditure out of income

If you can show that a gift you are making is one of a regular pattern of similar gifts and that you are making it out of your income (rather than from your savings or other capital), the gift will be exempt from IHT.

Gifts made under a legally binding agreement, such as a deed of covenant, will usually be treated as regular gifts. So too will premiums you pay for an insurance policy or contributions to a pension scheme that is for the benefit of someone else: for example, a policy on your life which would pay out to your children in the event of your death. If the gifts are not made under any formal agreement but you intend that they will be regular gifts, they can still qualify for the exemption. The first gift or two might not be treated as exempt at the time you make them but, once a regular pattern has been established, they can be reassessed as tax-exempt.

The gifts must be made out of your income, so you need to be able to show that you have enough income left to meet your day-to-day living expenses. The income can be from any source – a job, interest from investments, dividends from shares. However, not all receipts which you consider to be income are in fact income for this purpose. For example, if you have bought a 'purchased life annuity' (an investment where you swap a lump sum for a regular income usually payable for the rest of your life but not the type of annuity you buy as part of a pension arrangement), part of the 'income' you get counts as return of your capital so cannot be used to fund gifts under this IHT exemption. Similarly, some life insurance-based investments (such as with-profits bonds and single premium bonds) let you withdraw each year up to 5 per cent of the amount you have invested as an 'income' but again this is not income for the purpose of this IHT exemption.

Normally, gifts under this exemption are cash. If you make gifts which are not cash, you will have to be able to prove that the things you are giving were bought out of your income.

EXAMPLE 2.3

Stan, who is 73, would like to give some money to his grandson, Ed (aged 14), to help him later in life. Stan arranges a stakeholder pension scheme for Ed to which Stan pays £50 a month. Stan's payments count as normal expenditure out of income, so his gift to Ed is free of inheritance tax. The gift is also tax-efficient in other ways: the contributions are treated as being made after deduction of tax relief at the basic rate and the pension company claims back the relief to add to the scheme, so each £50 is boosted to £64.10 at 2005–6 tax rates; the investment grows largely tax-free; part of the eventual proceeds can be taken as a tax-free lump sum.

The main drawback from Ed's point of view is that he will not be able to touch the money until he reaches at least age 55 (the minimum age for drawing a pension from 2010 onwards) and, at that time, most of the proceeds must be taken in the form of a pension. That does not seem attractive to Ed at age 14. Later in life he will probably appreciate Stan's gift because pension contributions made so early in life have a long time to grow and can be expected to accumulate to a sizeable sum.

Gifts for the maintenance of your family

Money or things which you give to provide housing, food, education, or some other form of maintenance, for your husband or wife, ex-husband or ex-wife, ex-civil partner, children or a dependent relative are outside the IHT net.

As far as husband and wife are concerned, the normal exemption for gifts between married couples (see page 25) would usually apply rather than this exemption. But if either husband or wife are domiciled (see page 26) abroad, this exemption could be useful. This exemption will usually cover maintenance agreements made as a result of a marriage breakdown or dissolution of a civil partnership.

The definition of children is very wide, covering stepchildren, illegitimate and adopted children but it does not extend to grandchildren. Usually a child is considered to be adult when he or she reaches the age of 18 but, if he or she goes on to full-time education or training after that age, the IHT exemption carries on. This means, for example, that money you give a student son or daughter to support them while at university is exempt from IHT.

A 'dependent relative' can be any relative of you or your husband or wife who is unable to maintain him or herself because of old age or infirmity. It also includes your mother or mother-in-law, even if not elderly or infirm, if they are widowed, separated or divorced. As a concession, this exemption is also extended to gifts to your mother if she is unmarried, provided she is financially dependent on you.

Lottery syndicates and similar arrangements

There is no inheritance tax to pay on the transfer of winnings to members of a syndicate set up to share wins from schemes such as the National Lottery and football pools, provided the money is shared out according to an agreement that was drawn up in advance of the win. The agreement could be just oral but it is better to have a written agreement. So, if you and your family or friends often daydream about how you would give each other part of a really big win, it might be a good idea to draw up a formal arrangement now.

Yearly tax-free exemption

Every tax year, you can give away £3,000-worth of gifts without their counting in any way for IHT purposes. This exemption is in addition to the other exemptions, so a gift which qualifies for some other exemption does not count towards the £3,000 annual limit.

If you do not use up the full exemption one year, you can carry it forward to the next year – but not to any subsequent year. This means that, if you used none of last year's exemption, you could make up to £6,000-worth of gifts this year that qualify for the exemption. Gifts always use up the exemption for the tax year in which they are made first *before* using up any carried-forward exemption.

EXAMPLE 2.4

Ali gives his son, Jaffar, £20,000 to help him put down a deposit on a flat. Only part of the gift would count as a potentially exempt transfer (see page 69) because Ali has made no other gifts either this year or last. This means he can set the annual exemption for both years, 2 × £3,000 = £6,000 against the gift. So £6,000 of the gift is completely free of IHT.

Small gifts

You can make as many gifts as you like totalling up to £250 to each person, and these will be exempt. You cannot combine the small gift exemption with another exemption to give more than £250 to *one* person but you can, say, give £3,000 to one recipient and gifts of £250 to any number of *other* people.

This exemption will generally cover birthday and Christmas presents, and any other small gifts you make during the year.

Wedding gifts

As a parent, you can give up to £5,000 to the happy couple free of IHT. A grandparent (or other ancestor) can give up to £2,500. Anyone else can give up to £1,000. The bride and groom can give up to £2,500 to each other but this limit will not be relevant if both are domiciled in the UK, since the exemption for married couples will apply.

The exemptions apply to each giver: for example, assuming both sets of parents of the bride and groom were still living, the couple could receive a maximum of £20,000 from their parents without incurring IHT.

The exemptions under this section can also apply to a marriage settlement which aims to benefit the bride or groom, their children or the husbands or wives of their children.

At the time of writing, regulations had yet to be made but it was expected that, from 5 December 2005, gifts on the registration of a civil partnership would qualify for the same IHT exemptions as wedding gifts.

Potentially exempt transfers

A potentially exempt transfer (PET) is a gift from a person either to another person or to certain types of trust (see Chapter 7) that is not covered by some other IHT exemption. As long as the person making the gift survives for seven years after the date of the gift, there is no IHT to pay. If the giver dies within seven years, there may be an IHT bill. PETs are looked at in detail in Chapter 4.

EXAMPLE 2.5
Ali gives his son, Jaffar, £20,000. Ali sets his annual exemptions for this and last year against the gift, so £6,000 of it is completely free of IHT. The remaining £14,000 counts as a PET and will be free of IHT provided Ali survives for seven years after making the gift. But if he dies within that time, the gift will be reassessed as a chargeable gift and tax may then be due – see Chapter 4.

Combining CGT and IHT exemptions

Some types of gift are specifically exempt from both CGT and IHT: for example, gifts to charities and museums and gifts of national heritage property. Other gifts will be completely tax-free as long as they fall within an IHT exemption *and* you give cash or other assets which are not liable for CGT. Chapters 3 and 4 describe other situations in which either CGT or IHT may not be payable. You can sometimes combine the exemptions in these situations to ensure that your gifts are free of both taxes.

EXAMPLE 2.6
Jeffrey gives his son, Tom, £4,000 in cash as a wedding gift to help him and his new wife buy a home of their own. There is no CGT on a gift of cash and no IHT on a wedding gift of this size.

Jeffrey also wants to give his youngest daughter, Ruth, a gift of similar value. She decides she would like to have a watercolour – a family heirloom – which is valued at £4,500. This counts as a chattel (see page 20) and, since its value is less than £6,000, there is no CGT liability. The gift is a PET under the IHT rules and so, since Jeffrey is expected to live a good many years longer, the gift is likely to be completely free of IHT.

Chapter 3

Capital gains tax and gifts

AND STILL NO TAX TO PAY

'Congratulations!' Frederick raised his glass and drank his son's health. 'And now you are come of age, it's time you had some financial responsibility ... Happy birthday.'

Frederick handed an envelope to his son. Inside was a statement for £12,300-worth of unit trusts. 'I don't know what to say, Dad,' gasped Colin in surprise.

'Well, thank-you might be a start. It's not a trivial gift, you know – though at least I didn't have to pay any capital gains tax on it,' Frederick chuckled, with a satisfied smile on his face.

Capital gains are the profits you make as a result of something increasing in value during the time you have owned it. You are taxed on these gains when you dispose of the asset, which includes giving it away.

Big changes were made to the capital gains tax system from 6 April 1998. If you dispose of something you first started to own on or after that date, you need only concern yourself with the post–1998 rules. But if you started to own the asset before then, you also need to get to grips with indexation allowance (see page 37) which was an important part of the old rules.

No tax to pay?

Chapter 2 looked at gifts that are specifically exempt from CGT. But even if your gift is not covered by one of the exemptions – for example, if you are giving away shares, a second home or a valuable heirloom – there could still be no tax to pay, because:

- from 6 April 1998 onwards, your gain could have been reduced by taper relief, with the greatest relief given to the assets you have held the longest. Taper relief is especially generous if you are disposing of something which has counted as a 'business asset' during the time you owned it, for example, shares in an unlisted company
- increases in the value of an asset in line with inflation up to April 1998 are not taxed
- you reduce gains by deducting losses made on various other assets
- everyone has an 'annual exempt amount' – a tax-free slice of several thousands of pounds of gains which are automatically tax-free each year.

Your first step in working out what tax might be due is to calculate the basic gain on the asset you are giving away. What happens next will depend on when you first acquired the asset and the period over which you have held it.

The basic gain

- Take the 'final value' of the gift. This will usually be the price you would have received if you had sold the asset on the open market.
- Deduct the 'initial value'. This is the price you originally paid for it or its market value at the time you first became the owner.
- Deduct any allowable expenses. These are costs you incurred in acquiring and disposing of the asset (e.g. commission paid to a broker, the cost of an expert valuation or solicitor's fees, stamp duty paid on the purchase of a property) and any expenses associated with enhancing the value of the asset (e.g. adding an extension to a property) but not spending on maintenance and repairs.

Assets acquired on or after 1 April 1998

For an asset acquired on or after 1 April 1998, the result of the calculation above is your 'chargeable gain' (if the answer is greater than zero) or your 'allowable loss' (if the answer is less than zero).

Where you have made a chargeable gain, you must deduct any losses you have made during the same tax year in which the gift is

GIFTS BETWEEN HUSBAND AND WIFE OR BETWEEN CIVIL PARTNERS

There is no CGT on a gift between a husband and wife or between civil partners (see Chapter 2) and the transfer is said to be made on a 'no gain/no loss' basis. What this means becomes important if the recipient subsequently sells or gives away the asset, because in order to work out any CGT bill, you need to know about the following:

- **date of acquisition**. For CGT, the spouse or civil partner receiving the gift started to own the asset from the date of the gift
- **initial value**. The recipient is treated as if the value on that date is the initial value which applied to the spouse or civil partner making the gift plus any allowable expenses and/or indexation allowance the giver qualified for. In effect, the recipient has taken over the giver's allowable expenses and indexation allowance
- **taper relief**. The period of ownership of the spouse or civil partner making the gift is added to the recipient's period of ownership for the purpose of calculating taper relief.

EXAMPLE 3.1

Pete bought a paddock for £5,000 in May 1996. His indexation allowance for the period May 1996 to April 1998 is 0.063 × £5,000 = £315. In October 2005, he gives the paddock to his wife, Mel. In January 2006, Mel sells the paddock for £12,000. To work out whether CGT is due, Mel needs to do the following calculations:

- final value: £12,000
- deduct initial value: £5,315 (i.e. Pete's initial value plus Pete's indexation allowance and any allowable expenses)
- deduct Mel's allowable expenses: £300 in solicitor's fees
- this gives an indexed gain of: £12,000 – £5,315 – £300 = £6,385
- work out taper relief based on Pete's and Mel's combined period of ownership since April 1998, i.e. seven complete years plus a bonus year because Pete already held the paddock on 17 March 1998 – see page 38 – making eight years' taper relief in total.

made. You also deduct any losses brought forward from earlier tax years but no more than are needed to reduce your gains to the amount of the tax-free slice (see page 50 for more about losses). The resulting figure is your 'net chargeable gain'.

You do not necessarily pay tax on the whole of your net chargeable gain. The government wants to encourage people to hold investments for the longer term in the belief that this provides a healthier environment for British business. Therefore taper relief reduces the amount of your net chargeable gain with the largest reduction given to the assets you have held for the longest – see Table 3.1. For non-business assets, there is no reduction at all until you have held the asset for three years. The reduction then depends on the number of complete years since 6 April 1998 (inclusive) for which you have held the asset. The maximum reduction is given after ten complete years. Taper relief is more generous if the asset you are giving away counts as a business asset (see page 56).

Table 3.1 CGT taper relief for non-business assets

If you have held the asset for this many complete years after 5 April 1998:	Your net chargeable gain is reduced by this percentage:	Only this percentage of your gain counts as chargeable:	For example, a net chargeable gain of £5,000 is reduced to:
0	No reduction	100%	£5,000
1	No reduction	100%	£5,000
2	No reduction	100%	£5,000
3	5%	95%	£4,750
4	10%	90%	£4,500
5	15%	85%	£4,250
6	20%	80%	£4,000
7	25%	75%	£3,750
8	30%	70%	£3,500
9	35%	65%	£3,250
10 or more	40%	60%	£3,000

EXAMPLE 3.2

Carole bought a holiday cottage in May 1998 for £65,000. The buying costs amounted to £1,200. In August 1998, Carole added a conservatory to the cottage at a cost of £1,700. In June 2005, Carole gives the cottage to her niece, Becky. It is then valued at £125,000 and the costs incurred in making the transfer to Becky amount to £1,500. Carole is deemed to have made a chargeable gain on the gift as follows:

Final value of the cottage	£125,000
less initial value	£65,000
less allowable expenses (£1,200 + £1,700 + £1,500)	£4,400
Chargeable gain	£55,600
less allowable losses	£0
Net chargeable gain before CGT taper relief	£55,600
Number of complete years for which cottage held (May 1998 to June 2005)	7 years
Percentage taper	75%
Net chargeable gain after taper relief (75% × £55,600)	£41,700

CGT on gifts of assets acquired before 1 April 1998 but after March 1982

If you give away an asset which you started to own on or after 31 March 1982 but before 1 April 1998, work out the basic gain as on page 34. Divide your period of ownership into two:

- holding period 1: date of acquisition up to April 1998
- holding period 2: 6 April 1998 up to date when gift is made.

Holding period 1: indexation allowance

In respect of holding period 1 (date of acquisition up to April 1998), you can deduct indexation allowance. Take the initial value of the asset (see page 34) and each allowable expense and multiply each of these values by the appropriate indexation factor. Add the result together and the total is the indexation allowance.

The indexation factor for the initial value and each expense is derived from the change in the Retail Prices Index (RPI) since the expense was incurred up to 5 April 1998 (or, if earlier, the date on which the gift was made). This is described on page 42.

The effect of the indexation allowance is to strip out any gains which are simply the result of inflation – i.e. do not represent any real increase in your wealth. However, since 6 April 1995, the indexation allowance can at most wipe out the whole gain – it cannot be used to create or increase a loss for CGT purposes.

Deducting the indexation allowance from your basic gain gives you your 'indexed gain'.

Holding period 2: taper relief

Having found your indexed gain, you next work out how much taper relief you qualify for in respect of holding period 2 (6 April 1998 to date of gift) using the rules described on page 36 with one exception: you are allowed to add one extra year to the holding period for any non-business asset which you already owned on 17 March 1998 (the Budget day on which taper relief was announced).

EXAMPLE 3.3

On his 18th birthday on 1 September 2005, Colin is given a portfolio of unit trusts by his father, Frederick. Frederick originally bought the units in July 1991 for £4,700. They are now worth £12,300. As Frederick is disposing of the units, there could be a CGT bill. To work out whether he has made a chargeable gain, Frederick makes the following calculations:

Basic gain

Final value of units	£12,300
less initial value	£4,700
less fee paid to investment adviser at time units were bought	£150
	£7,450

Indexation allowance

Initial value and allowable expenses incurred at time of acquisition	£4,850
Indexation factor (see page 42)	0.215
Indexation allowance for period to April 1998 (0.215 × £4,850)	£1,043
Indexed gain (£7,450 − £1,043)	£6,407
less allowable losses	£0
Net chargeable gain before taper relief	£6,407

Taper relief

Number of complete years since 5 April 1998 for which asset held	7
Plus one year because asset acquired before 17 March 1998	8
Percentage taper (see page 36)	70%
Net chargeable gain after taper relief (70% × £6,407)	£4,484

EXAMPLE 3.4

In February 2005 Sylvia and Jeffrey decide to give their elder daughter, Hazel, an oil painting she had always liked. It has been in Jeffrey's family for several generations and in February was valued at £7,000.

The gift counts as a disposal of a chattel with a predicted life of more than 50 years. Its value is greater than £6,000, so there may be a CGT bill (see page 20) but special rules apply in calculating the chargeable gain: the gain will be the *lower* of either five-thirds of the excess of the disposal value over £6,000 or the gain (before deducting any losses or taper relief but after deducting any indexation allowance) worked out in the normal way.

When Jeffrey inherited the painting in February 1987, it was valued at £3,500. Jeffrey can claim an indexation allowance (see page 42) of 0.620 × £3,500 = £2,170. For simplicity, assume there are no allowable expenses. The two calculations are as follows:

Method 1

Final value	£7,000
less £6,000	£6,000
	£1,000
5/3 x £1,000	£1,667

Method 2

Final value	£7,000
less initial value	£3,500
less indexation allowance	£2,170
	£1,330

Method 2 gives the lower answer, so Jeffrey's chargeable gain is £1,330.

CGT on gifts of assets acquired before April 1982

Gains due to inflation were not always tax-free. The legislation taking them out of the CGT net is effective only from the end of March 1982 onwards. For an asset which you started to own before 1 April 1982, the sums are slightly different from those outlined in the previous section. There are two methods of calculating your chargeable gain, as follows:

- **Method 1** The initial value is usually taken to be the value of the asset on 31 March 1982, and the indexation allowance for the initial cost is based on inflation since that date. Any allowable expenses incurred before 31 March 1982 are ignored; allowable expenses after that date are indexed in the normal way
- **Method 2** If working out your chargeable gain using Method 1 would result in a higher CGT bill than taking into account the full period during which you have owned the asset including the pre-March 1982 period, you can instead work out the chargeable gain

based on the whole period. In this case, the initial value is the actual value at the time you first acquired the asset. The indexation allowance is worked out based on either the initial value or the asset's value on 31 March 1982 but adjusting for inflation only since March 1982.

If Method 1 and Method 2 both result in a gain, your chargeable gain will be the lower of the two amounts. If both methods give a loss, your allowable loss is the smaller amount. If one gives a gain and the other a loss, you are deemed to have made neither a gain nor a loss – there will be no CGT to pay but no loss to offset against gains on other assets. If Method 2 would, in any case, have produced neither a gain nor a loss, that method is used whatever the result of using Method 1 would have been. The comparison of the outcomes of Methods 1 and 2 is called the 'Kink test'.

You can choose to use just Method 1. If you do, *all* your assets will be covered by the election. The effect is as if you had sold all your assets on 31 March 1982 and immediately rebought them. It will usually be worth making this choice if the values of all or most of your assets were higher on 31 March 1982 than they were at the time you first acquired them.

EXAMPLE 3.5

Tom's grandmother, Emily, gives Tom some shares as a wedding present in June 2005. She originally bought them in 1979 for £1,500 and they are now worth £11,000. On 31 March 1982, they were valued at just £1,000. Emily's chargeable gain is worked out using Methods 1 and 2 as follows:

Method 1

Final value of shares	£11,000
less value of shares on 31 March 1982	£1,000
less indexation allowance for period March 1982 to April 1998 (see below)	£1,047
Chargeable gain (before losses and taper relief)	£8,953

Method 2

Final value of shares	£11,000
less initial value of shares	£1,500
less indexation allowance	£1,571
Chargeable gain (before losses and taper relief)	£7,929

Indexation allowance

Indexation factor for inflation from 31 March 1982 to April 1998	1.047
Indexation allowance using value at 31 March 1982 (1.047 × £1,000)	£1,047
Indexation allowance using initial value (1.047 × £1,500)	£1,571

The result is smaller using Method 2, so Emily's net chargeable gain is £7,929.

Working out your indexation allowance

Your indexation allowance is the appropriate indexation factor multiplied by the relevant initial value or allowable expense. The indexation factor depends on the month when you first acquired the asset or incurred the expense. Until April 1998, the factor also varied according to the month in which you disposed of the asset. But, since indexation allowance now runs only up to April 1998, there is just one set of indexation factors which applies to all disposals you make from April 1998 onwards. These are shown in Table 3.2. Look along the left-hand side to find the year in which you acquired the asset or incurred the expense; run your eye across to the column for the relevant month. This is the indexation factor you should use. See Example 3.6.

Table 3.2 Indexation factors for gifts or disposals you make from April 1998 onwards

	Jan	Feb	Mar	April	May	June	July	Aug	Sept	Oct	Nov	Dec
1982	–	–	1.047	1.006	0.992	0.987	0.986	0.985	0.987	0.977	0.967	0.971
1983	0.968	0.960	0.956	0.929	0.921	0.917	0.906	0.898	0.889	0.883	0.876	0.871
1984	0.872	0.865	0.859	0.834	0.828	0.823	0.825	0.808	0.804	0.793	0.788	0.789
1985	0.783	0.769	0.752	0.716	0.708	0.704	0.707	0.703	0.704	0.701	0.695	0.693
1986	0.689	0.683	0.681	0.665	0.662	0.663	0.667	0.662	0.654	0.652	0.638	0.632
1987	0.626	0.620	0.616	0.597	0.596	0.596	0.597	0.593	0.588	0.580	0.573	0.574
1988	0.574	0.568	0.562	0.537	0.531	0.525	0.524	0.507	0.500	0.485	0.478	0.474
1989	0.465	0.454	0.448	0.423	0.414	0.409	0.408	0.404	0.395	0.384	0.372	0.369
1990	0.361	0.353	0.339	0.300	0.288	0.283	0.282	0.269	0.258	0.248	0.251	0.252
1991	0.249	0.242	0.237	0.222	0.218	0.213	0.215	0.213	0.208	0.204	0.199	0.198
1992	0.199	0.193	0.189	0.171	0.167	0.167	0.171	0.171	0.166	0.162	0.164	0.168
1993	0.179	0.171	0.167	0.156	0.152	0.153	0.156	0.151	0.146	0.147	0.148	0.146
1994	0.151	0.144	0.141	0.128	0.124	0.124	0.129	0.124	0.121	0.120	0.119	0.114
1995	0.114	0.107	0.102	0.091	0.087	0.085	0.091	0.085	0.080	0.085	0.085	0.079
1996	0.083	0.078	0.073	0.066	0.063	0.063	0.067	0.062	0.057	0.057	0.057	0.053
1997	0.053	0.049	0.046	0.040	0.036	0.032	0.032	0.026	0.021	0.019	0.019	0.016
1998	0.019	0.014	0.011	–	–	–	–	–	–	–	–	–

EXAMPLE 3.6

In September 2005, Christina gives her daughter Michelle some jewellery which Christina inherited from her own mother in February 1990. She needs to work out what indexation allowance she can claim for the period February 1990 to April 1998. Using Table 3.2, she finds the year 1990 along the left-hand side and runs across to the column for February. The entry tells her that the indexation factor to use is 0.353.

You might need to work out the indexation factor for a period before April 1998 if you are now disposing of shares you acquired before then (see page 46). You can work it out from the Retail Prices Index (RPI). This index is the most commonly used measure of the level of prices in the UK. Table 3.3 lists the RPI from March 1982 up to April 1998. The latest RPI figure you will need for CGT calculations is that for April 1998.

To work out the appropriate indexation factor, take the RPI figure for the later month you are considering – call this R_D. Then take the RPI figure for the earlier month you are looking at or for March 1982, whichever is appropriate, and call this R_I. Now make the following calculation:

$$\text{Indexation factor} = \frac{R_D - R_I}{R_I}$$

Indexation factors are rounded to the nearest third decimal place.

EXAMPLE 3.7

Gerald had 1,000 shares in Megabucks plc which he had bought in June 1982. In March 1988, he bought a further 2,000 shares in the same company. The two purchases are pooled together to form a 'section 104 holding' (see page 46). Before the new shares can be added to the pool, Gerald must work out the indexation allowance clocked up for the 1,000 shares he already held over the period June 1982 to March 1988. He needs to know what indexation factor to use. From Table 3.3, he finds the RPI for June 1982 (81.85) and for March 1988 (104.1). The indexation factor is: (104.1 – 81.85) / 104.1 = 0.214.

Table 3.3 Retail Prices Index (Base: January 1987 = 100)

	Jan	Feb	Mar	April	May	June	July	Aug	Sept	Oct	Nov	Dec
1982	–	–	79.44	81.04	81.62	81.85	81.88	81.90	81.85	82.26	82.66	82.51
1983	82.61	82.97	83.12	84.28	84.64	84.84	85.30	85.68	86.06	86.36	86.67	86.89
1984	86.84	87.20	87.48	88.64	88.97	89.20	89.10	89.94	90.11	90.67	90.95	90.87
1985	91.20	91.94	92.80	94.78	95.21	95.41	95.23	95.49	95.44	95.59	95.92	96.05
1986	96.25	96.60	96.73	97.67	97.85	97.79	97.52	97.82	98.30	98.45	99.29	99.62
1987	100.0	100.4	100.6	101.8	101.9	101.9	101.8	102.1	102.4	102.9	103.4	103.3
1988	103.3	103.7	104.1	105.8	106.2	106.6	106.7	107.9	108.4	109.5	110.0	110.3
1989	111.0	111.8	112.3	114.3	115.0	115.4	115.5	115.8	116.6	117.5	118.5	118.8
1990	119.5	120.2	121.4	125.1	126.2	126.7	126.8	128.1	129.3	130.3	130.0	129.9
1991	130.2	130.9	131.4	133.1	133.5	134.1	133.8	134.1	134.6	135.1	135.6	135.7
1992	135.6	136.3	136.7	138.8	139.3	139.3	138.8	138.9	139.4	139.9	139.7	139.2
1993	137.9	138.8	139.3	140.6	141.1	141.0	140.7	141.3	141.9	141.8	141.6	141.9
1994	141.3	142.1	142.5	144.2	144.7	144.7	144.0	144.7	145.0	145.2	145.3	146.0
1995	146.0	146.9	147.5	149.0	149.6	149.8	149.1	149.9	150.6	149.8	149.8	150.7
1996	150.2	150.9	151.5	152.6	152.9	153.0	152.4	153.1	153.8	153.8	153.9	154.4
1997	154.4	155.0	155.4	156.3	156.9	157.5	157.5	158.5	159.3	159.5	159.6	160.0
1998	159.5	160.3	160.8	162.6	–	–	–	–	–	–	–	–

Shares and unit trusts

If you give away identical shares, unit trusts or other securities that you acquired all at the same time, the CGT rules apply in the same way as for any other asset. However, suppose you own shares in one company, all of the same type but bought at different times. Special rules are needed to identify which particular shares you are disposing of, so that you can use the correct initial value, taper relief and indexation allowance (if applicable) in your calculations.

For gifts and other disposals made on or after 6 April 1998, the shares, unit trusts or other securities which you give away are matched to the ones you own in the following order:

- shares you bought on the same day
- shares purchased within the following 30 days. This rule was introduced to curb a practice called 'bed-and-breakfasting'. You used to be able to realise a capital gain or loss by selling shares one day and buying them back the next – such a move could be very tax-efficient (see page 138). Now, you will need to leave at least 30 days between selling the shares and buying them back – a risky strategy when the stock market might move against you. However, there are alternative ways to bed-and-breakfast (see page 138)
- shares bought on or after 6 April 1998, identifying which are the most recent acquisitions first – this is called a last-in-first-out (LIFO) basis
- shares in your 'section 104 holding'. These are shares you acquired between 6 April 1982 and 5 April 1998 inclusive. These shares are pooled together. Your initial value and indexation allowance are worked out as a proportion of the values for all the shares in the pool – see Example 3.9. The calculation has to be reworked every time there is a change to the contents of the pool – for example, you buy, sell or give away shares. ('Section 104' refers to the part of the tax legislation which sets out the rules for this share pool)
- shares in your '1982 holding'. These are shares you acquired between 6 April 1965 and 5 April 1982 inclusive. Again, they form a pool and to value the shares you take a proportion of the value for the pool as a whole, which have to be recalculated every time the contents of the pool change. The indexation allowance is calculated only from 31 March 1982 based either on the actual purchases you made or on the value at 31 March 1982, unless you

have elected to have all your assets (including these shares) rebased to 31 March 1982 – see page 40

- shares you acquired before 6 April 1965, starting with the shares you bought most recently – i.e. LIFO basis. You can opt to have quoted shares treated as part of your 1965 pool instead.

An essential point to note about the rules for identifying shares (and unit trusts and other securities) is that you must keep accurate records of your share purchases and sales, recording the dates of transactions, quantity and price of the shares involved.

EXAMPLE 3.8

Connie received 300 Alliance & Leicester shares when the building society was demutualised in April 1997 and she bought further shares in the company as follows:

9 April 1998	1,700 shares
2 November 1999	500 shares
16 July 2000	700 shares

In October 2005, she decides to give half her Alliance & Leicester shares to her niece, Harriet. The 1,600 shares she gives away are matched in the following order:

16 July 2000	700 shares
2 November 1999	500 shares
9 April 1998	400 shares
Total	1,600 shares

Any subsequent gifts or other disposals would be matched against the remaining 1,300 shares bought on 9 April 1998 and then her original 300 shares.

EXAMPLE 3.9

In January 2006, Gerald gave his sister Dot 800 shares valued at £3,000. These were part of a holding which Gerald originally acquired in two lots: 1,000 shares for £1,500 in June 1982 and 2,000 shares for £4,000 in March 1988. The shares form a 'section 104 holding'. To work out if any

CGT is payable on the gift, Gerald needs to work out the initial value and indexation allowance he can claim. The key events for his section 104 holding can be set out as follows:

Date	Description of event	Number of shares in the section 104 holding	Value of the holding before indexation	Indexed value of the holding
June 1982	1,000 shares purchased at cost of £1,500	1,000	£1,500	£1,500
March 1988	Indexed value of pool. Indexation allowance June 1982 to March 1988 = 0.214 × £1,500 = £321 (see Example 3.7 on page 44 for how the indexation factor is calculated)	1,000	£1,500	£1,821
March 1988	2,000 shares purchased at cost of £4,000	3,000	£5,500	£5,821
April 1998	Indexed value of pool. Indexation allowance March 1988 to April 1998 = 0.562 × £5,821 = £3,271 (see Table 3.2 for the indexation factor). Rules now change: end of indexation, so no more indexation allowance can be added	3,000	£5,500	£9,092
January 2006	800 shares given away. Their value (£1,467 – see below) is subtracted from the value of the holding. Similarly the indexed value of the shares (£2,425) is deducted from the indexed value of the holding	2,200	£4,033	£6,667

The initial value of the shares given away is the relevant proportion of the value of the shares in the holding: 800/3,000 × £5,500 = £1,467. The same proportion of the indexed value of the holding is 800/3,000 × £9,092 = £2,425 which gives a maximum indexation allowance of £2,425 – £1,467 = £958 but bear in mind that the indexation allowance is capped at a lower amount if it would otherwise create or increase a loss.

The basic gain on the shares Gerald gives Dot is £3,000 – £1,467 = £1,533. He can subtract indexation allowance of £958 leaving an indexed gain of £575. Gerald has held the shares for seven complete years since April 1998 and qualifies for the bonus year, so he can claim eight years' taper relief. This means only 70 per cent of the gain is taxable. The chargeable gain is 70% × £575 = £402.

How much tax?

Yearly tax-free slice

If you are deemed to have made a chargeable gain on an asset you give away, there could be some tax to pay, but not necessarily. Everyone has a tax-free slice – more formally called the 'annual exempt amount'. This means that the first slice of chargeable gains which you make each year is tax-free. In 2005–6, you can have net chargeable gains of £8,500 before any CGT becomes payable. The tax-free slice for earlier years is shown in Table 3.4.

Table 3.4 Tax-free slice for capital gains

Tax year	Tax-free slice
1999–2000	£7,100
2000–1	£7,200
2001–2	£7,500
2002–3	£7,700
2003–4	£7,900
2004–5	£8,200
2005–6	£8,500

Claiming allowable losses

If you make a loss on something you give away or otherwise dispose of, you set the loss against gains you have made on other assets in the same tax year. You have no choice about this. Any capital losses made in the same year must be set against any gains to the extent that your gains are reduced to zero. This means that any taper relief and tax-free slice may then be wasted.

If your losses come to more than your gains for the tax year, you carry forward the unrelieved losses to future years. In general, you can never carry them back to earlier years – although, when you die, your executors can.

If your losses come to less than your gains for the tax year, you next deduct any losses you have brought forward from earlier years. Once again, you have no choice – you must set off any losses brought forward but, this time, only to the extent that your net chargeable gains are reduced to the amount of the tax-free slice. This means that, although taper relief may be wasted (see Example 3.10), your annual tax-free slice is not. Any losses not used up continue to be carried forward to be relieved in future years.

Since 6 April 1998, where you make a gift you deduct any losses you are claiming before applying the CGT taper and before deducting the tax-free slice. This means that losses, as well as gains, are reduced by the taper relief. But you do set off the losses in the way which benefits you most. This means, if you have made gains on several assets in the same year, setting losses against the gain(s) which qualify for the lowest taper relief – see Example 3.11.

EXAMPLE 3.10

In 2005–6, Sally has gains before taper relief of £9,100 and carried-forward losses of £1,300. The tax-free slice for the year is £8,500.

Sally must set enough of her carried-forward losses against the gains to reduce them to the level of the tax-free slice. In other words: £9,100 – £600 = £8,500. She qualifies for 10 per cent taper relief on her gains, reducing them to 90% × £8,500 = £7,650. But this is now £850 less than her tax-free slice for the year, so £850 of her reliefs have been wasted. She pays no tax on her gains and continues to carry forward the remaining £700 of losses.

If instead Sally had made gains of only £8,500 for the tax year, there would have been no tax to pay on them because they would be covered by the tax-free slice and she would have continued to carry forward the full £1,300 of losses.

EXAMPLE 3.11

In November 2005, Liam gives two plots of land to his son. The first was inherited in 1989. The gain on this plot after indexation allowance but before taper relief is £20,300. He qualifies for eight years' taper relief on this gain. This means the gain can be reduced by 30 per cent.

Liam bought the second plot in September 2000. The gain on this is £4,500 before taper relief. He has held the land for five complete tax years, which qualifies him for 15 per cent taper relief.

Liam is carrying forward losses of £3,000 which he made on share sales several years ago. Consider the impact of setting these losses against each gain:

Losses set against gain on plot 1

Gain on plot 1	£20,300
Less loss relief	£3,000
Gain on plot 1 before taper relief	£17,300
Less taper relief for plot 1 @ 30%	£5,190
Plus gain on plot 2	£4,500
Less taper relief for plot 2 @ 15%	£675
Chargeable gains after loss relief and taper relief	£15,935

Losses set against gain on plot 2

Gain on plot 2	£4,500
Less loss relief	£3,000
Gain on plot 2 before taper relief	£1,500
Less taper relief for plot 2 @ 15%	£225
Plus gain on plot 1	£20,300
Less taper relief for plot 1 @ 30%	£6,090
Chargeable gains after loss relief and taper relief	£15,485

Liam has lower chargeable gains and so pays less tax if he sets his carried-forward losses against the gain on plot 2 – in other words, the gain which qualifies for the lower rate of taper relief. This is because taper relief reduces the losses by less.

Working out the tax bill

If, after following these steps, you are left with a gain, there will be tax to pay. CGT is charged at three rates in 2005–6: the 10 per cent starting rate, the lower rate of 20 per cent and the higher rate of 40 per cent. To see which rate applies to you, add your taxable gains (after all the adjustments described above) to your taxable *income* for the year. The result of this sum tells you what rate of CGT is payable:

Table 3.5 Tax rate on chargeable gains 2005–6

This tax rate applies	If your gains plus taxable income equal:
10 per cent	Up to £2,090
20 per cent	From £2,091 to £32,400
40 per cent	More than £32,400

If your taxable income is below a threshold given in Table 3.5 and adding the gain to the income takes the total above the threshold, you will pay the lesser tax rate on part of your gain and the greater rate on the rest. For example, if you have taxable income of £31,500 in the 2005–6 tax year and taxable gains of £2,000 (a total of £33,500), you would pay 20 per cent CGT on £900 of the gain and 40 per cent CGT on the £1,100 of gain above the higher-rate threshold.

EXAMPLE 3.12

Frederick made a chargeable gain of £4,484 on the unit trusts he gives to Colin (see page 38). But after taking account of chargeable gains on other assets he has disposed of during the tax year, Frederick still has £4,500 of his tax-free slice unused. He can set this against the gift to Colin, which means there will be no CGT to pay.

EXAMPLE 3.13

In the 2005–6 tax year, Emily has net chargeable gains of £8,929. She deducts the tax-free slice of £8,500, leaving taxable gains of £429. Emily's taxable income for the year is £32,000. The tax on her gains is worked out as follows:

Slice of gains in excess of £32,400 threshold	£29
Slice of gain within basic-rate band	£400
CGT at 40 per cent on £29	£11.60
CGT at 20 per cent on £400	£80.00
Total CGT bill	£91.60

Hold-over relief

With a few gifts you make, you could face bills for both CGT and IHT at the time the gift is made. Alternatively, you might face a CGT bill and have to use some or all of an IHT exemption which could trigger an IHT bill on a later gift. 'Hold-over relief' lets you avoid this potential for a double tax bill. The way it works is that, instead of being treated as having realised a gain on the asset you give away, you – in effect – give away your CGT liability along with the asset. Gifts which qualify for this relief must be made between individuals or trusts. They include:

- gifts which count as chargeable gifts for inheritance tax purposes (see Chapter 4) or would do so if they were not covered by the yearly tax-free exemption (see page 29) or the tax-free slice (see page 64). Gifts which are potentially exempt transfers (PETs) (see page 69) do not qualify for relief, unless they become chargeable because the person making the gift dies within seven years
- gifts of national heritage property – land, buildings, a work of art and so on – though you will not need to claim hold-over relief if the property qualifies as exempt from CGT (see page 26)
- gifts to political parties (see page 27)
- gifts made from accumulation-and-maintenance trusts at the time a beneficiary becomes entitled to the trust property or a life interest in it (see Chapter 7).

Hold-over relief is not given automatically. If you are making a gift to a person, both you and that person jointly claim the relief using the form in HM Revenue & Customs (HMRC) – formerly known as the Inland Revenue – Helpsheet IR295. If you are putting the gift into trust, only you need claim.

Relief is given in the following way. The chargeable gain you have made on the asset up to the time of the gift is worked out. That amount is deducted from your total chargeable gains for the year – so you pay no CGT on the gain. The chargeable gain on the asset is also deducted from the recipient's initial value of the gift. This increases the likelihood of a chargeable gain when the recipient comes to dispose of the gift (though whether or not any tax would be payable then would depend on the availability of reliefs and exemptions, such as unused tax-free slice or further hold-over relief). For the purposes of calculating CGT taper relief when the recipient eventually disposes of the asset, the clock starts ticking from the date on which the recipient became the new owner of the asset.

Before 14 March 1989, hold-over relief applied to a much wider range of gifts, including those which counted as PETs under the IHT legislation. The restrictions now applying to the relief mean that it is mainly useful when you are making gifts to a discretionary trust (see page 113) or where you become entitled to receive property from such a trust.

Note, however, that there are rules to stop tax avoidance where you give to a trust property which is used as a home by one or more of the beneficiaries. The trustees cannot claim private residence relief (see p 21) for any period after 9 December 2003 if holdover relief had been claimed when the property was given to the trust unless the holdover relief claim is revoked.

Hold-over relief may be clawed back if the person receiving the gift ceases to be a UK resident within six years of the end of the tax year in which the gift was made. The recipient will then be liable for CGT on the held-over gain but, if he or she doesn't pay, the HMRC can seek to recover tax from the person who made the gift, which could land you with an unexpected CGT bill. If there is a possibility that the person to whom you are making the gift might move abroad, you could take out insurance to cover the possible CGT bill.

Giving away a business or business assets

Hold-over relief is also available when you give away assets used in your business or shares in an unlisted trading company. However, to counter tax avoidance, hold-over relief ceased to be available from 9 November 1999 onwards where shares or securities are transferred to any company.

Relief must be claimed, in most cases, jointly by both the giver and the recipient – use the form in HMRC Helpsheet IR295. It works by enabling the giver to deduct the gain which would otherwise be payable from their chargeable gains, and the recipient deducts the same amount from the initial value at which he or she receives the assets or shares.

If the assets concerned have not been used in the business for the whole time that they were owned by the giver, then the amount of hold-over relief available may be scaled down proportionately (and the relevant period of ownership includes any time before 31 March 1982).

If hold-over relief is available on the assets anyway because they are subject to an IHT charge (see above) then the IHT-related hold-over relief applies rather than the business-related relief. Similarly, if the assets or shares qualified for 'retirement relief' (which until April 2003 reduced or eliminated a CGT bill that would otherwise be payable when you dispose of your business in order to retire), this was given in preference to hold-over relief.

Hold-over relief can also be claimed on gifts of agricultural property. If the land or property is not currently in use as part of your business, then relief may still be granted if the property also qualifies for relief from IHT (see page 80).

If you give away or otherwise dispose of business assets, a higher than normal rate of taper relief applies in respect of periods since April 1998 during which you held the asset. Taper relief for business assets was made more generous for disposals from 6 April 2000 and again from 6 April 2002 – Table 3.6 shows the rates that apply from 6 April 2002 onwards.

Table 3.6 CGT taper relief for business assets

If you have held the asset for this many complete years after 5 April 1998:	Your net chargeable gain is reduced by:	Only this percentage of your gain counts as chargeable:	For example, a net chargeable gain of £5,000 is reduced to:
0	No reduction	100%	£5,000
1	50%	50%	£2,500
2 or more	75%	25%	£1,250

Business assets can be:

- something used in your business if you are a sole trader or partner
- from 6 April 2004 onwards, something used in a business carried on by some other individual or partnership
- something used by a 'qualifying company' (see below)
- something you are required to have as a result of your employment
- shares in a qualifying company (see below).

The definition of a qualifying company changed from 6 April 2000 onwards. Before that date, it meant:

- a trading company where you controlled at least 25 per cent of the voting rights, or
- provided you were a full-time officer or employee of the company, a trading company where you controlled at least 5 per cent of the voting rights.

From 6 April 2000 onwards, the definition has been widened so that now it means:

- any unlisted trading company
- a quoted trading company where you control at least 5 per cent of the voting rights, or
- provided you are an officer or an employee (full- or part-time), any quoted company whether a trading or non-trading company.

'Unlisted' means that none of the company's shares are quoted on a recognised stock exchange. For this purpose, shares traded on the Alternative Investment Market (AIM) count as unlisted. 'Trading company' is a company carrying on one or more trades, professions or vocations in order to make a profit. It excludes simply holding investments (except where they do not make up a substantial extent of the company's activities) but specifically does include letting out furnished holiday accommodation on a commercial basis.

If you give away an asset which counted as a non-business asset for part of the time you owned it, but a business asset for the rest of the time, you have to apportion any capital gain between the two periods and claim the relevant taper relief for each part – see Example 3.14. This can have the perverse effect of allowing more taper relief on an asset held for a shorter period of time than available on an asset held for a longer period – see Example 3.15.

If you have held a business asset for a long time and it is affected by the apportioning rules demonstrated in Example 3.15, you might want to look at resetting the taper relief clock. You can do this by giving the asset to a discretionary trust which you control. You claim holdover relief to transfer your gain to the trustees so no CGT is payable at the time of the gift. Under the holdover relief rules, taper relief restarts from the date the recipient (in this case, the trust) receives the gift so the whole period is now covered by business taper relief. When deciding whether it is worth resetting the taper relief clock you need to weigh up:

- **the tax saving**. As time goes by, an increasing proportion of the time you have held the asset will qualify for business taper relief, so the amount of any extra tax due because of the apportioning rules will fall, and
- **the cost of setting up a discretionary trust**. How much it costs will depend on the complexity of the trust and the value of the asset(s) involved, but you are probably looking at paying out at the very least £500.

EXAMPLE 3.14

Since 6 April 1998, Bella has held 3 per cent of the ordinary shares of Hammerson Ltd, an unquoted electronics company. Until 6 April 2000, this holding did not count as a business asset but from that date it does.

On 10 May 2005, Bella decides to give the shares to her grand-daughter, Phoebe. She realises a taxable profit of £12,000. For taper relief purposes, she has held the shares for seven complete years. This entitles her to 25 per cent taper relief at the non-business rate and 75 per cent at the business taper rate.

During five of these years (6 April 2000 to 5 April 2005), the shares counted as a business asset. Therefore, 75 per cent taper relief is applied to 5/7th of £12,000, reducing that part of the taxable gain to 5/7th × £12,000 × 25% = £2,142.

During the period 6 April 1998 to 5 April 2000 the shares counted as non-business assets. Therefore 25 per cent taper relief is applied to 2/7th of £12,000, reducing that part of the gain to 2/7th × £12,000 × 75% = £2,571.

Bella's taxable gain after taper relief is £2,142 + £2,571 = £4,713.

EXAMPLE 3.15

Bella's husband, Richard, also has a 3 per cent holding in Hammerson Ltd (see Example 3.13). Neither Bella nor Richard work for the company. They look at whether it would be more tax-efficient if Richard instead of Bella gave shares to Phoebe.

Richard first acquired his shares on 6 April 2000. Coincidentally, on 10 May 2005, Richard would also have a gain of £12,000 if he gave away the shares. The shares count as a business asset throughout the five complete years that Richard has held them and so qualify for 75 per cent taper relief. This reduces Richard's taxable gain to £12,000 × 25% = £3,000.

Even though Richard has not held Hammerson shares for as long as Bella, his taxable gain is significantly lower (£3,000 compared with Bella's £4,713). It would, therefore, be more tax-efficient for Richard to make the gift to Phoebe.

Where something is used partly for business and partly privately, the gain will be divided pro rata and the appropriate taper relief applied to each part.

If you are planning to give away your business or farm, you should seek advice from your accountant and solicitor.

Telling the taxman

If you get a full tax return

If you receive a full-length tax return (usually in April each year) asking about your income and capital gains, give the information asked for. As well as the main form and any other supplements you get, you will need the capital gains supplement. If it is not included in the package you are sent, request it from the HMRC Orderline★.

To avoid penalties, you must file your tax return no later than 31 January following the end of the tax year which is also the normal deadline for paying any tax due. But you might choose an earlier filing deadlines – see Table 3.7. For example, you can get your tax office to work out your tax bill for you, but it will guarantee to tell you the amount due in time for the 31 January payment deadline only if you send in your return by 30 September. If you send it in later, your tax office will still work out the tax due but might not tell you in time.

Employees and many pensioners pay most of their income tax through PAYE. If this applies to you and the total extra tax you owe including any CGT is less than £2,000 (this is the limit applying since 6 April 2000 and is changed only infrequently), you can opt to have the tax collected through PAYE instead of paying a lump sum on 31 January. This gives you more time to pay and spreads the bill in instalments across a year. For example, if you owe less than £2,000 tax for 2005–6, instead of paying a lump sum on 31 January 2007, you could pay through PAYE over the 2007–8 tax year.

Table 3.7 Deadline for telling the taxman if you get a full tax return

Do you want to work out your own tax bill?	Do you owe less than £2,000 tax and want to pay it through PAYE	Will you file your tax return by internet?	Deadline – date following end of tax year	Deadlines for gains you made in 2005–6 tax year
No	No	No	30 September	30 September 2006
		Yes	31 January	31 January 2007
	Yes	No	30 September	30 September 2006
		Yes	30 December	30 December 2006
Yes	No	No	31 January	31 January 2007
		Yes	31 January	31 January 2007
	Yes	No	30 September	30 September 2006
		Yes	30 December	30 December 2006

If you file your return by internet, the software will immediately work out and tell you how much tax you owe. You cannot use the free HMRC software because it does not cover the CGT supplement, so you'll need to buy a commercial software package. The HMRC★ website lists suitable packages that are available.

If you get a short tax return

If your tax affairs are fairly straightforward, you might be sent a short four-page tax return instead of the full return. The HMRC chooses whether to send you the short return based on your previous years' history, but it is up to you to check that the short return is suitable given your current tax situation and to get a full return if not.

You can still use the short return if you have made some capital gains and have tax to pay on them. But there is no place on the short return to report the gains. Instead you need to contact the HMRC Orderline★ for form R40(CG) which you then send back with the short return.

The final deadline for returning the short return is 31 January following the end of the tax year, but the HMRC encourages you to send it back by 30 September. The short return cannot be filed online. If you want to file online, you'll need to complete a full return instead.

If you don't get a tax return

You must tell your tax office about any taxable capital gains by 5 October following the end of the tax year in which you made the gains. Your tax office will normally then send you a full tax return to complete and this must be filed either by the normal 31 January deadline or within three months if you receive the return after 31 October.

If you have no tax to pay, there is no need to report any disposals to your tax office.

Keeping records

You are required to keep a record of any information needed to calculate your tax bill. The information may be original documents or copies and, by law, must be kept for one year following the date on which you filed your tax return with your tax office. Your tax office can ask to see these documents.

It is prudent to hold on to your records for longer than this, because, if you discover an error, you can go back up to five years from 31 January following the year of assessment to claim back tax overpaid.

Moreover, during the same period, the HMRC can open a 'discovery assessment' if it thinks your tax return did not contain all the information your tax office required to be sure that the correct tax assessment could be made. Following a tax case in 2004 (Langham v Veltema), this may apply if your return includes a valuation which will usually be the case where you are declaring a gift rather than the sale of an asset. Just including the valuation is not enough. To minimise the likelihood of a discovery assessment, you should use one of the additional information boxes on your return to give details of the valuation, including who carried it out, a statement that the valuer was independent and suitably qualified (if that was the case), and the basis on which the valuation was carried out. See the HMRC* website for more guidance.

The rules about keeping documents are different for businesses. If you are self-employed or a partner, you must keep any records relating to business gifts for five years from 31 January following the end of the tax year to which they relate. For information about the tax treatment of gains on gifts made by companies and the record-keeping requirements, talk to your accountant.

EXAMPLE 3.16

Unexpectedly, Emily does not receive a tax return for the 2005–6 tax year. However, she knows that she has some capital gains tax to pay. She must tell her tax office by 5 October 2006, so that it can send her a tax return to complete. Emily or her accountant should calculate the amount of CGT due and ensure that it is paid by 31 January 2007. Alternatively, Emily can ask her tax office to work out the tax bill but if the return reaches the office after 30 September 2006 it cannot guarantee to let Emily know the amount of CGT due in time for the 31 January 2007 payment date. To avoid any fine, Emily should pay an estimated amount by 31 January 2007 even if she does not know the exact bill by then.

Chapter 4

Inheritance tax on lifetime gifts

A TAX NO-ONE PAYS?

'Do you have to pay any inheritance tax when you give me the house in Kent?' asked Marie.

'It's not really your business,' sighed Frank, 'though if they taught anything useful in colleges these days, you'd know that there's no inheritance tax on a gift from one person to another – it's a PET. I suppose you think that's a furry animal.'

'As it happens I do know about PETs,' retorted Marie, 'and there could be a tax bill – what's more I could end up having to pay it. So it is my business.'

For many years inheritance tax had a reputation as a tax that mainly concerned rich people and, because of the many exemptions and loopholes, was a largely voluntary tax at that. When the Labour government came to power in 1997, it was widely thought that the lenient system would be overhauled and the days of exemptions such as the much loved PET (potentially exempt transfer) were numbered. In the event, the inheritance tax system itself has continued largely unchanged and received no mention at all in the Labour's 2005 election manifesto. However, much lifetime tax planning has been scotched by the introduction of the new pre-owned assets tax described in Chapter 5.

Chapter 2 listed the many exemptions from IHT for gifts you make during your lifetime. There are, however two types of gift that could result in an IHT bill during the giver's lifetime:

- gifts to or from a company
- gifts to a 'discretionary trust' (see Chapter 7).

Gifts from one person to another, which counted as PETs when they were made (see page 69) can also cause an IHT bill if the person making the gift dies within seven years. You must also be careful if you make 'gifts with reservation' – that is, giving away something from which you continue to benefit (page 74) – or make a series of transactions that could be construed as 'associated operations' (page 79).

Gifts which are taxable when they are made

The scope of inheritance tax

The forerunner of IHT was called capital transfer tax (CTT). The two taxes were virtually the same, with one very important difference: CTT applied to virtually *all* gifts, whereas under the IHT system, gifts between *individuals* (and certain types of trust) count as PETs. These are tax-free as long as the giver survives for seven years after making the gift. However, even under the present system, some gifts – that is, those which are *not* between individuals (and certain trusts) – can prompt an immediate tax bill. In tax language, such gifts are called 'chargeable transfers' and they comprise mainly gifts involving companies and gifts to discretionary trusts. In this book, chargeable transfers are also referred to as 'chargeable gifts'.

How a chargeable transfer is taxed

IHT does not apply to each gift you make in isolation. It is based on all the chargeable transfers you have made over the last seven years. Adding all these gifts together gives you a 'cumulative total' – called your 'running total' in this book. The first slice of the running total – up to £275,000 for the 2005–6 tax year – is tax-free. You pay tax only on gifts which take you above that limit. The tax-free slice is normally increased each tax year broadly in line with price inflation but the changes have sometimes been more erratic. Exceptionally, the tax free slice for the next couple of years has already been announced (but could be subject to further change). Table 4.1 shows the amounts for recent years.

The IHT rate on lifetime gifts is set with reference to the rate of tax which may apply to your estate when you die (see Chapter 11). The death rate for the 2005–6 tax year is 40 per cent; the lifetime rate is half this, in other words 20 per cent.

Table 4.1 Rates of inheritance tax

| Tax year | Tax-free slice | Rate of tax on running total in excess of the tax-free slice | |
		Death rate	Lifetime rate
1998–9	£223,000	40%	20%
1999–2000	£231,000	40%	20%
2000–1	£234,000	40%	20%
2001–2	£242,000	40%	20%
2002–3	£250,000	40%	20%
2003–4	£255,000	40%	20%
2004–5	£263,000	40%	20%
2005–6	£275,000	40%	20%
2006–7	£285,000	40%	20%
2007–8	£300,000	40%	20%

Tax due on a lifetime gift can be paid either by the person (or trust or company) making the gift or by the person (or trust or company) receiving the gift. If the person making the gift pays, the tax itself counts as part of the gift, which increases the value of the transfer to be taxed. A gift where the giver pays the tax is called a 'net gift'; if the recipient pays the tax, it is called a 'gross gift'. You can work out how much tax is due on a net or gross gift using the calculators below and overleaf.

CALCULATOR FOR INHERITANCE TAX ON A NET GIFT 2005–6

A What is your running total before making the gift (including any tax paid by you)?

B Work out the tax due on your running total:
If **A** is £275,000 or less, the tax due is 0.
If **A** is more than £275,000, the tax due is 20% × [**A** – £275,000].

C Subtract **B** from **A**. This gives you your net running total.

D Enter value of gift – use the amount the recipient will receive.

E Add **C** and **D**. This gives you your new net running total.

F Work out the tax due on your new running total:
If **E** is £275,000 or less, the tax is 0.
If **E** is more than £275,000, the tax due is 25% × [**E** – £275,000].

G Subtract **B** from **F**. This is the amount of tax (to be paid by the giver) on the current gift.

CALCULATOR FOR INHERITANCE TAX ON A GROSS GIFT 2005–6

A What is your running total before making the gift (including any tax paid by you)?

B Work out the tax due on your running total:
If **A** is £275,000 or less, the tax due is 0.
If **A** is more than £275,000, the tax due is 20% × [**A** – £275,000].

C Enter the current gift – use the amount you are giving.

D Find your new running total by adding **C** and **A**.

E Work out the tax due on your new running total:
If **D** is £275,000 or less, the tax due is 0.
If **D** is more than £275,000, the tax due is 20% × [**D** – £275,000].

F Subtract **B** from **E**. This is the amount of tax (to be paid by the recipient) on the current gift.

EXAMPLE 4.1

Frederick has a grown-up daughter, Louise, who has a learning disability. She lives largely independently and has a modest income from a job in a supermarket but she would not be able to cope with large sums of money or complicated planning for the future.

Frederick wants to make sure that Louise will always be financially secure and to provide a 'last resort' emergency fund which would also be available to his son Colin if the need arose. Frederick decides to set up a discretionary trust for the benefit of his children, making himself and his sister the trustees who will decide when Louise or Colin need help and how much help they should receive. (For more about discretionary trusts, see Chapter 7.)

Frederick sets up the trust in October 2005 with a gift of £70,000. He will pay any tax due on this, so it is a net gift. As Frederick has not used any of his annual exemption of £3,000 for 2005–6 (see page 29), only £67,000 counts as a chargeable transfer. Over the seven years from November 1998 to October 2005, he has made other chargeable transfers of £220,000. He uses the calculator for net gifts (see page 65) to work out his inheritance tax position as follows:

A	Frederick's running total before making the gift (including any tax paid by him)	£220,000
B	Tax due on his running total: If **A** is £275,000 or less, the tax due is 0 If **A** is more than £275,000, the tax due is 20% × [**A** − £275,000]	£0
C	Subtract **B** from **A**. This gives you Frederick's net running total	£220,000
D	Enter value of gift – the amount the trust will receive	£67,000
E	Add **C** and **D**. This gives Frederick's new net running total	£287,000
F	Tax due on his new running total: If **E** is £275,000 or less, the tax is 0 If **E** is more than £275,000, the tax due is 25% × [**E** − £275,000] (i.e. $\frac{1}{4}$ × £12,000)	£3,000
G	Subtract **B** from **F**. This is the amount of tax (to be paid by Frederick) on the gift to the trust.	£3,000

Frederick's gift to the trust is made up of the £70,000 plus £3,000 he pays in tax – £73,000 in total.

EXAMPLE 4.2

Suppose, in Example 4.1 above, that Frederick decided to pay £70,000 into the trust, but to leave the trust to pay any tax. In this case, the chargeable transfer of £67,000 would be a *gross* gift. Using the calculator for gross gifts (see opposite), the inheritance tax position would be:

A Frederick's running total before making the gift (including any tax paid by him)	£220,000
B Tax due on his running total: If **A** is £275,000 or less, the tax due is 0. If **A** is more than £275,000, the tax due is 20% × [**A** – £275,000]	£0
C Enter the current gift – the amount Frederick is giving	£67,000
D Frederick's new running total is found by adding **C** and **A**	£287,000
E Tax due on his new running total: If **D** is £275,000 or less, the tax due is 0. If **D** is more than £275,000, the tax due is 20% × [**D** – £275,000]. (i.e. 20% × £12,000)	£2,400
F Subtract **B** from **E**. This is the amount of tax (to be paid by the trust) on the gift to the trust.	£2,400

The trust would receive £70,000 but £2,400 would have to be used to pay the IHT bill due on the transfer leaving £67,600 in the trust fund.

Death within seven years

Tax on a lifetime gift which is a chargeable transfer is usually charged at a rate of 20 per cent (in 2005–6). But, if the person making the gift dies within three years, the gift is reassessed and tax is charged at the full death rate current at the time of death (i.e. 40 per cent for 2005–6). If the giver dies more than three years but less than seven years after making the gift, the gift is still reassessed for tax but at less than the full death rate due to the effect of IHT taper relief. Table 4.2 shows the rates which would apply.

The extra tax due will be charged to the person who received the gift but, if they cannot or will not pay, the giver's estate must pay the bill.

Table 4.2 New tax rate if giver dies within seven years of making a gift

Years between gift and death	% of full death rate which applies	% rate of tax on the gift (at 2005–6 rates)
Up to 3	100	40
More than 3 and up to 4	80	32
More than 4 and up to 5	60	24
More than 5 and up to 6	40	16
More than 6 and up to 7	20	8
More than 7	0	no extra tax

At first sight, you might assume that there will never be any extra tax to pay if the giver dies more than five years after making the chargeable transfer, since the rate of tax which would then apply (16 per cent assuming 2005–6 rates) is lower than the 20 per cent rate at which tax is paid on lifetime gifts. However, the position is not so simple: in reassessing the gift, it is looked at in relation to the running total at the time the gift was made; since PETs may also be reassessed (see below) when the giver dies, a PET made within the seven-year period but before the chargeable transfer being considered would increase the running total. Also, bear in mind that the original tax on the gift was charged at the tax-free slice and rates applicable at the time of the gift, whereas tax due on reassessment is charged at the tax-free slice and rates applicable at the time of death – and a change in rates may result in extra tax becoming due. Equally, a relaxation in IHT rates may seem to imply a reduction in the tax bill, but none of the tax paid at the time the gift was made is refundable – see Example 4.3 on page 71. For a summary of tax-free slices and tax rates applicable in earlier years, see Table 4.1 on page 65.

Potentially exempt transfers (PETs)

Most of the gifts that you make during your lifetime are free of IHT. Even if they are not covered by one of the specific exemptions outlined in Chapter 2, they will count as potentially exempt transfers (PETs). As the name suggests, these gifts are exempt but with a proviso: the giver must survive for seven years after making the gift. The purpose of this rule is to prevent people escaping tax on their estates by giving away their possessions shortly before death.

If the giver does die within seven years of making a gift, the gift loses its exempt status and is reassessed as a chargeable gift. This has two effects, which are quite separate though unfortunately often confused:

- first, because the PET is now treated as chargeable, the taxman steps back in time and asks: at the time this gift was made, given that we now know it is chargeable, should any tax have been paid? What happens if the answer is 'yes' is described under 'How the PET is taxed' below
- second, because the PET has become a chargeable gift, it enters into your running total, which may mean that extra tax becomes due on subsequent chargeable gifts, later PETs being reassessed and the estate left at the time of death – see Example 4.3 opposite.

How the PET is taxed

If the giver dies within seven years, the PET is treated as if it had originally been a chargeable transfer. Of course, this does not necessarily mean tax is due, because:

- in the tax year you made the gift, you might not have used your yearly £3,000 tax-free exemption (see page 29). And, if you had not used the exemption in the previous year either, you might have the scope to give up to £6,000 in that tax year in chargeable gifts without having any tax to pay
- as with any other gift which might be taxable, it is not looked at in isolation. It is included in your running total over the seven years up to the date of the gift in question. Only if the running total exceeds the relevant tax-free slice will any tax become due. In the case of a reassessed PET, the relevant tax-free slice is the amount in force at the time of death (not at the time the gift was made) – i.e. £275,000 if the giver died in the 2005–6 tax year.

It is important to note that PETs up to seven years before death are reassessed and gifts in the seven years up to the making of the PET are looked at in deciding whether tax is due. This means that gifts made during the 14 years before death could be relevant.

If the running total up to the making of the reassessed PET does come to more than the tax-free slice at the time of death, then IHT is due at the rates current at the time of death – i.e. 40 per cent in 2005–6.

However, if the giver died more than three years after making the gift, the amount of tax payable is reduced by the effect of IHT taper relief. Table 4.3 shows the effect of this relief.

Table 4.3 How IHT taper relief reduces tax on a reassessed PET

Years between making the PET and death	% of full death rate which applies	Effective % rate of tax on the gift (at 2005–6 rates)
Up to 3	100	40
More than 3 and up to 4	80	32
More than 4 and up to 5	60	24
More than 5 and up to 6	40	16
More than 6 and up to 7	20	8
More than 7	0	no tax

Bear in mind that taper relief only reduces any tax due on the reassessed PET. If there is no tax payable on the PET (for example, because the running total including the PET is less than the tax-free slice), then taper relief has no relevance. And taper relief cannot be used to reduce tax on the estate of the deceased giver, even if that tax bill was created or increased because of the inclusion of the reassessed PET in the running total up to the time of death.

Who pays the tax?

Any tax which becomes due on a reassessed PET is first charged to the person who received the gift. If he or she cannot or will not pay, the late giver's estate must pay the bill. It is possible to take out insurance to cover the potential tax bill on a PET (see page 206).

EXAMPLE 4.3

Godfrey dies on 1 January 2006 leaving an estate of £250,000. He made the following gifts during his lifetime (assuming the annual tax-free exemptions have already been used in each case):

| 1 January 1996 | Chargeable transfer | £100,000 paid into a discretionary trust |
| 1 January 1998 | Chargeable transfer | £70,000 paid into a discretionary trust |

1 February 1999	Chargeable transfer	£68,000 paid into a discretionary trust
1 June 2001	PET	£80,000 given to nephew, John

On his death, chargeable transfers and PETs made within the seven years before death – i.e. in the period 2 January 1999 to 1 January 2006 – are reassessed as follows:

- **chargeable transfer made on 1 February 1999.** Tax was originally paid in 1998–9 on a running total of £100,000 + £70,000 + £68,000 = £238,000. The tax-free slice then was £223,000 (see Table 4.1) and the trust paid tax at 20 per cent on the £15,000 of the February 1999 gift which exceeded that slice – i.e. tax of 20 per cent × £15,000 = £3,000. When the gift is reassessed on Godfrey's death, there is no tax to be paid because the running total of £238,000 is less than the tax-free slice in force at the time of death – i.e. £275,000. However, no refund is allowed of the tax already paid in Godfrey's lifetime

- **PET made on 1 June 2001.** No tax was charged on the PET at the time it was made. When it is reviewed on Godfrey's death, the PET becomes the top slice of £80,000 on a running total of £100,000 + £70,000 + £68,000 + £80,000 = £318,000. Earlier gifts have used up £238,000 of the tax-free slice of £275,000. £37,000 of the PET exhausts the remaining tax-free slice. This leaves £43,000 to be taxed at the death rate of 40 per cent. So tax is initially calculated as 40% × £43,000 = £17,200. However, taper relief applies because the PET was more than three years before Godfrey's death. Only 60 per cent of the tax is payable – i.e. 60% × £17,200 = £10,320.

Although more properly the subject of Chapter 11, it is worth noting here what impact the reassessed chargeable transfers and PETs have on tax on the estate. The estate counts as the top slice of £250,000 on a running total of £68,000 + £80,000 + £250,000 = £398,000. The earlier gifts use up £148,000 of the £275,000 tax-free slice. And £127,000 of the estate uses up the remaining part of the tax-free slice. This leaves £123,000 of the estate to be taxed at 40 per cent – i.e. 40% × £123,000 = £49,200. Note that taper relief is not relevant to this tax bill which is payable in full – by the estate, unless the will specifies otherwise.

Fall in value

There is some tax relief if the value of a reassessed PET or chargeable transfer has fallen since the time it was first made. Whoever is paying the tax is allowed to deduct the fall in value from the original value of the gift. Bear in mind, however, that the original value of a gift was the loss to the giver not the value to the recipient, so even a large percentage fall in the value of the item in the recipient's hands might have only a small impact on the value of the item for IHT purposes (see Example 4.4). The fall-in-value relief is not given automatically; the person paying the tax must make a claim to the Capital Taxes Office.*

EXAMPLE 4.4

In September 2003, Dorothy gave her niece, Charlotte, one of a pair of rare antique vases. As a pair, the vases had a market price of £110,000 but individually they were each worth only £40,000. The value of the gift was the loss to Dorothy. In other words, the difference between the market price of the pair and the price of the remaining vase: £110,000 – £40,000 = £70,000. The gift counted as a PET and so there was no tax to pay.

In February 2006, Dorothy dies and Charlotte receives a demand for tax on the gift of the vase. She has the vase valued by a local dealer who puts a market price of only £35,000 on the vase now. Charlotte agrees to the reduced value of the gift which is worked out as the original loss to the giver less the fall in value: £70,000 – £5,000 = £65,000.

Tax now due on the gift is calculated as follows. Just before she made the gift to Charlotte, in September 2003, Dorothy's cumulative total of gifts, including other PETs that have become chargeable since her death, came to £213,000. Adding the value of the vase brings the total to £213,000 + £65,000 = £278,000. This is £3,000 more than the 2005–6 tax-free slice of £275,000, so IHT is payable at 40% × £3,000 = £1,200. As fewer than three years have passed since Dorothy made the gift, taper relief does not apply.

Protection from IHT on a PET

Life insurance can be used to protect the person receiving a PET from a possible IHT bill (see page 206 for how this would work). The insurance could be taken out by the person making a PET, in which case the insurance would itself count as a gift but might qualify for one of the IHT exemptions (see Chapter 2). Another option would be for the person receiving the PET to pay premiums him or herself for a term insurance policy based on the life of the giver.

Life insurance can also be used in just the same way to protect the recipient of a gift that counts as a chargeable transfer from the possibility of an extra tax bill, should the giver die within seven years.

For more information, seek advice from an insurance broker* or an independent financial adviser.*

Gifts with reservation

What is a gift with reservation?

Problems can arise if you give something away but continue to benefit from it in some way. A 'gift with reservation' occurs in the following circumstances:

- if the person to whom you give the gift does not really take possession of it: for example, you might give a valuable painting to someone but carry on hanging it in your home
- if you carry on deriving some benefit from the thing you give away unless you pay a full market rate – or the equivalent in kind – for your use of the asset. This might occur, for example, if you give your home to your children but you retain the right to live in part of the property rent-free. (See Chapter 14 for more about this.)

In most cases, special inheritance tax rules apply to gifts like these. See page 76 for gifts which are not affected.

A gift might not be a gift with reservation at the time you make it, but can become a gift with reservation later on if you subsequently start to use it or benefit from it – see Example 4.5.

EXAMPLE 4.5

Mburu gives his niece a painting that continues to hang in his house but pays his niece a full commercial rent for the use of the picture which takes it outside the gift with reservation rules (see page 77). But the rent is not reviewed and, after five years, it ceases to be a commercial amount. At that stage, the gift becomes a gift with reservation and the painting once more forms part of Mburu's estate for inheritance tax purposes.

How a gift with reservation is taxed

Unless the gift counts as a chargeable transfer, there is no IHT to pay when the gift with reservation is made but there may be later on. The special rules come into operation at the time the person who made the gift dies. If, at the time of death, the giver still benefited from the gift with reservation, the possessions they gave are treated as if they are still part of the giver's estate and were given away only at the time of death (see Chapter 11).

If the giver stopped benefiting from the possessions some time before his or her death, the gift with reservation is treated as a PET made at the time the giver's benefit stopped. Provided that this was more than seven years before death, IHT will not apply. On the other hand, if that time was within the seven years before the giver's death, the normal PET rules apply and there may be an IHT bill on the gift. But, in the event that the giver had unused yearly exemption for the year in which the gift stopped being a gift with reservation, it is the HMRC's (controversial) view that the exemption cannot be set against this PET.

If the gift with reservation counted as a chargeable transfer, IHT may have been paid when the gift was made – this would apply, say, to a gift you made to a discretionary trust. The special rules still apply when the giver dies but other rules prevent IHT being payable twice over on the same gift. For example, suppose you give £10,000 to a discretionary trust designed to benefit your whole family, including yourself. Because you are a beneficiary of the trust, you are still able to benefit from the £10,000, so it counts as a gift with reservation. As a gift to a discretionary trust, it is a chargeable transfer on which IHT may be payable. But, if you continue to be a beneficiary of the trust right up to the time you die, the £10,000 will continue to be deemed as part of your estate and treated as if it was given outright to the trust only on the date of your death. At that time, the gift may again give rise to an IHT bill but special rules give relief against the double charge (though not against other tax charges relating to the trust, see Chapter 8).

Gifts outside the gift-with-reservation rules

Gifts made a long-time ago

The gift with reservation rules do not apply to any gifts made before 18 March 1986, the date on which the rules were introduced.

Gifts which are exempt from inheritance tax

If the gift is covered by certain of the exemptions outlined in Chapter 2 at the time the gift is made, the gift with reservation rules do not apply. The exemptions are:

- gifts between husband and wife, and from 5 December 2005 onwards gifts between civil partners (but see below)
- gifts to charities and certain other bodies
- gifts of national heritage property
- gifts to political parties
- gifts to housing associations
- small gifts (up to £250 per person)
- wedding gifts.

Note that the above list does not include all types of exempt lifetime gift. In particular, the gift with reservation rules can apply even though a gift is exempt at the time it is made because it is 'normal expenditure out or income' or covered by the £3,000 yearly exemption.

For gifts made from 20 June 2003 onwards, the law was changed so that the gift with reservation rules do apply to gifts between husbands and wives or gifts between civil partners in the following circumstances:

- the gifted asset(s) are put into a trust giving your spouse or civil partner an interest in possession
- the interest in possession later ends before the giver's death, and
- the spouse or partner then neither becomes the outright owner of the property nor gets a further interest in possession in it.

These 2003 rules were introduced specifically to stop complex tax avoidance arrangements known as 'Eversden schemes'. For general information about trusts and what an 'interest in possession' is, see Chapter 7.

Gifts that benefit your spouse or civil partner

There is no gift with reservation if your husband, wife or civil partner rather than you uses or benefits from the item you give away. But you must take care to ensure that there is no way in which you could be construed as potentially benefiting – for example, if it is a gift of money, it should not be paid into an account which your spouse or civil partner holds jointly with you.

Gifts you pay to use

A gift of land or chattels (possessions, including antiques, paintings, books, and so on) is not a gift with reservation if you continue to use or benefit from it but pay the full market rent for doing so. For example, you might give a son or daughter a piece of furniture but continue to keep it at your home. If you pay to insure it and pay your child an appropriate rent based on an independent, professional valuation of the item, you should normally be outside the gift with reservation rules. A gift can also be outside the rules if you give full payment in kind for any benefit you retain.

Gifts you share without benefiting by more than your share

Without triggering the gift with reservation rules, you are allowed to give away part of land or property – for example, part of your home – and share it with the co-owner(s) provided you do not benefit in any way from the share you've given away – for example, you would have to bear your full share of the bills. See Chapter 14 for more information.

Gifts that are separated from the part you keep

If you can carve up a possession which you intend to give away so that you can keep a distinct part of it that forms a separate asset in its own right (a process called 'shearing'), you can give away the remainder without the part you retain counting as a gift with reservation – see Example 4.6.

However, these days you will be caught by the gift with reservation rules if you apply shearing to gifts of land or property by, for example, splitting your ownership into a lease that you keep and a freehold that you sell (called a lease-carve-out or 'Ingram scheme'), because of anti-avoidance rules that came into effect in 1999. Ingram schemes set up before 9 March 1999 continue successfully to fall outside the gift with reservation rules.

EXAMPLE 4.6

Sybil invests a lump sum in a school fees plan designed to pay fees for her grandson, Harry. The arrangement allows for the policy to return a lump sum to Sybil if Harry were to die before finishing his education at the school. The payment of school fees is the gift from Sybil to Harry and the right to the refund is not deemed to be part of the gift, so there is no gift with reservation.

Reservation of benefit due to infirmity

The gift with reservation rules will not apply if the benefit or use you derive from land you gave away has arisen because of unforeseen changes which mean you can no longer take care of yourself because of old age, illness or disability. This could apply if, say, you give the family home to your children and you move out – perhaps to somewhere smaller and more manageable. If later, you have to move in with the children so that they can care for you, this will not trigger the gift with reservation rules. For the exception to apply the person who receives the gift must be a relative of the giver or the giver's husband, wife or civil partner.

The tracing rules

In general you cannot get around the gift with reservation rules simply by swapping the gift for something else, because special rules enable the HMRC to trace the passage of the gift. For example, if you give your son a house, he sells the house, buys another and lets you live in the new property, there is still a gift with reservation.

The tracing rules do not apply to outright gifts of cash, but this does not mean you can escape the gift with reservation regime. For example, suppose you give your son a lump sum which later he uses to buy a holiday home that you also use. The HMRC cannot use the tracing rules to track the conversion of the cash into a property that you use. But the HMRC could instead challenge you under the associated operations rules (see opposite) to establish that there is a gift with reservation.

Gifts with reservation and the pre-owned assets tax

If you use or benefit from something you have given away and you have managed to arrange it in a way that escapes the gift with reservation rules do not congratulate yourself too soon. From 6 April 2005 onwards, you might have to pay the pre-owned assets tax which can apply to things you gave away as long ago as 1986, the year when the gift with reservation rules were introduced. See Chapter 5 for details.

Gift with reservation rules and capital gains tax

The gift with reservation rules have no impact at all on CGT. For CGT purposes, your gift is effective at the time you make it regardless of whether it counts as a gift with reservation for inheritance tax purposes.

This means that the gifted asset is not part of your estate at death for CGT purposes, so the exemption from CGT at death is not relevant. Any increase in the value of the asset between the time you make the gift and the time you die is a capital gain built up in the hands of the recipient on which tax may become due when the recipient eventually disposes of the asset.

Associated operations

You might be tempted to side-step the inheritance tax rules by making a series of transactions – for example, splitting one gift into several or cascading the gifted asset through various different types of trust – but in most cases this will not work. The HMRC can decide the transactions are 'associated operations' and treat them all as is they form a single direct gift made on the date of the last transaction.

For example, if you wanted to give your son or daughter a pair of tables together valued at £7,000 but individually valued at £3,000, you might imagine you could give one table in 2005–6 (a gift worth £7,000 – £3,000 = £4,000) and the second in 2006–7 (a gift worth £3,000) covering each gift with your yearly tax-free exemption (assuming carried forward exemption was also available from 2004–5 to cover the first gift). But HMRC could count this as a single gift worth £7,000 made in 2006–7.

The associated operations rules have effectively stopped some complex arrangements that tried to use a series of devices to circumvent the gift with reservation rules.

Giving away the family business

If you pass on your business or farm during your lifetime, you may qualify for relief against IHT on the value of the transfer. Basic details of the schemes are given in Chapter 11, which looks at passing on your business or farm in your will. The application of the scheme is broadly the same in the case of lifetime gifts, with one important exception, outlined below.

Whether your gift of business or agricultural property counts as a PET or as a chargeable transfer, the relief will be clawed back, if:

- you die within seven years of making the gift, and
- the recipient no longer owns the business or farm, and
- the recipient does not fully reinvest the proceeds in – in the case of business property relief – a new business, or – in the case of agricultural property relief – a new farm.

Relief will also be clawed back if the recipient dies before you and no longer owns the business or farm.

In view of this clawback, it is extremely important that you plan carefully and that you take expert advice from your accountant★ and a solicitor,★ before making a gift of part or all of your business or farm.

Telling the taxman

You do not have to tell the tax authorities about any lifetime gifts you make which count as PETs but you should keep a record of them. Put a copy of the record where it would be found by whoever would handle your estate if you were to die – for example, in the same place as your will. It would be the responsibility of that person to pass these details on to the Capital Taxes Office so that PETs could be reassessed.

If you make gifts which count as chargeable transfers – i.e. gifts to discretionary trusts or involving companies – you do not need to tell the tax office, provided:

- your total chargeable transfers during the year come to no more than £10,000, and
- your running total of gifts during the last ten years – probably the government intended to reduce this to seven years but so far the change has been overlooked – comes to no more than £40,000.

If you have made a chargeable transfer that should be reported, you need to complete **form IHT100,** which is available from the Capital Taxes Office.★ Normally, you must send in the completed form within 12 months of the end of the month in which you made the gift but tax will usually have to be paid before this.

In the case of lifetime chargeable gifts, IHT is normally due to be paid six months after the end of the month in which the gift was made. But, if the gift was made in the period 6 April to 30 September inclusive, tax is due on 30 April of the following year.

Should extra tax become payable on a chargeable gift, or should the PET become chargeable because of the death of the giver within seven years of making the gift, the tax is due six months after the end of the month in which the death occurs. In some limited cases, it may be possible to pay the tax in ten equal yearly instalments.

Chapter 5
Pre-owned assets tax

ONE FOR THE POAT

'I've been looking at these equity release schemes,' sighed Molly. 'But they all seem such poor value. I have to sell a huge chunk of my home to get not much in return.'

'Why not sell to me?' suggested her grandson, Dan. 'You know I'm doing really well these days and I could easily afford it. In fact, it would be a good investment for me – and I could give you a much better deal.'

'I did mention that as an idea to the financial adviser,' replied Molly. 'But he said I'd have to pay some new income tax charge – pre-owned something or other.'

When it comes to inheritance tax planning, an ideal situation would be to give away something so that it no longer formed part of your estate for tax but still carrying on using the thing as if you hadn't given it away at all. In general law, you can do this – ownership can be legally transferred to someone else – but for inheritance tax purposes such a gift is not normally effective because of the gift with reservation rules (see page 74).

However, tax advisers are clever people and, over the years, a variety of schemes grew up which got around the gift with reservation rules. Two – Ingram schemes and Eversden schemes – were briefly mentioned in the last chapter. For many years, these and other avoidance schemes were typically used only by people with fairly substantial wealth. But, as rising house prices during the 1990s and early 2000s brought many 'ordinary' people potentially into the inheritance tax net, some schemes started to be marketed more widely.

The HMRC had for many years countered each scheme as it arose with challenges in the courts and changes to the law. But generally each HMRC success in stopping future use of a scheme left a trail of successful tax avoiders who had bolted before the stable door was closed. The HMRC decided on a new tack and introduced the pre-owned assets tax (POAT or sometimes abbreviated to POT).

A tax with a past

POAT is an extremely unusual tax for two reasons:

- it is an income tax being used to plug the holes in a completely different tax, namely inheritance tax
- it is 'retroactive'. The government points out that POAT does not go back and reassess you for tax for previous years and, on that basis, insists that this is not a 'retrospective' tax. But the point is debatable. New tax measures normally apply only to actions taken on or after the date the measures come into effect. By contrast, POAT imposes a tax charge now on actions you took in the past.

The government has also warned that it is prepared to make further use of retroactive legislation so that actions you take now that success-fully save tax cease to be effective once the law is changed. This means that the scope for lifetime inheritance tax planning is now severely restricted because any scheme which is successful in saving inheri-tance tax on your estate is likely to draw the HMRC's attention and may result in some other compensating tax charge.

Who has to pay POAT?

POAT is an income tax on the benefits received by a former owner of an asset. 'Benefit' includes, for example, occupying land, using the asset or receiving income from it. Three types of assets are affected: land (meaning buildings as well as just land), possessions (which the HMRC calls 'chattels', covering for example furniture, paintings, jewellery, books) and intangible assets (see the Box opposite). In the case of land or possessions, POAT may affect you if you are able to use or benefit from:

- an asset you have disposed of at any time after 17 March 1986 (called the 'disposal condition'), or

- an asset owned by someone to whom you have given money within the last seven years in order to directly or indirectly fund their acquiring the asset (called the 'contribution condition'). You are not treated as having made any contribution if you only acted as guarantor for a loan taken out by the person.

Although POAT was introduced to tackle problems with inheritance tax avoidance, the scope of POAT is much wider because it can apply to other types of disposal, not just gifts. However there are a number of exemptions as set out in Table 5.1 overleaf.

In addition, POAT does not apply if the person who made the gift and receives the benefit is not resident in the UK. If you are resident in the UK but your domicile (the place you consider to be your permanent home) is elsewhere, POAT can apply only to assets you have in the UK not elsewhere in the world.

'INTANGIBLE ASSETS'

You may also be caught by POAT if you put 'intangible assets' – for example, cash, shares, insurance policies, other investments – into a trust and, under the income tax anti-avoidance settlement rules, income from the trust is taxed as if it were your own (see page 96) or would be if there were any income. For the purpose of POAT, 'trust' does not include a bare trust (see page 118) and you are not caught if any benefit is enjoyed by your husband, wife or civil partner, but not you.

EXAMPLE 5.1

Jack and Angela sold the family home to their daughter, Lizzie and her husband, at a knock-down price and bought themselves a bungalow. After Jack died, Angela's health deteriorated and now she can no longer cope on her own. She moves back into the family home so that Lizzie can look after her. Although Angela is now using the home she sold at less than its full value, this is caught by neither the inheritance tax gift with reservation rules nor POAT because the reason for her use was unforeseen and due to her old age and ill health.

Table 5.1 Transactions to which POAT does not apply

Transactions involving land, possessions or intangible assets

- The yearly benefit you get from all your transactions caught by POAT, before deducting anything you pay the owner(s), comes to no more than £5,000. (If it exceeds £5,000, the whole amount not just the excess is taxable.) See Example 5.3 on page 90.
- Where the assets are still part of the giver's estate for inheritance tax purposes.
- A gift caught by the inheritance tax gift with reservation rules (see page 74).
- A gift where you have opted to be treated as if the gift with reservation rules apply – see page 88.
- Where legislation specifically allows the gift to be exempt from the gift with reservation rules because it is exempt from inheritance tax (see list on page 76), you pay full market rent for your benefit (see page 77), or you share the asset and benefit no more than your fair share (see page 77).

Transactions involving land or possessions

- Disposal of the whole of the asset at arm's length to someone not connected to you[1] or, if to someone who is connected to you, on arm's length terms. You can however retain rights for yourself if they can be carved out as a separate asset in the same way as applies under the gift with reservation rules (see page 77).
- Disposal of part of the asset at arm's length to someone not connected with you.[1] This exempts, for example, an equity release scheme where you sell part of your home to a commercial company.
- Disposal of part of the asset to someone who is connected with you[1] on arm's length terms provided the transaction took place before 7 March 2005. This exemption could cover an informal equity release scheme where you had sold part of your home to a relative in return for cash or income.
- Disposal of part of the asset on arm's length terms on or after 7 March 2005 where the amount paid to you is not in cash or assets readily convertible to cash. This could cover a situation where you gave part of your home to someone who had moved in to be your carer in recognition of their caring services to you.
- Transfer to your husband, wife or civil partner or to a trust giving them an interest in possession (see page 111) for life.
- Transfer under a court order to a former husband, wife or civil partner or to a trust giving them an interest in possession (see page 111) for life.
- Where the reason for the disposal is the maintenance of your family.
- Where the disposal is an outright gift covered by the inheritance tax yearly allowance (see page 29) or the small gifts exemption (see page 30).
- Outright cash gift used to buy land or possessions where gift made at least seven years before your use of or benefit from the asset started.
- Where your use of the land started only because you were no longer able to care for yourself because of old age or infirmity. See Example 5.1.

[1] For the purpose of POAT, a 'connected person' includes your husband, wife, civil partner, children, brother, sister, grandparent (and their parents, grandparents and so on), grandchild (and their children and so on down the line), uncles, aunts, nieces, nephews and trusts of which you are the settlor.

How POAT works

The benefit you are deemed to receive from an asset you have given away is added to your other income for the year and income tax is charged in the normal way. (POAT works in a very similar way to income tax on the value of fringe benefits that you receive through your job.) The benefit you are deemed to get depends on the type of asset concerned:

- **land**. The full market rent you would otherwise have to pay. If you benefit from only part of the property, the benefit is a proportion of the full market rent equal to the value of the part you benefit from divided by the value of the whole property. You can deduct any rent you actually pay to the owner

- **possessions (chattels)**. The market value of the asset multiplied by an official interest rate published by HMRC. The interest rate is changed from time to time but usually set for a year at a time and in 2005–6 was 5 per cent. For example, if the item was valued at £50,000, the yearly benefit would be 5% × £50,000 = £2,500. As with land, the benefit is scaled down if you use only part of the possession and you can deduct any amount you actually pay the owner for your use of the asset

- **intangible property**. The market value of the trust property multiplied by the official interest rate (5 per cent in 2005–6) less income tax or capital gains tax you already pay on the property under various tax rules. (This is a complex area. Contact any adviser who set up or helps you run the trust for further information.)

The value of an asset is generally the value it could be expected to fetch if sold on the open market (without any reduction that might occur because of putting the whole property on the market at one time). Assets must be valued on the first day of the tax year (6 April) or, in the case of a new transaction, the date the asset first came within the POAT regime. Land and possessions need be valued only once every five years with each valuation applying unchanged for the whole five year period. This means, where a valuation takes place at a time when asset prices are low, the POAT charge for the next five years is also low, but there could be a large jump at the next valuation if asset prices are then much higher.

Your options under POAT

If you have a transaction which is caught by POAT, you have four options:

- **pay the yearly POAT charge**. Bear in mind POAT is a charge on a benefit not actual income, so to pay POAT you will need to have actual income or other resources you can dip into
- **pay the full market rent to the owner of the asset for your use of it**. Again, you will need to have enough income or other resources to afford this option
- **unscramble the transaction so that it returns to your estate or becomes subject to the inheritance tax gift with reservation rules**. The relevant exemption in Table 5.1 will then apply and so no POAT will be due. However, inheritance tax may be due on the asset concerned when you die. Unscrambling will not necessarily be possible. Under the transaction legal ownership of the asset concerned has normally passed to someone else. They may be unwilling or unable to give the property back. In addition, unscrambling may incur costs and capital gains tax (CGT) charges
- **without unscrambling the transaction, opt to be treated as if the inheritance tax gift with reservation rules apply**. This means no POAT is payable but inheritance tax may be due on the asset when you die. Making this election affects only the inheritance tax position; for CGT purposes, you continue to have disposed of the asset on the date the transaction took place. Any increase in the value of the asset between the date of the transaction and the date of death accrues in the hands of the new owner and may be liable to CGT when they dispose of the asset. By contrast, if the asset had been part of your estate, any taxable gain would have been wiped out by the exemption from capital gains tax for assets given away on death. You have until 31 January following the end of the tax year in which you first became subject to POAT to make this election. If you miss this deadline, the opportunity to make the election is lost for good (apart from a few exceptional excuses that HMRC might accept as ground for a late election). Once the election is made and the deadline passed, the election becomes irreversible.

If the benefits you get from all the assets caught by POAT comes to no more than £5,000, the first exemption listed in Table 5.1 applies, so there will be no POAT to pay. In that case, you might decide to stay within the POAT regime, but consider how the value of the asset concerned might change in future. If it could have risen considerably by the next valuation, you may then have to start paying POAT.

Paying the owner a full market rent could be a good option if you can afford it and you would, in any case, like to pass on more of your wealth to the owner. For example, you might have given your home to your children under a scheme which got around the gift with reservation rules and you can now pass them a regular sum each year in the form of rent without any inheritance tax implications. However, the rent will count as taxable income in the hands of your children.

Coming back within the gift with reservation rules (either by unscrambling or election) would not cause an inheritance tax problem if your estate at death would in any case be less than the tax-free slice (£275,000 in 2005–6).

EXAMPLE 5.2

In 2000, Lily transferred her home to her son, Peter, using a 'double trust scheme'. Under the scheme, she sold her house, then worth £450,000, to a trust under which Lily has an interest in possession (see page 111) letting her live in the home for life. The trust did not give Lily cash for the sale but instead gave her an IOU. Lily gave the IOU to a second trust of which her son, Peter, is the only beneficiary. On her death, the trust will sell the home and pay off the IOU, thus passing the value of the home to Peter. Because of the interest in possession, the trust property will be part of Lily's estate for inheritance tax (see page 122) but this will comprise the value of the home at the time of death less the IOU, so there will be little or no inheritance tax due.

Although Lily sold her whole home to the trust, it was not an arm's length transaction to an unconnected person, so the scheme is caught by POAT. The full market rent for living in the home would be £1,000 a month, so Lily is taxed on a deemed benefit of £12,000 a year. If she is a basic rate taxpayer, this would mean a tax bill of 22% × £12,000 = £2,640 in 2005–6.

Lily cannot afford to pay this amount of extra tax each year, so she opts to be treated as if the gift with reservation rules apply to her continued occupation of the house. This means that the value of the home will count as part of her estate for inheritance tax purposes when she dies.

EXAMPLE 5.3

Molly, like many pensioners, is 'cash-poor, asset-rich'. She struggles to manage on her pensions but lives in a valuable home. She has been thinking about taking out a home reversion scheme, whereby she would sell part of her home to a company for a lump sum but retain the right to live in the home until she dies (or, if necessary, moves permanently into care).

Her grandson, Dan, suggests that instead of going to a reversion company, he could buy a share of her home and give her a better deal than a company. If Molly and Dan had made such an arrangement before 7 March 2005, there would have been no problem. But, from that date onwards, such arrangements are caught by POAT and Molly will become liable to tax each year on her benefit from living in the part of the home she sells to Dan if it exceeds the £5,000 threshold at which POAT becomes due. They work out if this will be the case.

Molly's home is worth £300,000. Dan is willing to pay her the full £150,000 for a half share. A local estate agent advises that the rent they could charge if they let out the home would be £450 a month. This comes to £5,400 a year and so Molly's benefit from using the half the home that was sold would be 50% × £5,400 = £2,700. This is less than the POAT threshold, so Dan and Molly decide to go ahead with the scheme.

Telling the taxman

You must declare any liability for POAT on your tax return. If you do not receive a tax return, tell your tax office* by 5 October following the end of the tax year in which the liability started and you will be sent a form.

If you want opt out of POAT by electing to be treated as if the gift with reservation rules apply, use form IHT500 available from HMRC* and send it in no later then 31 January following the year in which the liability to POAT starts. For example, if you are liable for POAT from 6 April 2005 onwards, you must make the election by 31 January 2007.

Chapter 6

Income tax and gifts

WHOSE TAX IS IT ANYWAY?
'I don't believe this,' Michael exploded, waving the tax assessment he had just opened. 'The Revenue have charged me income tax on Rebecca's savings account.'

Rebecca looked on quizzically. 'But you opened the account for me, Daddy. Isn't it mine any more?'

Apart from the relatively few occasions when the pre-owned assets tax applies (see Chapter 5), there is no income tax as such on a gift. However, making a gift can affect the income tax position of either giver, recipient or both. In the case of gifts to individuals (or trusts), the impact is not always welcome. But, where you make a gift to charity, you may qualify for tax relief. If you are aware of the types of gift that affect income tax, the pitfalls to watch out for and the reliefs available, you are then well placed to arrange your giving in the most tax-efficient way.

Gifts between husband and wife or civil partners

Independent taxation

An important date in the tax calendar was 6 April 1990, because, from the 1990–1 tax year onwards, 'independent taxation' was introduced. A married couple had up to then been treated as a single unit for tax purposes but now husband and wife are each treated as individuals responsible for their own tax. This means that:

- you are taxed on your own income, regardless of your spouse's income
- you claim your own tax allowances to set against your income
- you have your own tax-free slice for capital gains tax (CGT) purposes. (You also have your own inheritance tax – IHT – running total and exemptions, but this was the case even before independent taxation was introduced.)

Before independent taxation, it mattered little from an income tax point of view whether it was you or your husband or wife who owned the family assets – house, savings, chattels. It seems amazing in this age of equality that any income from such assets used always to be treated as that of the husband even if legally it belonged to the wife. Nowadays, the system is much fairer: your individual tax bills will take account of income from the assets that each of you in fact owns. This means that who owns what is important and rearranging the family assets – for example, through gifts between husband and wife – could reduce the income tax bill of the family as a whole. Bear in mind that there is no CGT or IHT to pay on gifts between husband and wife but the pattern in which you hold the family assets could affect IHT later on (see Chapter 13).

From 5 December 2005 onwards, same-sex couples who have registered their relationship as a civil partnership are treated in exactly the same way for tax as married couples.

EXAMPLE 6.1

In August 2005, Ray inherits a substantial portfolio of corporate bonds and government stocks from his late aunt. The portfolio produces a healthy income which Ray welcomes but he is dismayed at having to pay tax on it at his top rate of 40 per cent. His wife, Joyce, has no income or savings of her own, so it makes sense for Ray to give some of his investments to her. He transfers enough so that Joyce receives an investment income of around £4,895 – the amount of her unused personal allowance in 2005–6. No IHT or CGT is payable on the gift from Ray to Joyce.

Although some of the investments pay out income with some tax already deducted, Joyce is able to claim the tax back, so the income is tax-free in her hands.

Jointly owned assets

You may well have bank accounts, savings accounts and investments that are jointly held by you and your husband, wife or civil partner. In England and Wales there are two ways of holding assets jointly: under a 'joint tenancy' or as 'tenants in common'. These are legal terms which can apply to any type of asset and not only to the way you share a home. (Different arrangements apply in Scotland – see page 96.)

Under a joint tenancy, you and your spouse or civil partner both own the whole asset, you have identical interests in it, and you cannot sell or give away the asset without the agreement of the other person. In the event of one of you dying, the other automatically becomes the sole owner of the asset (though the deceased person's share still counts as part of his or her estate).

Under a tenancy in common, you and your spouse or civil partner both have the right to enjoy or use the whole asset, but you each have your own distinct share in the asset and the shares need not be equal. On your death, your share of the asset does not automatically pass to your husband, wife or civil partner and you can leave it to anyone you choose.

Some solicitors advise that you need a formal, signed and witnessed deed in order to switch from a joint tenancy to a tenancy in common. In fact, that is not the case. The law simply requires that one joint owner gives the other notice *in writing*. The notice does not have to be in any particular form – a letter would do – nor do you have to use any particular words. But your intention must be clear. To make matters doubly clear, you might consider drawing up a joint statement which you both sign.

EXAMPLE 6.2
Richard and Chris are registered civil partners and own their home as joint tenants but they realise that they could plan their tax affairs more efficiently if they each had a distinct half-share in the home as tenants in common. To achieve this, Richard sends Chris a letter as follows:

3 Tosca Drive
Hampton
Lancs
DT56 6PP
29 March 2006

Mr Chris Jones
3 Tosca Drive
Hampton
Lancs
DT56 6PP

Dear Chris,

Please accept this letter as notice of my desire to sever as from today the joint tenancy in our property known as 3 Tosca Drive, Hampton, Lancs DT56 6PP now held by us as joint tenants both at law and in equity, so that from now on this property shall belong to us as tenants in common in equal shares.

Yours sincerely,

Richard

Richard Brown

Switching from a tenancy in common to a joint tenancy does require a formal deed, which a solicitor can draw up for you.

For income tax purposes, the HMRC will at first assume that any assets you hold jointly are held under a joint tenancy. This means that you will each be treated as receiving half of any income from the asset. If you want the income to be treated differently, you need to send your tax office a completed **form 17** setting out how the income is to be shared between you. You can get form 17 from your usual tax office* or a local tax enquiry centre.*

However, be warned that the way the income is split for tax purposes *must* reflect the actual shares that you and your spouse or civil partner have in the income-producing asset. You cannot just choose the most convenient income split if it does not match the real shares and you cannot choose one split for income purposes and another for capital. Joint bank and building society accounts are almost always held as joint tenants, so can only ever be held on a 50–50 basis, but of course there's nothing to stop you transferring cash to your husband, wife or civil partner so they can pay into an account in their own name. If, exceptionally, you do hold an account as tenants in common, you must send the HMRC proof of this arrangement at the time you submit **form 17**.

In the case of other assets, you do not need to send in proof with form 17 but, if requested to do so, you should be prepared to provide the HMRC with proof of the shares you each have in an asset and thus your share of the income. The proof might be copies of application forms or documents you signed when you first had the asset or copies of deeds or letters stating the relative shares.

Consider giving some of your assets to your husband, wife or civil partner or giving away part of your share of an asset, if to do so would mean that together you pay less tax, as in the following circumstances:

- if one of you pays income tax and the other does not, give income-producing assets to the non-taxpayer (as in Example 6.1 on page 92). But note that since April 1999 non-taxpayers can no longer reclaim the tax already deducted from income from shares, share-based unit trusts and similar investments. In 2005–6, this type of income is paid with tax at 10 per cent already deducted. Higher-rate taxpayers have extra to pay but for all other taxpayers there is neither more tax to pay nor any tax to reclaim

- if one of you pays tax at the higher rate and the other pays tax at the basic or starting rate, give income-producing assets (including shares, unit trusts and cash that can be invested in a bank or building society account) to the taxpayer paying at the lesser rate. Income from most investments is paid with tax (at the savings rate of 20 per cent or at the dividend rate of 10 per cent in 2005–6) already deducted. Starting- and basic-rate taxpayers have no further tax to pay, but higher-rate taxpayers must pay extra tax

- if one of you has income tax allowances that are being reduced because your income exceeds a given threshold, give enough income-producing assets to the other, so that the allowances are restored to the full amount. This may affect you if you are receiving married couple's allowance (available to couples where husband and/or wife was born before 6 April 1935) or age-related personal allowance (available to anyone aged 65 or over)

- if one of you regularly uses up your capital gains tax-free slice but the other does not, give assets whose value is expected to rise to the person with the unused slice.

Joint assets in Scotland

In Scotland, jointly owned assets are nearly always held as tenants in common – i.e. with each person owning a distinct share of the asset. However, if the owners have agreed on it, there can be a 'survivorship destination clause' written into the ownership documents. Like joint tenancy in England and Wales, the survivorship destination clause ensures that the share of a co-owner who dies automatically passes to the remaining owner(s) – even if the will stipulates that something different should happen. Note that the clause can only be cancelled with the consent of all the owners and it requires a formal deed which can be drawn up by a solicitor.

Anti-avoidance rules

There are tax rules that aim to catch the artificial transfer of income from one person to another. They operate where a 'settlement' comes into being. A settlement is any transfer where there is an element of 'bounty' – in other words, you do not get your full money's worth in return for the transfer. Trusts – see Chapter 9 – are examples of settlements, but so too can be many other types of arrangement, including informal gifts.

If a gift you make is treated as a settlement, any income from this will continue to be treated as yours if either of the following applies:

- you or your husband, wife or civil partner can benefit from the gift or income from it
- the gift was to your own child who is unmarried and under the age of 18 (except that income which does not exceed £100 a year can be treated as that of the child).

The rules do not normally apply to an outright gift between husband and wife or civil partners provided there are no strings attached.

Following a case in 2005 (often referred to as 'Arctic Systems'), the courts have confirmed as correct a revised approach by the HMRC to situations where a husband and wife or civil partners each hold shares in a family company where only one of them does most or all of the work that produces the income of the company. Typically companies have been set up like this in the past because some dividends then flow to the non-working spouse who generally pays tax at a lower rate than the working spouse, so reducing the overall amount of tax paid by the family. Since the non-working spouse is the legal owner of the shares and may well share the risks of the company by, for example, having put in capital, it was thought that this was a legitimate tax-saving arrangement. However, the HMRC now argues that dividends paid to the non-working spouse or civil partner are in effect a gift from the working spouse caught by the settlement rules and should be taxed as the working spouse's income. This is not a change in the law, but reflects the way the law should always have been interpreted, so the HMRC may seek back taxes. The court ruling is being appealed. If you think you might be in this situation, get advice from an accountant.

The anti-avoidance rules mean that you can't reduce the family income tax bill by, say, shifting assets to your children. Unfortunately, they also catch genuine gifts you might want to make to your child – for more information, see Chapter 15. However, bear in mind that currently the rules apply only to income, not capital gains – and not to some types of tax-free income. So, for example, gifts to children can still be effective provided that, instead of producing income, they generate capital gains.

However, as part of a package of measures generally aimed at simplifying the taxation of trusts (see Chapter 8), the government is proposing that the anti-avoidance settlement rules currently applying to income should be extended to capital. If this change goes ahead (possibly from 6 April 2006), capital earned by a gift you give to your child could in future also be taxed as yours if it comes to more than a given amount.

The anti-avoidance rules also catch gifts you put into trust if you or your husband, wife or civil partner are actual or potential beneficiaries – see Chapter 8.

EXAMPLE 6.3
Michael had not realised, when he opened a building society account for his daughter Rebecca, that income from the £20,000 he had placed in the account would count as his own for tax purposes.

He decides to close the account and put £1,000 into a National Savings Children's Bonus Bond for Rebecca and the rest into a growth unit trust for her (see Chapter 15 for more information).

Gifts to charity

Provided you use one of the special schemes available, you can claim a reduction in your income tax bill or get tax relief added to your donation when you give cash to charity. The schemes are: gift aid, payroll giving and community investment tax relief. You can also claim income tax relief if you make gifts of shares or property to charity. Details of how these schemes work are given in Chapter 16.

Chapter 7

Trusts

PLANNING FOR THE FUTURE

Ruth and David have become grandparents for the first time. 'I want to give the baby a nest egg for her future,' David explains to his solicitor. 'Of course, she's too young to handle money now, but I can put it in trust, can't I?'

'Yes, indeed,' replied the solicitor. 'You probably require what is known as an accumulation-and-maintenance trust. That would enable her to receive the money when she is adult, but gives the option to use it for her benefit in the meantime. Let us have a look at your precise circumstances and wishes.'

Trusts are legal arrangements that let you give away assets but retain some control over how they are used. They are also frequently used as a way of reducing inheritance tax (IHT) that might otherwise be payable on death. Trusts can be set up during your lifetime or under a will. (Trusts are also sometimes referred to as 'settlements' though for tax purposes 'settlement' includes many other types of arrangement.)

What is a trust?

A trust is an arrangement where the legal owners of assets (which can be things, money, land, buildings and so on) hold, and must use, them for the benefit of someone else. There are three conditions that must be met for the creation of a trust: the intention to create it must be clear from the words used, the trust property must be identified, and it must be clear who is to benefit from the trust. (In Scotland, there is a further requirement that trust assets or evidence of their ownership is physically delivered to the trustees or alternatively that the trust is registered in the Books of Council and Session.) It is common to set out this information and other conditions in a written deed, but trusts can, and do, come into being without anything being put into writing.

There are three main participants in a trust:

- **the settlor (called the truster or granter in Scotland)** This is the person who gives away the assets to be placed in the trust. A trust may have more than one settlor and this does not have to be an individual. For example, the settlor could be a company or another trust
- **the trustees** There is usually more than one trustee (see below) and these are the legal owners of the trust property. So the property is registered in their names, and they are responsible for holding it safely and accounting for it. The settlor can be a trustee, so too can a beneficiary
- **the beneficiaries** There might be one beneficiary or more. These are the people who will – or might – share the trust property and any income from it. Beneficiaries can be individuals, companies, charities or other bodies. Different beneficiaries may have different rights – see below for more information. The settlor can be a beneficiary of the trust, but this has tax implications – see Chapter 8.

Why use a trust?

A trust can be useful in many situations, for example:

- **giving to children** You might want to make a gift now to a child to be available to him or her later, for example, when they reach an age you specify
- **maintaining control** The person you want to benefit might not be good at handling money, for example, they have learning difficulties or a tendency to be spendthrift
- **giving to a group** Maybe you want to give to a group of people that is not yet complete – for example, your grandchildren including those yet to be born

- **retaining flexibility** Perhaps you're not sure at this stage who should benefit from your gift or you want to be able to change who benefits or the amount they get if circumstances change. Provided you specify the range of potential beneficiaries now, you can leave these decisions until later
- **separating income from capital** This lets you specify that someone will have your assets in the end but, in the meantime, someone else has the income from them or the use of them. This can be particularly useful in family situations – for example, if you want a widow or widower to be financially secure but ultimately want your children (maybe from a former marriage) to benefit
- **giving on special occasions or in set circumstances** You might want to make a gift only on the occasion of some possible but indeterminate event, such as a marriage or birth. Similarly, you might want someone to benefit now but for your gift to pass to someone else if, say, the first beneficiary goes bankrupt
- **maintaining confidentiality** A beneficiary does not have to know that you have arranged a gift to be made at some future time. Similarly, a beneficiary in receipt of income or capital from a trust does not have to know who the settlor was
- **tax-efficiency** Sometimes a gift into trust can save you tax, or avoid tax problems that would arise with an outright gift. See Chapter 8 for a detailed discussion of the tax treatment of trusts.

How do you create a trust?

It is best to use a formal, written trust deed that makes your intentions crystal clear. This is not a job for the DIY enthusiast – get professional help either from a solicitor★ or an accountant,★ tax adviser★ or independent financial adviser (IFA)★ (who can advise on the appropriate trust and explain the pros and cons but will normally use a solicitor to draw up the deed itself). Creating a trust in this way can be costly, so check that the benefits warrant the financial outlay.

Life insurance products are very often used in conjunction with trusts. They can be particularly suitable because they pay out on death and special tax rules enable capital to be drawn from a policy during your lifetime without immediate tax implications (see page 205). As a result, many life insurance companies can provide you with off-the-shelf trust documents that let you very simply, and usually at no extra cost, opt to have a life policy written in trust (see Chapter 13). You can either arrange this direct with the insurance company or through an IFA.*

More about the participants

The settlor

The settlor makes the gift to the trust and specifies what he or she wants the trust to do, who the beneficiaries are, and what powers the trustees will have.

However, there are some constraints on what, as settlor, you can do. For example, the law generally sets the maximum lifetime of a trust – usually 80 years – and the maximum period over which income can be accumulated within a trust before it has to be paid out to one or more beneficiaries. Many statutory rules come into play only if your trust deed fails to specify what should happen. Provided a solicitor draws up the deed for you, there should be no nasty surprises.

It is usual – but not required – that the settlor appoints the first trustees. It is common for a settlor to want to retain some control over the trust property and the decisions concerning it. There are various ways of approaching this:

- even though you are the settlor, you can also be a trustee. But be aware that you are bound by the terms of the trust just like any other trustee
- obviously, at the outset, you should choose trustees who you think are sympathetic to your aims. And, if the deed is worded appropriately, you can retain the right to appoint new trustees in future. This will help you to ensure that the trustees remain sympathetic
- you can give the trustees an expression of your wishes. This needs to be carefully written so that it does not legally bind the trustees (since this could alter the nature of the trust with consequent tax implications).

The settlor can be a beneficiary of the trust, in which case it becomes a 'settlor-interested trust'. This may seem tempting as it could give you an opening to get your money or assets back if circumstances change, but there are serious tax drawbacks, as described in Chapter 8.

The beneficiaries

As described below, there are two main types of trusts: those with an interest in possession and those without. In an interest-in-possession trust, there are two types of beneficiary:

- **life interest (called life rent in Scotland)** A beneficiary with a life interest is called a life tenant (life renter in Scotland) and is entitled to the income produced by the trust assets or to the use of the assets (for example, the right to live in a home owned by the trust). But a life tenant has no right to the trust assets him or herself so, for example, the trustees cannot give this beneficiary the trust assets or the proceeds of selling them
- **reversionary interest** A beneficiary with a reversionary interest (sometimes called a 'remainderman') will eventually become entitled to the trust assets but only when the life interest comes to an end.

Where there is no interest in possession, the trustees may have discretion to distribute income, capital or both to the beneficiaries who might be named individuals or people within a specified 'class' such as your grandchildren.

If you are the settlor and a beneficiary of the trust is your own child who is unmarried and under the age of 18, any income paid out to the child or used for his or her benefit (for example, to pay school fees) will count as your own income for tax purposes. Except in the case of bare trusts, this does not apply if the income is accumulated within the trust. See Chapter 8 for details.

Beneficiaries might have a contingent interest so that they benefit only when a particular, specified event takes place, such as reaching a particular age, outliving someone else, or perhaps if the current beneficiary becomes bankrupt.

A trust might have a single beneficiary or many. Unless the trust deed specifies otherwise, multiple beneficiaries share an interest in equal shares. For example, if a life interest is given to two beneficiaries, and the trust deed does not say otherwise, they will each receive half the income from the trust.

Modern trusts are often flexible, giving the trustees the power to change the beneficiaries after the trust has been set up. For example, a trust might initially give a life interest to one person but give the trustees the power to revoke this and assign the interest to someone else. Trusts that give the trustees these very wide powers are often called 'flexible trusts' or 'flexible power of appointment trusts'.

As a beneficiary, you have the right to inspect the trust deed and rules, the general records of meetings and the trust accounts. But you do not have any right to see records of the reasons behind the decisions of trustees in exercising their discretionary powers.

Beneficiaries do not have the right to alter the actions or decisions of trustees, provided that the trustees have acted within their powers. But, if as a beneficiary you believe the trustees are in breach of their duties – for example, by failing to look after the trust assets properly, investing them unsuitably, or making decisions that conflict with the powers in the trust deed – you can take court action to challenge the actions of the trustees.

If certain conditions are met, the beneficiaries can direct the trustees to hand over the trust property and the trust then comes to an end. The conditions are that: all the beneficiaries can be identified, there is no possibility of further beneficiaries (for example, children who have not yet been born), they have all reached age 18 and are all of sound mind.

The trustees

If a trust holds land, the maximum number of trustees is four. There is no minimum, but as two trustees are required to give a valid receipt for the proceeds from selling land, two is the practical minimum. (The exception is where there is a sole corporate trustee.) For trusts not holding land, there is no minimum or maximum number but more than four trustees of a family trust would be unusual.

Anyone can be a trustee, provided they are at least 18 years old and of sound mind – even someone who is bankrupt or has been convicted of a serious offence. However, a court can remove trustees it deems to be unfit. Beneficiaries can be trustees, though usually this is not a good idea as trustees should not normally profit from a trust and should be wary of acting if they have a conflict of interest. (However, in some types of trust – for example, pension schemes – it is normal for some of the trustees to be beneficiaries.)

Usually, the settlor appoints the first trustees. If you set up a trust in your will, it is normal to appoint the same people to be executors of the will and trustees of the trust, but you can choose different people if you want to.

Someone cannot be forced to act as a trustee. Having taken on the job they can usually resign, but this may be subject to either a replacement being found or at least two trustees remaining (or a single corporate trustee).

The trust deed may specify how trustees are to be appointed – for example, the deed may name one or more people as 'appointers' who have the job of choosing trustees as and when the need arises. If not, the remaining trustees have the power to appoint new trustees when required. If the last trustee dies, his or her personal representative inherits this power.

Usually there is no automatic right of the beneficiaries to remove a trustee – the beneficiaries would have to ask a court to do this.

Being a trustee is an onerous task, not to be taken on lightly. As a trustee, various Acts of Parliament (in particular the Trustee Act 1925 and, in England and Wales, the Trustee Act 2000) give you certain powers and also impose duties. In several areas, these are often varied by the rules of the particular trust, so an important first job as a trustee is to read the trust rules and make sure you understand them. Some of the main statutory powers and duties are briefly outlined below.

The trustees' powers
Advancement
The power to give ('advance') capital to a beneficiary, subject to the rules of the trust and rights of other beneficiaries.

Maintenance
The power to use the income of the trust for the maintenance, education or benefit of a beneficiary. This clearly applies where a beneficiary has the right to receive the trust income. It can also apply to a beneficiary who has the right to receive trust assets, say, at a given age – in the meantime, they may have the right to income earned by those assets.

Charging
Trustees are not allowed to profit from their role but they can set reasonable expenses against the trust income or capital. In addition, professional trustees – such as solicitors or a bank – can be paid a reasonable sum for their services.

Delegation

Trustees generally can delegate any of their administrative functions (managing investments, paperwork, keeping assets safe etc.), but they may not delegate their distributive functions, such as:

- deciding how the trust assets should be distributed among the beneficiaries
- deciding whether expenses etc. should be paid out of income or capital (since this affects the distribution of the trust assets between beneficiaries with an interest in the income and those with an interest in the capital)
- appointing new trustees.

(The rules for charitable trusts are a little different.)

Individual trustees can delegate to someone else under a power of attorney for a maximum period of 12 months, but remain responsible for the actions of the person they appoint.

Insurance

Trustees may – but do not have to – insure trust property. However, their duty to take reasonable care – see opposite – may require them to arrange insurance.

Investment

In England and Wales, trustees have very wide powers to make any kind of investment but they must take heed of the 'standard investment criteria':

- the investments chosen or retained must be suitable for the trust
- there must be a range of different investments appropriate to that trust.

For example, unless the trust had very short-term aims, it would not be suitable for all its resources to be invested in a building society savings account.

Trustees have a duty to get and consider investment advice when choosing or reviewing investments, unless they can show this would be unnecessary or inappropriate. For example, it might be excessive for a trust with just a few hundred pounds of assets to get investment advice but essential and appropriate for a trust with, say, £50,000.

The Trustee Act 2000 does not apply to Scotland or Northern Ireland. Instead, the earlier Trustee Investments Act 1961 continues to apply. This restricts trusts to a much more limited range of investments unless the trust deed specifically gives the trustees wider investment powers.

Sale

Trustees have extensive powers to sell any trust property and are under a duty to obtain the best price.

Duties of trustees

Conflicts of interest

You should be wary of becoming a trustee if there is or might be a conflict of interest between you and any beneficiary. If a conflict arises after you have taken on the role, you should disclose it to your fellow trustees.

New trustees

You should read the trust documents to make sure you understand the objectives of the trust, the rights of beneficiaries, whether any of those rights have been assigned to someone else, your powers, the nature and whereabouts of any trust property and other assets.

If you are joining an already established trust, you should also check as far as possible that the existing trustees have not committed any breach. Although you cannot be held responsible for the actions of other trustees prior to your joining them, you could be liable if you fail to take reasonable steps to recover any losses their actions caused.

Duty to take reasonable care

In carrying out most of their powers and duties, trustees must exercise reasonable care. This means exercising such care and skill as is reasonable given any special knowledge or experience. Professional trustees – such as solicitors and banks – are under a higher duty than an ordinary, lay trustee. The latter is normally required to act as an ordinary prudent businessman or businesswoman would. This rule must be interpreted within context so, for example, when making investment decisions, a lay trustee is required to act as if he or she was investing for other people whom he or she felt morally obliged to support. Investing in, say, traded options might be prudent for someone investing their own money and given their own circumstances. It would usually not be when the aim was to provide for their children.

Ensure assets are correctly distributed
The trustees must ensure that the right people get the trust assets. In particular, if a beneficiary has assigned an interest to someone else, that other person's claim to the assets should be carefully checked before the assets are handed over to them.

Ensure fairness between beneficiaries
This is especially tricky where some beneficiaries have an interest in income and others in capital. For example, you need to consider how expenses are set off and how to strike the right balance between income-producing investments and those offering capital growth.

Comply with the terms of the trust
You must act in accordance with the trust deed and rules and any legal requirements. In general the rules of a trust can be changed only with the agreement of all the beneficiaries who must all be adults and capable of making such decisions or with the permission of the court.

Provide information and accounts
If they ask, you must provide beneficiaries with information about the trust and its investments, copies of accounts and access to title deeds and any other documents. There is no general requirement to have accounts audited. You are allowed to charge the reasonable cost of producing such documents. You must also allow beneficiaries to inspect the minutes but you are not under any duty to explain the reasons for trustees' decisions.

Duty to act jointly
The law requires that trustees' decisions must be unanimous. However, this can be and often is over-ridden by the individual trust's rules to allow majority voting.

Duties to act without reward and not to profit from the trust
This is the general rule. However, the Trustee Act 2000 gives trustees the power to make reasonable payments to professional trustees (see

page 105) and usually the individual trust's rules will include a charging clause.

Duty not to purchase trust property
If you are a trustee, neither you nor your husband or wife (or a company in which either of you has an interest) should buy assets from the trust. Even if you paid a fair price, the beneficiaries can declare the purchase void and require the assets to be resold. The rules of the individual trust may over-ride this rule.

Duty to consult the beneficiaries
If the trust holds land and all the beneficiaries are adults, the trustees should consult the beneficiaries before taking decisions affecting the land.

Choosing the appropriate trust

There are four main types of trust: bare trusts, interest-in-possession trusts, discretionary trusts, and accumulation-and-maintenance trusts (which are in fact a special type of discretionary trust that benefits from favourable IHT treatment as long as special rules are kept). Which type of trust will best suit your needs is dictated in part by the characteristics of each type of trust. Of great importance, however, is your tax position and the tax treatment of the different trusts.

The tax treatment of trusts is undoubtedly complex and there are numerous pitfalls for the unwary. The wording of the trust deed and the powers of the trustees can be crucial in assessing which tax regime applies. You are strongly advised to take advice from a solicitor* before deciding on whether or not to use a trust and which type would be appropriate, and you should ask a solicitor to draw up the trust deed. (In DIY books about wills, some of the pro forma wills provided include clauses for setting up trusts. Use these only if you are certain that the pro forma will selected reflects your wishes. If in doubt, consult a solicitor. Never try to adapt the wording of one of these wills if it does not quite match your circumstances.)

The main types of trust

Bare trust

How does it work?

This is the simplest type of trust, requiring very little administration. Someone holds assets as nominee for someone else – for example, a parent or some other relative holds investments given by the parent to their child as outlined in Chapter 16. Property is transferred to the bare trustee who holds it for the beneficiary and uses it in accordance with his or her instructions. So, provided the beneficiary is aged 18 or more (or is married if younger), he or she can call for the income and/or capital at any time and the trustee has no right to withhold it. For tax purposes, the beneficiary – not the trustee – is treated as the owner of the trust property.

Pros and cons

A bare trust is not a complex trust to administer. Tax on the trust property will generally be lower than if it were held in, say, an accumulation-and-maintenance trust. Watch out if you are a parent making a gift to your child to be held in a bare trust. Income from any gifts made on or after 9 March 1999 is taxed as yours not the child's, even if it is not paid out, unless it comes to no more than £100 – see Chapter 15. Income from gifts from other sources – for example, from grandparents – counts as that of the child. And, under current rules, any capital gains, whatever the source of the investments, are taxed as the child's. This can make a bare trust more tax-efficient than other trust options in suitable cases. Against this, you must balance the drawbacks. Once the trust is set up, you cannot change the beneficiaries or the shares in which they own the trust property. The settlor has no control at all over the use of the trust property once a child has reached his or her majority. The trust property is part of the beneficiary's estate when he or she dies – if the beneficiary is under the age of 18 (16 in Scotland) at the time of death, he or she would die intestate (see Chapter 10) since he or she would be too young to have made a will.

Possible uses

*   Making a gift of property to a child – e.g. a share in a family business – which the child does not yet have the legal capacity to hold because of his or her young age.
*   Building up a nest-egg for a child to have on reaching age 18. (But, for children born on or after 1 September 2002, consider also the child trust fund – see Chapter 15.)

EXAMPLE 7.1

Nichola invests £10,000 for her niece, Angela. Although Nichola is the nominal owner of the investments they are held on bare trust for Angela. Income from the investments is treated as Angela's but she pays no tax on it because it falls within her personal allowance. When Angela reaches 18 (or sooner if she gets married), she can demand that the investments are transferred into her own name.

Interest-in-possession trust

Also known as a 'life-interest trust' or 'fixed-interest trust'.

How does it work?

One or more beneficiaries have the right to receive income earned by the assets in the trust as that income arises. Alternatively they have the right to use the assets held by the trust, for example, the right to live in a house. Eventually – for example, on the death of the life interest beneficiaries, at a given date or when a specified event, such as marriage, occurs – the assets in the trust are distributed. The person or people who receive the assets are said to hold the 'reversionary interest'. The beneficiaries who receive the income (or use of the assets) need not be the same as the beneficiaries who have the reversionary interest, though they could be. For example, you might specify in your will that your share of the family home be put into trust, giving your husband or wife a life interest so that he or she could continue living there as long as desired but giving the reversionary interest to your children so that they would inherit on the death of your spouse. See also Example 7.2.

Pros and cons

Interest-in-possession trusts are not as flexible as discretionary trusts or accumulation-and-maintenance trusts. Nevertheless, they have been popular in the past particularly because they enjoyed more advantageous capital gains tax (CGT) treatment than other types of trust. But, from 6 April 1998, the CGT treatment of interest-in-possession trusts was brought into line with the tax treatment of other types of trust. You should be wary of choosing an interest-in-possession trust if you might want to alter the people who benefit from the trust income or the shares the beneficiaries have in it. Such alterations will usually count as gifts from one beneficiary to another under the IHT rules.

Possible uses

- Where you eventually want to pass on assets to one or more people but need to provide for someone else in the interim – see Example 7.2.
- Where you do not want the beneficiary to have full control of the assets in the trust or you want to defer handing over control until a later date.
- If you want to give to children, usually an accumulation-and-maintenance trust would be a better choice. However, you could adapt an interest-in-possession trust to suit gifts to children by, for example, specifying that income should be held for the child(ren) until they reach age 18. In effect, this is combining a bare trust (see page 110) with the interest-in-possession trust.

EXAMPLE 7.2

David's will stipulates that, on his death, a large part of his assets should be placed in trust. The trustees would invest the assets as they saw fit and the income from them (and use of his former share of the family home) should go to his wife during her lifetime. On his wife's death, the assets are to be shared equally between their three children. David has drawn up his will in this way, first, to guard against his widow being short of money during her lifetime and, secondly, to ensure that his children will eventually receive his assets even if his widow remarries.

Discretionary trust

How does it work?

If a trust is not a bare trust or an interest-in-possession trust, it is by default a discretionary trust. That said, the distinguishing features are usually that income can be accumulated within the trust to be paid out later or to be paid out at the discretion of the trustees and that there is usually more than one beneficiary. Often there will be a 'class' of beneficiaries, such as your children or your grandchildren, not all of whom have to be born at the time the trust is set up.

Pros and cons

Although discretionary trusts are very flexible, they are treated less favourably for tax purposes than either interest-in-possession trusts or accumulation-and-maintenance trusts.

Possible uses

- Where you want to be able to alter the people (or bodies) who will benefit under the trust.
- Where you want to be able to alter the proportions in which the beneficiaries share in income and/or capital from the trust.

EXAMPLE 7.3

John had been ill for some time and, knowing that he did not have long to live, he checked his will and brought it up to date. He was a widower and had six sons whose ages ranged from 22 to 30. Two of the sons had good, secure incomes, while three had not settled down to careers yet but had only minor financial problems. The sixth son was generally in financial difficulties – largely of his own making.

John wanted to be fair to all his boys but was not happy with the idea of just sharing out his assets between them. They did not all have the same need and the youngest son in particular would be likely to squander any inheritance. John wanted a solution which would ensure that help was available to all his sons if they needed it but would protect the assets otherwise. He decided to set up a discretionary trust in favour of all the sons. He appointed his own two brothers (the sons' uncles) as trustees and gave them discretion to make payments and loans from the trust fund to the sons if or when, in the trustees' opinion, such help was warranted. After ten years (by which time John felt the boys should all take responsibility for themselves), the remaining trust assets were to be distributed equally among them.

Accumulation-and-maintenance trust

How does it work?

This is a special type of discretionary trust but, provided certain rules are kept, it escapes the worst of the unfavourable tax treatment normally applying to discretionary trusts. The rules include:

- one or more of the beneficiaries must become entitled to either the income or capital from the trust on or before reaching age 25
- in the run-up to the entitlement above coming into effect, no beneficiary can have an interest in possession. Instead, income from the assets in the trust must be accumulated, except that it can be used to pay for the maintenance, education or other benefit of one or more of the beneficiaries
- the trust can exist for a maximum of 25 years, unless all the beneficiaries have a common grandparent, in which case the life of the trust can be longer (adopted children and stepchildren are treated in the same way as other children of a family for the purpose of this test)
- although the beneficiaries can be a group, such as all your grandchildren, there must be at least one member of the group living at the time the trust is set up. (However, if there is just one member and that person dies before any others are born, the trust can continue.)

Pros and cons

The accumulation–and–maintenance trust is flexible and tax-efficient but only for gifts to children. Unlike a direct gift or a bare trust (see page 110), the trust property is not part of a beneficiary's estate if he or she dies.

Under the anti-avoidance rules, if you are the settlor and income or capital from the trust is used to pay for the maintenance or education of, or to otherwise benefit, your own child who is under age 18 and unmarried, the payments will be taxed as your income unless they come to no more than £100. However, income and gains that remain within the trust to be accumulated are not taxed as the parent's income, so this is a tax-efficient way of building up a nest-egg for your own child. For more information about gifts to children, see Chapter 15.

Possible uses

- Where you want to be able to alter the people who will benefit under the trust, e.g. by allowing for children who are as yet unborn.
- Where you want to be able to alter the proportions in which the beneficiaries share in income and/or capital from the trust.
- Where you want to make gifts as a parent to your child(ren) without income added to the gift being treated as yours (see Chapter 6). But be aware that this advantage is lost if the income is paid out instead of being accumulated within the trust.
- Building up a nest-egg for children and grandchildren.
- Paying school fees.

EXAMPLE 7.4
David set up a trust to accept a gift for his first granddaughter, Jemima. Bearing in mind that there might be more grandchildren to come, he established an accumulation-and-maintenance trust in favour of all his grandchildren. For the present, he has settled £25,000 in the trust but can add more later if he wishes. Jemima is to become entitled to a lump sum from the trust when she reaches age 21. In the meantime, money can be paid out – to pay for school fees, say – at the discretion of the trustees, who are David and his wife, Ruth.

Other special types of trust

Accumulation-and-maintenance trusts are just one type of discretionary trust which qualifies for special treatment. There are others. Most are outside the scope of gift planning (they include, *inter alia*, pension schemes, compensation funds and unit trusts). Two may be of use:

- **charitable trusts** If you want to give large amounts (say, at least £10,000) to a range of charities, setting up your own charitable trust could be worth considering. A charitable trust benefits from tax advantages and as a trustee you can decide which good causes your trust will fund. Setting up your own charitable trust is usually a complicated business for which you will need the help of a solicitor★. Once the trust deed is drawn up, it has to be sent to the Charity Commission★ which, in conjunction with HMRC, will decide whether the trust qualifies as a charity. If so, money, shares and property you put into the trust can qualify for income tax relief in the same way as other gifts to charity (see Chapter 16) and most income and all gains earned by the assets in the trust build up tax free. A simpler way to set up your own charitable trust is to use the ready-made scheme offered by the Charities Aid Foundation (CAF)★

• **disabled trusts**   For assets placed in trust on or after 10 March 1981, mainly for the benefit of someone who is incapable of looking after their own property because of mental disorder or someone who is receiving attendance allowance, the disabled person is treated as if he or she has an interest in possession. This means that the more favourable interest-in-possession tax rules apply rather than those for discretionary trusts. In addition, back-dated to 6 April 2004, trustees of a disabled trust may jointly elect with the disabled person for the trust to pay tax as if the trust income and gains were received direct by the disabled person, so making use of the person's allowances and starting rate tax band. The election must be made by 31 January falling one year and 10 months after the end of the first tax year from which the election is to apply (for example by 31 January 2007 if the election is to start from 6 April 2004). Once made, the election cannot be reversed.

A special type of interest-in-possession trust can also be useful if you want to make a gift to someone but you have real doubts about whether he or she can be trusted to act responsibly. This is a 'protective trust'. Basically, the beneficiary is entitled to the income from, or use of, the trust assets for as long as he or she behaves responsibly. But if a specified event occurs – for example, the beneficiary becomes bankrupt – the interest in possession ceases. The trust then automatically converts into a discretionary trust and the trustees decide how best to use the assets for the maintenance and support of the original beneficiary and/or his or her family.

Chapter 8
Taxation of trusts

The tax treatment of trusts is crucial to any decision regarding the use of a trust as a way of making gifts. Unfortunately, it is also complex. Since 1991, governments have been consulting on ways to simplify the taxation of trusts but the issue has been thorny and progress slow. At long last, the present government has put together a package of measures, some of which have come into force and others of which are likely to take effect from April 2006, which aim to make trusts more transparent (so that the tax paid by trustees more closely reflects the tax beneficiaries would pay if they received income or benefits direct), deter the use of trusts for tax avoidance, and avoid penalising those who are forced to or need to use trusts (for example, children inheriting under the intestacy rules – see Chapter 10 – and disabled people). Once all the measures are in place, they aim to form a coherent package. They include:

- since 6 April 2004, increasing the tax rates which discretionary trusts pay on income and gains to match the top personal tax rates
- backdated to 6 April 2004, allowing trusts for vulnerable people (disabled people and minor children) to be taxed as if income and gains went directly to the vulnerable person
- from 6 April 2005, introducing a £500 basic-rate tax band for most discretionary trusts to reduce the number of small trusts required to submit annual tax returns
- from a future date, possibly 6 April 2006, introducing 'income streaming' for discretionary trusts, so that trustees pay tax at the basic rate (or savings rate or 10 per cent dividend rate, depending on the type of income) on income received by the trust that is paid out to beneficiaries by 31 December following the tax year in which the income arose. The £500 basic-rate tax band (see above) would apply to other income over and above any streamed income

- from a future date, possibly 6 April 2006, anti-avoidance legislation covering 'settlements' (which includes trusts but also many other types of arrangement) is to be harmonised so that the same rules apply to capital gains as already apply to income. One effect of this would be that, where a gift from a parent to a child produces capital gains, the gains would be taxed as those of the parent if they exceed a set amount
- from a future date, possibly 6 April 2006, for income tax and capital gains tax purposes, there will be three categories of trust: settlor-interested trusts, bare trusts and general trusts. The tax treatment of these three categories is summarised on page 134.

This chapter describes the tax position of trusts as it stands in the 2005–6 tax year.

Bare trusts

Putting a gift into trust

Unless you can use one of the exemptions described in Chapter 2, your gift into a bare trust counts as a potentially exempt transfer (PET), so there is no IHT to pay provided you survive for at least seven years – see page 69. No special rules apply regarding capital gains tax (CGT) – check the ordinary rules in Chapters 2 and 3 to see if any CGT will be payable.

The trust's tax position

The trust does not have a separate tax identity from the beneficiary. Income and gains from the trust property are treated in the same way as if the property were owned directly by the beneficiary. This means that income is taxed at the beneficiary's top rate after taking into account allowances and any other deductions. The exception to this is where the assets in the trust are a gift from a parent to an unmarried child under age 18 and the gift was made on or after 9 March 1999. If such income exceeds £100 a year, it is treated as that of the parent. This applies whether the income is accumulated or paid out. Income from a gift made by a parent before 9 March 1999 is taxed as that of the child provided it is accumulated and not paid out.

Gains are taxed at the beneficiary's top rate after taking account of the yearly tax-free slice.

Payments to beneficiaries

Where, as is usual, tax has already been paid as income and gains arose (see above), there is no further tax to pay when payments are made to the beneficiary or used for his or her benefit.

The exception is where the assets in the trust are a gift from a parent to an unmarried child under age 18 and the gift was made before 9 March 1999. In this case, provided income was accumulated within the trust, it will have been treated as that of the child. But, once paid out to the child, or used for the child's benefit, it becomes taxable as that of the parent if the income exceeds £100.

When the bare trust ends

The trust property has been treated as owned by the beneficiary throughout. Therefore there is no change when the beneficiary takes outright possession of the trust property.

EXAMPLE 8.1

Angela is the beneficiary of a bare trust containing £10,000 capital. This was a gift from her father made before 9 March 1999. The capital has earned approximately £400 a year income and a small amount of capital profit. Both are well within Angela's 2005–6 tax allowances of £4,895 personal allowance against taxable income and £8,500 against chargeable gains. On reaching age 18, Angela intends to ask the trustee, Aunt Nichola, to carry on acting as trustee but to advance Angela regular sums to support her while she is at university. This will be taxed in the same way as if accumulated within the trust. On finishing her university course, Angela intends to take outright possession of the remaining trust property (if any). As she is already treated as the outright owner, no transfer takes place and so there is no IHT.

Interest-in-possession trusts

Putting a gift into trust

If you make a gift which is placed in an interest–in–possession trust (and none of the exemptions in Chapter 2 apply), you are treated as if you had made a potentially exempt transfer (PET). No IHT is charged provided you survive for seven years after making the gift (see page 69 for more details). If you die within seven years, the trustees will normally be liable for the tax due. No special rules apply in respect of CGT, so check the ordinary rules to see if tax will be payable (see Chapters 2 and 3).

The trust's tax position

Income from the assets in the trust may be paid either direct to the beneficiaries or first to the trustees who then pass it on to the beneficiaries.

The trustees are responsible for tax on income earned by the trust assets. Tax may be payable at any of three rates, depending on the type of income involved (rates apply to 2005–6):

- on dividends, distributions from share-based unit trusts and similar investments, the rate is 10 per cent
- on savings income (for example, interest from savings accounts or, corporate bonds or distributions from unit trusts investing in bonds), tax is charged at the savings rate of 20 per cent
- on any other income, tax is charged at the basic rate which is 22 per cent.

Example 8.2 on page 123 shows how this can work out in practice.

Until 5 April 1998, an interest-in-possession trust was also liable for CGT on any capital gains but only at the basic rate. No further CGT was payable if capital was paid out to a beneficiary. Therefore, the low rate of CGT on the trust's gains made this form of trust particularly attractive where a beneficiary was a higher-rate taxpayer (who would normally be taxed on gains at a rate of 40 per cent). The government, worried that interest-in-possession trusts were being set up purely for tax-avoidance reasons, closed the loophole. Since 6 April 1998, interest-in-possession trusts have been brought into line with discretionary trusts (including accumulation-and-maintenance trusts): gains realised by all these trusts are now taxable at a uniform special 'rate applicable to trusts' (RAT). In 2005–6, this is 40 per cent. The first slice of gains each tax year is tax-free. The tax-free slice for a trust is usually set at half the rate for an individual – i.e. £4,250 in 2005–6 – but see box opposite.

Payments to beneficiaries

Income paid out to beneficiaries is broadly treated as if it had been received directly by them. This means three different treatments may apply, depending on the type of income:

- dividends and similar income are received net of tax at 10 per cent and accompanied by a tax credit. Since 6 April 1999, non-taxpayers cannot reclaim this tax credit. Starting- and basic-rate taxpayers have no further tax to pay. Higher-rate taxpayers must pay further tax of 22.5 per cent on the grossed-up amount of the dividend – see Example 8.3 on page 123
- savings income is paid net of tax at 20 per cent. Non-taxpayers can reclaim this. Starting-rate taxpayers can reclaim half the tax deducted. Basic-rate taxpayers have no further tax to pay. Higher-rate taxpayers must pay extra tax of 20 per cent on the grossed-up amount of the interest – see Example 8.3
- all other income is paid with tax at the basic rate already deducted. Non-taxpayers can reclaim all the tax deducted and starting-rate taxpayers can reclaim 12 per cent. Higher-rate taxpayers have extra tax of 18 per cent to pay on the grossed-up income. See Example 8.3.

CAPITAL GAINS TAX-FREE SLICE IF YOU SET UP MORE THAN ONE TRUST
Where you put money or assets into more than one trust on or after 7 July 1978, the annual tax-free slice for capital gains is divided between the trusts. But the minimum tax-free slice for each trust is one-fifth. For example, if you set up two trusts, each has a tax-free slice of 1/2 × £4,250 = £2,125 in 2005–6. If you set up five or more trusts, each has 1/5 × £4,250 = £850. In making this adjustment, trusts are included whether or not they are in fact capable of producing any capital gains, but some types of trusts are ignored, for example, trusts for people with disabilities, occupational pension schemes and retirement annuity contracts (but not personal pensions).

There may be arrangements for beneficiaries to receive income direct from the trust investments instead of the income passing through the hands of the trustees. In this case, the beneficiary accounts for tax direct to the HMRC.

If you receive payment of capital from the trust, you cannot reclaim any CGT paid by the trust even if you are a non-taxpayer, starting- or basic-rate taxpayer. Equally there is no extra CGT to pay if you are a higher-rate taxpayer.

When the interest in possession ends

If you have an interest in possession, you are treated, for tax purposes, as owning the assets in the trust – the reversionary interest is ignored. If there is more than one beneficiary, you are treated as owning the trust assets in proportion to your shares in the income from them. When your interest in possession ends, you are deemed to make a gift of the assets to the beneficiary who holds the reversionary interest (or, if applicable, the beneficiary who takes a subsequent life interest). Provided you are 'giving' the assets to an individual or to an appropriate type of trust, the gift counts as a PET and no tax is payable as long as you survive for seven years (see page 69). If the assets pass, say, to a discretionary trust, the gift counts as chargeable and there may be an immediate IHT bill, depending on your running total of gifts during the last seven years (see page 64).

If, when the trust ends, you become entitled to receive the trust property outright, there is no IHT liability. In most cases there is also no IHT if the property passes back to the settlor (or his or her spouse) when the interest in possession ends.

If a beneficiary's interest in possession ends during his or her lifetime, the beneficiary is deemed to be disposing of the trust assets and there may be CGT to pay. There is no CGT liability when a life interest ends on the death of the beneficiary holding the interest.

A reversionary interest in an interest-in-possession trust is treated as a separate asset from the interest in possession and counts as 'excluded property' for IHT purposes, which means that it is completely outside the IHT net. This can be useful, since a gift of a reversionary interest cannot create an IHT bill (see Example 8.4) There is no CGT on the gift of a reversionary interest provided you are the beneficiary for whom the interest was created or, if not, you did not buy the interest.

EXAMPLE 8.2

Molly was left a life interest in a trust set up by her husband, Charlie, who died several years ago. The trust holds a mix of investments: some property and various shares and bonds. In 2005–6, the income and tax position of the trust was as follows:

Income

Income from property (before deduction of tax)	£4,000
Dividends from shares (net of 10% tax credit)	£1,800
Interest income (net of 20% savings tax)	£3,200

Tax

Tax at 22% on property income (22% × £4,000)	£880
Tax at 10% already deducted from dividends (10/90 × £1,800)	£200
Tax at 20% already deducted from interest (20/80 × £3,200)	£800
	————
Total tax paid	£1,880
Income after tax (£4,000 – £880 + £1,800 + £3,200)	£8,120

EXAMPLE 8.3

All the income from the trust in Example 8.2 is paid out to Molly in 2005–6. Molly has income from other sources too and is a higher-rate taxpayer. Her trust income is treated for tax as follows:

Income from property Molly receives £3,120 from which tax at 22 per cent has already been deducted. She grosses this up by doing the following sum: 100% / (100% – 22%) × £3,120 = £4,000. Higher-rate tax on this is 40% × £4,000 = £1,600. Tax of £880 has already been paid, so Molly must now pay £1,600 – £880 = £720

Income from shares Molly receives £1,800 in dividends plus a tax credit for £200. She grosses up the dividends by doing the following sum: 100% / (100% – 10%) × £1,800 = £2,000. Higher-rate tax on this is 32.5% × £2,000 = £650. Tax of £200 has already been paid, so Molly must now pay £650 – £200 = £450

Interest income Molly receives £3,200 from which tax at 20 per cent has already been deducted. She grosses this up by doing the following sum:

100% / (100% − 20%) × £3,200 = £4,000. Higher-rate tax on this is 40% × £4,000 = £1,600. Tax of £800 has already been paid, so Molly must now pay £1,600 − £800 = £800.

In total, Molly has further tax of £720 + £450 + £800 = £1,970 to pay on her trust income. This leaves her with a net sum of £8,120 − £1,970 = £6,150.

EXAMPLE 8.4

When Charlie died, he left part of his assets (some £150,000 in total) in trust, giving his wife, Molly, a life interest and his daughter, Pru, the reversionary interest in the trust property. The life interest means Molly receives the income from the trust property for the rest of her life. The reversionary interest means, when Molly dies, the trust hands over all the trust property to Pru and, at that point, the trust ends. Pru is in her thirties and has children of her own. Her husband has a well-paid job and the family is financially comfortable. Pru doesn't need the trust property and would prefer that her father's assets passed to her children. So she decides to release her reversionary interest in the trust and give it to the children. There is no IHT to pay on Pru's gift to her children, because reversionary interests are excluded from the IHT regime.

Discretionary trusts

Putting a gift into trust

A gift put into a discretionary trust counts as a chargeable gift for IHT (unless you can claim one of the exemptions in Chapter 2) and can create an immediate tax bill (see page 64). Whether or not you have to pay any tax depends on whether you can claim an exemption (for example, the yearly tax-free exemption of £3,000) or, if not, on your running total of chargeable gifts during the previous seven years. If the gift when added to your running total is less than your tax-free slice (£275,000 in 2005–6), there will be no immediate IHT bill. Note that, if you set up other trusts on the same day, they can mean the trust has to pay extra IHT later on – see below. Try to avoid setting up other trusts on the same day as a discretionary trust.

CGT may be due on the gift, if you are giving assets other than cash, but you can claim hold-over relief (see page 53).

The trust's tax position

There is a 'periodic charge' for IHT on the value of the trust property. This charge is made on the tenth anniversary of the setting-up of the trust and at ten-year intervals after that. The amount of tax due is worked out as follows:

- *add* up the value of the trust at the time of the tax charge *and* any gifts made by the settlor (i.e. the person who set up the discretionary trust) to other trusts (apart from charitable trusts) set up on the same day at their value on that day. To this, *add* the value of chargeable gifts made by the settlor in the seven years up to the date of the trust starting
- work out the tax due on that total amount by *deducting* the tax-free slice and *multiplying* by the lifetime rate of 20 per cent (in the 2005–6 tax year)
- *divide* the tax due by the value of everything owned by the discretionary trust. This gives you the 'effective rate of tax'
- take 30 per cent of the effective rate (i.e. *multiply* by 0.3). This gives you the rate at which tax will be charged on the trust property.

This means that the *highest* rate of tax that will have to be paid is 30 per cent of the lifetime rate of 20 per cent – that is, 6 per cent – and the rate could be as low as nothing at all.

If money or assets are paid out of a discretionary trust, an 'interim charge' for IHT is made and must be paid by the trustees. The charge is worked out by multiplying the full ten-year charges by 1/40 for each three-month period during which the property was in the trust since the last periodic charge to IHT. (The procedure is slightly different for payments made before the first ten-year period is up.) This interim charge is also called an 'exit charge'. The tax charge is scaled down similarly in the case of property added to the trust after the start of the relevant ten-year period.

EXAMPLE 8.5

Peter set up a discretionary trust on 1 May 1995, paying £80,000 into it. That day, he also set up an interest-in-possession trust in favour of his daughter and paid £50,000 into that. His cumulative total of chargeable gifts over the seven years before 1 May 1993 was £40,000.

On 1 May 2005, the first ten-year IHT charge becomes payable on the discretionary trust, which is now valued at £230,000. The tax due is worked out as follows:

Current value of discretionary trust	£230,000
plus original value of other trust set up on 1 May 1993	£50,000
plus Peter's seven-year running total up to 30 April 1993	£40,000
	£320,000
less tax-free slice	£275,000
	£45,000
Tax @ 20% on £45,000	£9,000
Effective rate of tax (£9,000 ÷ £230,000)	3.9%
30% × effective rate	1.17%
IHT due on the trust (1.17% × £230,000)	£2,700

EXAMPLE 8.6

In Example 8.5, if Peter had set up the interest-in-possession trust on the day after setting up the discretionary trust, the periodic charge at the discretionary trust's ten-year anniversary would have been lower – in fact, there would have been no charge at all because the value of the trust property and running slice up to the date the trust was created would come to less than the tax-free slice:

Current value of discretionary trust	£230,000
plus Peter's seven-year running total up to 30 April 1993	£40,000
	£270,000
less tax-free slice	£275,000
	£0
Tax @ 20% on £0	£0
Effective rate of tax	0%

The trustees are also responsible for paying income tax on any income received by the trust. This is paid at the 'rate applicable to trusts' (RAT) which is set at two rates, depending on the type of income involved (rates are for 2005–6):

- on dividends from shares, distributions from share-based unit trusts and similar investments, tax is paid at a rate of 32.5 per cent
- on other income, tax is paid at 40 per cent.

Until 5 April 2005, these rates applied to all income however small. But, from 6 April 2005 onwards, all trusts liable for the RAT benefit from a £500 basic-rate band. In 2005–6, income falling within the basic rate band is taxed at 10 per cent (dividends), 20 per cent (savings income) or 22 per cent (other income). The band is set first against income taxed at 22 per cent, any band remaining is set next against income taxed at 20 per cent and lastly against the 10 per cent income. Many trusts will receive income with the correct amount of tax already deducted and have no further tax to pay and the aim of the measure is to remove the need for small trusts in this position to submit a tax return each year. The government estimates that around one-third of eligible trusts have income no higher than the basic rate band and so will no longer have to pay the RAT on any of their income. Many will need to complete a tax return only every five years or so.

Except where the income paid out is covered by the £500 basic rate band, trustees must effectively account for extra tax when they pay out dividend income to beneficiaries. This is because, since 6 April 1999, the trustees cannot count the tax credit on dividends the trust has received as part of the tax it deducts from payments to beneficiaries (see below). Where a trust has accumulated funds or other income out of which to pay this extra tax, it might still pass on the full after-tax amount of dividend income. But a trust without alternative funds will be forced to reduce the amount of dividend income it can pass on to beneficiaries. See Example 8.8.

CGT on any taxable capital gains is also payable by the trustees at the RAT of 40 per cent in 2005–6, though the trust can set a tax-free allowance (usually £4,250 in 2005–6 but see box on page 121) against the first slice of gains.

Payments to beneficiaries

Unlike an interest-in-possession trust (see page 119), income paid out from a discretionary trust is treated in just one way, regardless of the source of income. It is all paid out with tax at a notional rate of 40 per cent already deducted. As a beneficiary, you receive the net income plus a 40 per cent tax credit. The sum of the two counts as gross income which is taxable but you set the tax credit against your tax bill. This means that, unless you are a higher-rate taxpayer, you can claim a refund of part or all of the tax.

On the face of it, you might think that this opens up a way of reclaiming tax on dividends and similar income from April 1999 onwards (when such tax generally ceased to be reclaimable). In practice, this is not the case. As outlined above, from April 1999 onwards, in most cases, the trustees must effectively pay extra tax when such income is distributed. This means that, unless the trust has other funds available to meet the tax bill, it can afford to pass on to beneficiaries less of the dividend income it receives. So, indirectly, you do feel the impact of tax on dividends ceasing to be reclaimable.

If you receive a payment of capital from the trust, there is no CGT for you to pay and you cannot reclaim any CGT paid by the trust. Note that, once income has been accumulated within the trust, the payment of it to a beneficiary will normally count as a payment of capital.

When the trust ends

When the discretionary trust comes to an end, an 'exit' charge is made on the whole of the trust property as if it were any other payment from the trust (see above).

EXAMPLE 8.7

Some years ago, Jaspar and Anne set up a discretionary trust in favour of their grandchildren. The trust holds a mix of investments: some property and various shares and bonds. In 2005–6, the income and tax position of the trust (before making any payments to beneficiaries) was as follows:

Income

Income from property (paid without tax deducted)	£4,000
Interest from savings (net of 20% savings tax)	£3,200
Dividends from shares (net of 10% tax credit)	£1,800

Tax

Tax at 22% on property income within the £500 basic rate band (22% × £500)	£110
Tax at 40% on remaining property income (40% × £3,500)	£1,400
Tax at 20% already deducted from interest (20/80 × £3,200 = £800) Additional tax on interest: 40% of grossed-up amount (100/80 × £3,200 = £4,000) less tax already paid (£800)	£800
Tax at 10% already deducted from dividends (10/90 × £1,800 = £200) Additional tax on dividends: 32.5% of grossed-up amount (100/90 × £1,800) less tax already paid (£200)	£450
Extra tax due	£2,760

Income after tax

£4,000 + £3,200 + £1,800 – £2,760	£6,240

EXAMPLE 8.8

If the trust in Example 8.7 accumulates its dividend income, the amount available for accumulation in 2005–6 is as follows:

Dividend income received by the trust	£1,800
Non-reclaimable tax credit at 10%	£200
Grossed up dividend	£2,000
Additional tax due: 32.5% × £2,000 less tax credit	£450
Amount of income available for accumulation (£2,000 – £200 – £450)	£1,350

But further tax may become due if dividend income is paid out to a beneficiary. For example, if the trustees decide to pass on the £1,350 they could otherwise accumulate to a beneficiary, they need to account for the 40 per cent tax credit that would accompany the payment: £1,350 × 40/60 = £900. Against this, they can set the £450 tax already paid but not the non-reclaimable £200 tax credit. So, the trustees have to pay the Inland Revenue an extra £450. If they do not have, or do not wish to use, other funds to meet this bill, they must reduce the amount they pay to the beneficiary.

If the trustees want to limit the payment to the beneficiary plus the extra tax bill to the amount they could otherwise accumulate, they should pay the beneficiary £1,080. The tax credit on this is 40/60 × £1,080 = £720. The extra tax due is £720 − £450 = £270. This can be paid out of the £1,350 otherwise available for accumulation, leaving £1,350 − £270 = £1,080 to fund the distribution to the beneficiary.

EXAMPLE 8.9

The trustees in Example 8.8 decide to use the dividend income to pay out £1,080 plus a tax credit of £720 to one of the beneficiaries, Jenny. Whether she can reclaim tax depends on her tax situation:

- if Jenny is a non-taxpayer, she can reclaim the full tax credit of £720, bringing the total she receives to £1,800. In other words, she gets the amount of net dividend payment to the trustees but not the non-reclaimable tax credit
- if Jenny is a starting-rate taxpayer (i.e. she pays tax at 10 per cent in 2005–6), she can claim back tax equal to 40% − 10% = 30% of the grossed-up payment of £1,800, which comes to £540. This brings the total she gets to £1,080 + £540 = £1,620. In other words she has paid tax of 10% × £1,800 = £180
- if she is a basic-rate taxpayer (i.e. she pays tax at 22 per cent in 2005–6), Jenny can claim back tax equal to 40% − 22% = 18% of the grossed-up payment of £1,800, which comes to £324. This brings her total receipts to £1,080 + £324 = £1,404. In other words, she has paid tax of 22% × £1,800 = £396
- if she is a higher-rate taxpayer (i.e. she pays tax at 40 per cent in 2005–6), the tax credit exactly balances the tax due, so Jenny cannot reclaim any tax but also has no further tax to pay.

Accumulation-and-maintenance trusts

Putting a gift into trust

Although accumulation-and-maintenance trusts are a special form of discretionary trust, the tax rules are much more favourable. A payment into an accumulation-and-maintenance trust counts as a PET (see page 69) – assuming none of the exemptions in Chapter 2 apply – and so there is no tax to pay provided you survive for seven years after making the gift.

Normal CGT rules apply to a gift to an accumulation-and-maintenance trust, so you will need to check whether there is any CGT to pay (see Chapters 2 and 3).

The trust's tax position

An accumulation-and-maintenance trust is not subject to the periodic charge regime – that is, there is no IHT to pay on the value of the trust during the lifetime of the trust nor is there any IHT charge when payments are made to beneficiaries.

The income and capital gains tax position of the trust is the same as for other discretionary trusts – see page 127.

Payments to beneficiaries

The rules are the same as for other discretionary trusts (see page 128).

Bear in mind that, if you set up an accumulation-and-maintenance trust for your own child, any income paid out to your child under the age of 18 (and unmarried) or used for his or her benefit will count as your income for tax purposes if it exceeds £100 a year. Any capital paid out will be treated in the same way to the extent that it can be matched against income accumulated within the trust (and may in future be taxed in the same way regardless of whether it can be matched to income – see page 134). But you can avoid income being taxed as yours if you leave all the income and capital to accumulate within the trust.

When the trust ends

There is no IHT charge, provided one or more beneficiaries have become entitled to the trust property (or dies before becoming entitled). The trustees may need to pay CGT on any capital gains – this cannot be reclaimed by the beneficiaries. Amounts received by beneficiaries are treated as described under 'Payments to beneficiaries' on page 128.

However, if the income-and-accumulation trust comes to an end in other circumstances – for example, if it simply reaches the end of its 25-year lifespan without any beneficiaries having become entitled to the property, there will normally be an IHT bill. The amount of tax due depends on how long the trust has existed – see HMRC Leaflet IHT16, *Settled property*, for further information. After a full 25 years, the charge would be 21 per cent of the trust property. The charge can be avoided if, before the 25 years are up, you ensure that a beneficiary is given an interest in the trust property – this can either be an interest in possession or to the capital.

Situations when the normal tax rules do not apply

Settlor-interested trusts

A settlor-interested trust is one in which the settlor has a 'retained interest'. If this applies, both income and capital gains made by the trust will be taxed as those of the settlor. Often this will mean a higher tax bill. You will be treated as having a retained interest if you or your husband, wife or civil partner can in any circumstances benefit from the trust either now or at some future time.

The definition of retained interest is very widely drawn, so you will be caught by the rules not simply if you or your husband or wife is a named beneficiary of the trust, but even if you might become a beneficiary only because of some seemingly unlikely circumstances, for example:

- the trust says your grandchild will become entitled to the trust property provided he or she reaches age 25 but you fail to say what happens if he or she does not reach that age. In that case, the property would automatically revert back to the settlor, so you are a potential beneficiary and have a retained interest
- a trust is set up for your children and remoter issue but the trustees have the power to give the trust property to any other trust that includes the children and remoter issue as beneficiaries. This

would not exclude a trust that also included you or your husband, wife or civil partner as additional beneficiaries, so again you are deemed to have a retained interest.

Note, too, that if you are both the settlor and an actual or potential beneficiary under the trust, the gift with reservation rules apply (see page 74). This means that the trust property continues to count as part of your estate for IHT purposes until you cease to be able to benefit or you die, whichever happens first. Unlike the retained interest rules, the gift with reservation rules do not apply if your husband, wife or civil partner (but not you) is a beneficiary.

If you have an interest in the trust but have managed to set it up using a scheme that avoids the gift with reservation rules, the pre-owned assets tax (POAT) – see Chapter 5 – might instead apply. See Chapter 13 for guidance on whether some of the most popular types of scheme are caught by POAT.

Other situations when income from a trust is treated as that of the settlor

If you are the settlor and you or your husband, wife or civil partner enters into various loan and repayment arrangements with a trust, the income may be treated as yours for tax purposes rather than as income of the trust.

If the income of a trust of which you are the settlor is paid out to, or used for the benefit of, your unmarried children under the age of 18, it is taxed as your income unless it comes to no more than £100 a year. This will also apply to capital from the trust if there is available trust income to match the payment (and may in future be extended to any capital – see page 134). In the case of a bare trust even undistributed income will be taxed as that of the parent if it exceeds £100 and results from a parental gift into the trust made on or after 9 March 1999.

Changes on the horizon

As part of its package of measures to simplify the taxation of trusts (see page 117), the government is proposing that for income tax and capital gains tax purposes, trusts should fall into three categories, each with its own tax rules, as follows. At the time of writing, the measures are the subject of further consultation and so could change from the outline given here. It is expected that the new regime may come into force from 6 April 2006.

Settlor-interest trusts

As now, income from a trust where you or your husband, wife or civil partner have a retained interest would be taxed as your income. However, under current rules this usually means tax at the basic rate if you are a basic rate taxpayer. Under the new rules, tax would in that situation be due at the basic rate, savings rate or 10 per cent dividend rate depending on the type of income involved. First, the trustees would pay tax on any income at the rate applicable to trusts. You, as settlor, would then claim back tax if the income would have been taxed more lightly in your own hands.

Payments from the trust to beneficiaries (other than you) would be treated as if they were payments direct from you to the beneficiary. You would be able to claim any reliefs available on the payments, for example, gift aid relief (see Chapter 16) if the beneficiary was a charity.

The capital gains position would be the same as now – in other words, capital gains would be taxed as gains of the settlor. Losses made by the trust may not be set of against personal gains of the settlor.

Bear in mind that a gift from a parent to a child is caught by the anti-avoidance 'settlements' legislation and so currently treated as a settlor-interest trust for income tax purposes. This means that income (unless it comes to no more than £100 a year) is treated as income of the parent not the child. Under the new regime, this treatment would apply to capital gains as well as income.

Bare trusts

As now, income and gains would be taxed as if they were received direct by the beneficiary (unless, in the case of a gift from a parent to a child, the anti-avoidance settlements legislation applied – see above).

General trusts

This would cover interest in possession trusts, discretionary trusts and accumulation and maintenance trusts. A common tax regime would apply to all, but with some opportunities to opt for different treatment.

Interest in possession trusts would be taxed in basically the same way as now. The main change would be for discretionary trusts and accumulation and maintenance trusts where all income received by the trust would initially be taxed at the basic rate, savings rate or 10 per cent dividend tax rate, depending on the type of income. Where the income was paid out to a beneficiary by 31 December following the end of the tax year, the income would flow through the trust with no further tax adjustment (called 'income streaming').

Beneficiaries would receive the income with a tax credit at the appropriate rate for the type of income.

Income in excess of the £500 basic rate band (see page 127) and not paid out by 31 December would become subject to the rate applicable to trusts. Subsequent payments of this income to beneficiaries would be paid with a 40 per cent non-reclaimable tax credit. This means beneficiaries would have no further tax to pay but would not be able to reclaim any tax if their personal tax rate was lower.

Capital gains would be taxed in the same way as now.

The new rules for trusts for vulnerable people (see page 117) would be available, so these trusts could opt for tax on income and gains to be based on the circumstances of the vulnerable person, taking into account their personal allowance and, if applicable, the starting rate of tax.

Table 8.1 Which type of trust?

	Bare Trust	Interest-in-possession	Discretionary	Accumulation-and-maintenance
IHT status of gift when trust set up	PET	PET	Chargeable gift	PET
IHT regime once trust up and running	Does not apply	Favourable	Unfavourable	Favourable
Trust pays tax on income at:[†]	Beneficiary's own rate	22%, 20% and 10%	40% and 32.5%	40% and 32.5%
Trust pays tax on gains at:[†]	Beneficiary's own rate	40%	40%	40%
Can build up income within trust	Yes	Not usually	Yes	Yes
Can easily alter who benefits	No	No for income, yes for capital	Yes	Yes
Can easily alter the shares of the beneficiaries	No	No for income, yes for capital	Yes	Yes
Other				Only for minors

[†]2005–6 rates and rules.

Chapter 9

Lifetime gift planning

SKIP THE COUNTRY

'I'd like to give Jake the paddock. The trouble is now that the local council has included it in the development plan, it's worth such a lot. I'll have a massive capital gains tax bill to pay,' groaned Patrick. 'There's only one thing for it,' soothed his wife, Jenny. 'We'll have to flee the country – become tax exiles. But we'll have to stay away for at least five years.' 'Jenny, you're up to something ...' Patrick had belatedly spied the stack of maps and travel guides.

If you want to make gifts during your lifetime, most will be free of inheritance tax (IHT) either because of some specific exemption or because they count as potentially exempt transfers (PETs) (and so are tax-free provided you survive for seven years). Therefore your main concern is how to give without triggering an unnecessary capital gains tax (CGT) bill or creating income tax problems. Following the tips in this chapter can help but, if your affairs are complex, it is advisable to get help from an accountant* or other tax adviser.*

For a detailed look at making gifts of your home, gifts to children or gifts to charity, see Chapters 14, 15 and 16, respectively.

Give exempt assets

If you can, give away things which are outside the scope of CGT – for example, cash or personal items worth less than £6,000 – see Chapter 2.

Use your tax-free slice

If you are planning to make a gift within the next few years and it's showing a fairly sizeable gain on which you would face a hefty CGT bill, consider making use of your tax-free slice between now and the year in which you make the gift. You can dispose of a certain amount of chargeable assets, which would otherwise be taxable, each year without having to pay CGT – the tax-free slice for 2005–6 is £8,500.

New-style bed-and-breakfast

Instead of wasting your CGT tax-free slice in years when you are not making any gifts (or other disposals), a widely used ploy used to be to sell assets, most commonly shares, and buy them back again the next day – a practice called 'bed-and-breakfasting'. This realised the gain (or loss) on the asset for tax purposes, using up your tax-free slice for the year (or providing a loss to offset against other gains) and gave a new, higher initial value for calculating future gains on the asset.

However, the 1998 Budget brought traditional bed-and-breakfasting to an abrupt end. From 17 March 1998 onwards, any shares or similar assets which are sold and repurchased within a 30-day period are matched and any gain or loss which would otherwise have been realised is ignored for CGT purposes.

You could still bed-and-breakfast in the old way but leaving more than 30 days between the sale and repurchase. However, this would be a high-risk strategy, since the stock market could move dramatically over a month. Alternative ways to realise gains or losses while keeping your assets largely unchanged include:

- 'bed-and-ISA' your shares. This means selling the shares and immediately buying them back within the shelter of an Individual Savings Account (ISA). An ISA must be taken out through an approved ISA manager (e.g. a stockbroker)
- if you are married or in a civil partnership, sell your shares and ask your husband, wife or civil partner to buy the same shares immediately. Ownership has changed but at least the shares are still in the family
- sell your shares and simultaneously buy a 'call traded option' which gives you the right to buy the same company's shares at a fixed price on or before a set future date. This is a relatively expensive exercise because you must pay a premium for the option

- sell the shares in one company and buy back shares in another company which is expected to perform in a similar manner – usually shares in a company of similar size in the same sector. Deciding which shares are reasonably well-matched could be tricky.

Before attempting new-style bed-and-breakfasting, you would be wise to discuss the various possibilities with a stockbroker.*

Use your husband's, wife's or civil partner's tax-free slice

If your husband, wife or civil partner does not use his or her tax-free slice (£8,500 in 2005–6) and you have a gift to make on which there is a sizeable gain, you might be able to reduce the CGT bill by first giving part or all of the asset to your husband or wife. Gifts between husband and wife or between civil partners are normally tax-free (see page 23). Note, however, that the gift must be genuine and you cannot attach any conditions – e.g. insisting that he or she gives away the asset subsequently in accordance with your wishes. Therefore you need to be confident that you and your husband, wife or civil partner have genuinely similar views and aspirations about making gifts to the recipient.

Skip the country?

In the past, CGT was payable only if you were resident and/or ordinarily resident in the UK during the tax year in which you realised a chargeable gain. However, following changes in 1998, you can now still end up with a CGT bill even if you are living abroad.

For anyone who ceases to be resident from 17 March 1998 onwards and for anyone who becomes UK resident again from 6 April 1998 onwards, any gifts or other disposals he or she makes while abroad will be free of CGT only if he or she has been not resident and not ordinarily resident in the UK for five complete tax years or more.

Where your period abroad comes to less than five complete tax years, gains realised in the tax year in which you leave the UK will be taxable in that year. Gains realised while abroad will be taxed in the tax year of your return.

The tax statutes say very little about what the terms 'resident' and 'ordinarily resident' mean though, at the time of writing, the government was reviewing this and considering possible changes to the legal definitions of residence and domicile. In the meantime, a body of case law has developed. Under present rules, you will always count as resident for a tax year if you spend 183 days or more in the UK during the tax year and, if you spend fewer days there, you may still count as resident. You will usually count as 'ordinarily resident' if you live in the UK year after year, even if you are away temporarily. The main way in which someone who normally lives in the UK can count as not resident and not ordinarily resident is to go and work full-time abroad, provided the following conditions are met:

- your absence from the UK and your contract of employment both last at least a whole tax year
- you can make visits back home (e.g. for holidays) but the time spent in the UK must not add up to more than 183 days in any one tax year and, over the whole period abroad, must average only 91 days per tax year or less.

By concession, a husband, wife or civil partner accompanying their spouse while he or she works abroad can also count as resident or non-resident. For more information about residency status, see HMRC booklet IR20, *Residents and non-residents*, available from tax offices★ and the HMRC★ website.

Taking a decision to work abroad just so that you can avoid CGT may seem a drastic step. But, looked at from another perspective, if you do find yourself doing a stint working overseas, it would be an excellent time to consider making any gifts which could give rise to a large CGT bill.

EXAMPLE 9.1

Jenny is a fashion designer, working for an international firm. Usually she is based in London but in March 2005 she is posted to the USA. Her husband Patrick decides to go with her. The posting is due to last for a minimum of two years but can be extended thereafter on an annual basis. Jenny will have nine weeks' holiday a year when she can make visits back home. Provided Jenny continues to work abroad for at least five years, this would be an ideal opportunity to give their son, Jake, a piece of land which Patrick owns. The former paddock has been given development land status in the council's local plan which has boosted its value from a few thousand pounds to £300,000. Despite its high value, there is no CGT to pay on the gift, provided Patrick remains non-resident and not ordinarily resident for five whole tax years.

Don't forget hold-over relief

Hold-over relief (see Chapter 3) lets you, in effect, give away your CGT bill along with the asset which is the subject of your gift. One of the circumstances in which you can claim hold-over relief is where the gift counts as a chargeable transfer for IHT. Making your gift to a discretionary trust would fit the bill. Provided you make sure that the gift is covered by one of the IHT exemptions (see Chapter 2) or falls within your tax-free slice (£275,000 for 2005–6), there will be no IHT on the gift. However, make sure that a gift into trust suits your intentions and that you fully understand the tax position of the trust (see Chapter 8). Get advice from a solicitor.★

Gifts to children

It is difficult for a parent to make a gift to his or her child without income paid to the child or used for the benefit of the child counting as the parent's income for tax purposes. However the new child trust fund offers one route. See Chapter 15 for details of this and other ideas.

Part 2

Inheritance

Whether you are writing your own will or sorting out someone else's will, please note that it is important to consult a legal adviser if substantial sums of money are involved and/or the situation is at all complex.

Chapter 10

Making a will

WILLS ARE IMPORTANT

'Now, Mr Hope' – the solicitor's face became more serious – 'I take it you have made a will?'

'Well, no,' replied Richard, 'but my affairs are very straightforward. Everything would go to my wife – after all, the children are grown up.'

'Precisely, Mr Hope. Without a will, only part of your estate would pass to your wife. Your children would also benefit. Your wife might need to sell the home and there would certainly be a number of unnecessary costs. I would strongly advise you to make a will.'

A will is a legal document which says how your possessions (your *estate*) are to be dealt with when you die. Even if your estate is small and your intentions regarding it extremely simple, you should still make a will. If you do not, a number of problems can arise, as follows:

- your survivors may waste time trying to find out whether or not you did write a will; it may take them a long time to trace all your possessions; and they may have to spend time and money tracing relatives
- if there is no will, it may take longer and cost more to 'prove' the estate (an administrative process which has to be completed before your estate can be 'distributed' – that is, handed on – to your heirs)
- without a will, your next of kin (often a wife, husband or civil partner) will usually be appointed to sort out your affairs. At the time of bereavement, he or she may prefer not to take on this role and you may, in any case, have friends or relatives who would be more suited to the task

- the law will dictate how your estate is passed on and this may not coincide with your wishes
- the law may require that various trusts are set up. The terms of these trusts may be overly restrictive and, especially where small sums are involved, unnecessarily large expenses may be incurred
- your heirs may have to pay inheritance tax (or more tax) than would have been the case had you used your will to pass on your possessions tax-efficiently (see Chapter 13).

Apart from avoiding these problems and ensuring that your possessions are given away as you would choose, a will can be used for other purposes too: you can appoint guardians to care for young children; and you can express your preferences about funeral arrangements and any wishes about the use of your body for medical purposes after death.

Note that the rules relating to wills and intestacy in Scotland and Northern Ireland differ in a number of respects from the rules for the rest of the UK – see pages 154 and 155. The rules described here apply to England and Wales.

Definitions

Three types of player are involved in a will:

- **testator/testatrix**   The man or woman whose will it is. You must be aged 18 or over (and of sound mind) to make a valid will
- **beneficiary**   A person or organisation left something ('benefits') under a will
- **personal representative**   The person, people or organisation that sees that your estate is distributed following your death. If you have not made a will, they are your *administrators* and they will distribute your estate in accordance with the law. If you have made a will, they are your *executors* and they will try to ensure that the instructions in your will are carried out.

Dying without a will

If you die without making a will ('intestate') the law dictates how your estate will be passed on (with the exception of joint assets held under a 'joint tenancy' – see page 93 – which pass automatically to the surviving co-owners). The law aims, in the first instance, to protect your immediate family – husband, wife, civil partner and children. This might coincide with your wishes but, even if it did, it still might not result in your estate being used as you had expected or would have wished. Furthermore, people who are not formally part of your family – for example, an unmarried partner – have no automatic rights under the intestacy laws (though they might still have a claim against your estate – see page 152).

CIVIL PARTNERS
From 5 December 2005 onwards, same-sex couples in the UK will be able to register their relationship as a civil partnership. The intestacy laws for England, Wales and Northern Ireland have been amended to treat civil partners in the same way as married people. The intestacy laws for Scotland have been amended to give civil partners some of the rights accorded to married people.

Where part or all of your estate would pass to your spouse or civil partner under the intestacy rules, this will only happen if he or she survives you by at least 28 days. This 'survivorship provision' (which is a common device used in wills) makes sure that, in cases where you and your spouse or civil partner die within a short time of one another (for example, as a result of a road traffic accident), the relatives of each of you benefit from your respective estates rather than everything going to the relatives of the second to die. Bear in mind that a person under 18 cannot make a valid will, so the estate of child who dies – including any assets held under a bare trust for the child – would be subject to the intestacy rules.

The intestacy laws assume that all your possessions could be sold by your personal representative to convert your whole estate into cash which would then be distributed according to the rules described below. In practice, the possessions would not necessarily be sold and could be passed on intact but problems can arise where there is a large possession – for example, the family home – if it needs to be split between two or more beneficiaries. The intestacy laws operate as follows.

If you are survived by a spouse or civil partner and no children

Your husband, wife or civil partner is entitled to all your *personal chattels* (i.e. personal possessions, such as clothes, furniture, jewellery and private cars). If your estate is valued at £200,000 or less, your husband, wife or civil partner also inherits the whole estate. (See Chapter 12 for guidance on valuing your estate.)

If your estate is valued at more than £200,000, your spouse or civil partner gets the whole lot, provided you had no living parents or brothers or sisters at the time of your death. If you are survived by parents, brothers or sisters, your spouse or civil partner is entitled to a fixed sum of £200,000 (plus interest at a set rate from the date of death until the date the payment is made) plus half of whatever remains. The remainder goes to your parents or, if they are dead, to your brothers and sisters. Chart 10.1 summarises the position.

The £200,000 limit was set in 1993 and, at the time of writing, was under review. The proposal was to increase it to £650,000 from a future date (probably in 2006).

Chart 10.1 Who inherits if you leave a spouse/civil partner and no children

Is your estate worth more than £200,000?	→	NO →	Husband/wife/civil partner inherits whole estate
↓ YES ↓			
Do you have parents? ↓ NO ↓	→	YES →	Husband/wife/civil partner gets £200,000 (with interest) plus half the remaining estate. Your parents inherit the rest.
Do you have brothers or sisters? ↓ NO ↓	→	YES →	Husband/wife/civil partner gets £200,000 (with interest) plus half the remaining estate. Your brothers and sisters (or their children) share the rest.
Husband/wife/civil partner inheritswhole estate			

EXAMPLE 10.1

Jeremy and Ali had been married for ten years when tragically Jeremy died in a road accident. He was only 36 and, though he had several times thought about making a will, he had not got around to doing it. His estate was valued at £250,000 and he would have left everything to Ali but under the intestacy laws the estate was divided between Ali and his parents as follows:

Ali's share

Fixed sum	£200,000
plus interest	£4,940
plus half the remaining estate	
(i.e. £250,000 – £204,940) ÷ 2	£22,530
Total	£227,470
Jeremy's parents' share	£22,530

If you are survived by children

If you leave children, but no husband, wife or civil partner, the inheritance position is simple: your children share your estate equally. Note that 'children' includes offspring from your most recent marriage, any previous marriages, adopted and illegitimate children. However, it does not include stepchildren.

If you are survived by a husband, wife or civil partner, he or she is entitled to all your personal possessions. And, if your estate is valued at £125,000 or less, he or she also inherits the whole of that.

If your estate is valued at more than £125,000, your husband, wife or civil partner receives a fixed sum of £125,000 (plus interest at a set rate from the date of death until the date payment is made) and a life interest in half of the remaining estate. A life interest gives him or her the right to the income from that part of the estate (or use of it in the case of, say, a house) but he or she cannot touch the capital. (Note that the husband, wife or civil partner can decide to take an appropriately calculated lump sum from the estate in place of a life interest.) The rest of the estate passes to your children to be shared equally between them. They also become entitled to the capital bearing the life interest when your husband, wife or civil partner dies. (Note that children can inherit capital outright only once they reach the age of 18, so they have an income entitlement up to that age.) Chart 10.2 summarises the position.

The £125,000 limit was set in 1993 and, at the time of writing, was under review. The proposal was to increase it to £350,000 from a future date (probably in 2006).

Chart 10.2 Who inherits if you leave children

Do you have a husband, wife or civil partner? → NO →		Your children inherit equal shares in the estate
↓		
YES		
↓		
Is your estate worth more than £125,000? → NO →		Husband/wife/civil partner inherits whole estate
↓		
YES		
↓		
Husband/wife/civil partner gets £125,000 (with interest) plus life interest in half the remaining estate (which passes eventually to your children). Your children inherit the rest.		

EXAMPLE 10.2

Alan died leaving an estate valued at £250,000. Of this amount £200,000 represented his half-share in the family home (which he and his wife, Julia, owned as tenants in common – see page 93). However, he had made no will. Under the intestacy rules Julia and his only child inherited the estate in the following shares:

Julia's share

Capital: fixed sum	£125,000
plus interest	£3,090
Total capital	£128,090

Remaining estate (£250,000 – £128,090)   £121,910
So Julia also gets income/use from half of
£121,910 i.e. £60,955

Child's share

Capital now   £60,955
Capital to be set aside for future (Julia has life interest)   £60,955

Unfortunately, Julia's outright inheritance of £128,090 and interest in a further £60,955 come to less than the value of the family home. In order to comply with the intestacy rules requiring capital of £121,910 in total to be set aside for the child, part of the family home must be held in trust for the child.

Chart 10.3 Who inherits if you leave no near-relatives

Are you survived by your parents?	→ YES →		Your parents inherit equal shares in your estate
↓ NO ↓			
Do you have any brothers or sisters?	→ YES →		Your brothers and sisters inherit equal shares in your estate[†]
↓ NO ↓			
Are you survived by any grandparents?	→ YES →		Your grandparents inherit the estate in equal shares
↓ NO ↓			
Do you have any uncles or aunts?	→ YES →		Your uncles and aunts inherit the estate in equal shares[‡]
↓ NO ↓			
Your estate passes to the Crown			

[†] If a brother or sister has died before you, their offspring, if any, inherit instead. If you have no full brothers or sisters, any half-brothers or half-sisters will share the estate instead.
[‡] If any uncle or aunt has died before you, their offspring inherit instead. If you have no full uncles or aunts, any half-uncles or half-aunts share the estate instead.

If you are survived by no near-relatives

If you leave no husband, wife or civil partner and no children, the intestacy rules rank your heirs in the order in which they will inherit your estate.

If you have no relatives who are eligible to inherit (see Chart 10.3), your estate passes to the Crown in *bona vacantia* (which literally means 'unclaimed goods'). The Crown may make ex gratia payments if your dependants or distant relatives make an application to it. It is important to realise that such claimants have no *right* to receive anything – payments are at the discretion of the Crown. Applicants who are most likely to succeed include the following:

- someone who had a long, close association with you: for example, an unmarried partner or someone who lived with you as a child
- someone whom you clearly intended to benefit under a will that was invalid for some reason.

EXAMPLE 10.3
Harold died aged 89 without making a will. He was an only child. His wife and parents died before him and he himself had no children. But his Uncle Jack (who died long ago) had two children, Jean and Richard, who are both still living. They each inherit half of Harold's estate.

Partial intestacy

Your will should cover all your assets. If you do not specify how part of your estate is to be used, that part will be subject to the intestacy rules even though the rest of your estate is disposed of in accordance with the will.

Problems caused by intestacy

The main problems of intestacy arise where you are survived by a partner (either married or not) and/or you have children. Unless you make a will, you cannot be certain that they will be adequately provided for in the event of your death.

If you are not married to your partner, he or she has no automatic right of inheritance in the event of your death. However, he or she will be able to claim a share of your estate under the Inheritance (Provision for Family and Dependants) Act 1975 if they lived with you as husband, wife or civil partner throughout the two years prior to your death. If that condition does not apply and if they can show that they were being partly or wholly maintained by you when you were alive, they may still be able to claim support from your estate. In either case, a claim must usually be made within six months of permission being granted to distribute the estate. It will then be considered by the courts, which is generally a lengthy and often costly procedure.

If you are married or in a civil partnership, there is a tendency to assume that your husband, wife or civil partner will automatically inherit everything. The foregoing sections have shown that this is by no means certain. And, even if you are happy for your husband, wife or civil partner and children to share your assets, the practical application of the intestacy rules may be very distressing to your survivors. Where the estate must be shared between your spouse or civil partner and children, or shared with other relatives, your husband, wife or civil partner has the right to claim the family home as part or all of his or her inheritance (provided he or she lived there with you prior to your death). If the home is worth more than the amount he or she is entitled to inherit, your husband, wife or civil partner can 'buy' the excess from the estate. But if he or she does not have sufficient resources to be able to do this, the home may have to be sold so that the cash raised can be split as required by the intestacy provisions.

Minors cannot inherit directly under the intestacy laws, so any assets passing to these children must be held in trust. The trustees will be required to invest the assets in accordance with the Trustee Act 2000 (see page 106) assuming the law of England and Wales applies. Fortunately, this gives the trustees very wide investment powers. They may be required to obtain professional advice. This could be unduly costly if only a relatively small sum is involved. In Scotland and Northern Ireland, the more restrictive investment rules of the Trustee Investments Act 1961 apply. This could mean an unduly high proportion of the trust fund being held as deposits, gilts and other bonds, and the trustees will be required to get investment advice unless they stick to a narrow range of investments largely made up of National Savings & Investments products.

Assets continue to be held in trust until the child reaches age 18, at which point he or she takes over direct ownership of the assets. This might be earlier than you would have wished – in a will, you could require assets to be held in trust until a later age.

Tax and intestacy

Although intestacy might mean your estate is not passed on as you would have wished, it does in fact impose a certain amount of tax-efficiency. This is because the rules require a share of your estate above the fixed amounts to be passed to people other than your husband, wife or civil partner, so using up some or all of your inheritance tax-free slice. This can save up to £110,000 inheritance tax (in 2005–6) on the subsequent death of your husband, wife or civil partner – see page 199.

Intestacy in Scotland

The law in Scotland works differently for those who die without making a will, as follows. The amounts stated apply from 1 June 2005 onwards. Lower amounts applied before that date.

- **If you were married with no children** Your husband or wife has 'prior rights' to the family home (provided it is in Scotland) up to a value of £300,000, furniture and household effects up to £24,000 and a cash sum up to £75,000. He or she also has 'legal rights' to half the remaining 'moveable estate' (i.e. excluding land and buildings). See below for the remaining estate.
- **If you were married with children** Your husband or wife has prior rights to the family home up to £300,000, furniture and effects up to £24,000 and a cash sum up to £42,000 plus legal rights to share one-third of the remaining moveable estate. The children also have legal rights to share one-third of the moveable estate between them. See below for the remaining estate.
- **If you had a civil partner and no children** Your civil partner has legal rights to half your moveable estate.
- **If you had a civil partner and children** Your civil partner has legal rights to one third of your moveable estate. The children also have a legal right to share a third of the moveable estate between them.
- **If you had children but no husband, wife or civil partner** The children have legal rights to half the moveable estate.

- **The remaining estate** Whatever remains after meeting the prior rights, the legal rights and, in the case of partial intestacy, bequests under a will is known as 'the dead's part' and is distributed in the following order of priority:

  - children
  - if there are both parents and brothers and sisters, half the remainder goes to the parents, half to the brothers and sisters
  - brothers and sisters, if there are no parents
  - parents, if there are no brothers and sisters
  - husband or wife
  - uncles and aunts (or, if they have died, their children)
  - grandparents
  - brothers and sisters of grandparents (or, if they have died, their children)
  - remoter ancestors, going back one generation at a time
  - the Crown.

Intestacy in Northern Ireland

The law is also different in Northern Ireland for those who die without making a will.

- **If you were married or in a civil partnership with no children** Your husband, wife or civil partner inherits all your personal effects plus the first £200,000 of your estate and half of any residue. The remainder passes to parent(s) or brother(s) and sister(s) if there are no parents still living. If there are no children, no parents and no brothers or sisters (or nephews or nieces), then your spouse inherits your whole estate.
- **If you were married or in a civil partnership with children** Your husband, wife or civil partner inherits all your personal effects plus the first £125,000 of your estate plus half of any residue if there is one child, or one-third of the residue, if there are two or more children. The remainder of the estate passes to the child(ren) – in trust if they are aged under 18.
- **If you had children but no husband, wife or civil partner** The estate is divided equally between the children.
- **If you had no children and no husband, wife or civil partner** Your estate goes to your relatives, starting with parents but extending to very distant relatives if no closer ones survive you.

Drawing up a will

In many people's minds, making a will is inextricably linked with using a solicitor but this need not be so. Provided your personal circumstances are not overly complicated and you understand what you are doing, there is no reason why you should not write your own will. A number of books and kits are available to help you do this: for example, *Wills and Probate* available from Which? Books.* The main advantage of writing your own will is, of course, the saving in solicitors' fees. But a simple will, for example involving only personal (no business) assets in the UK, with everything left to your husband, wife or civil partner, need not cost much even if you do go to a professional. If your affairs are more complex, you should be wary of the DIY route.

A will, to fulfil its purpose, must record your intentions clearly and unambiguously and should include contingency plans to cover the possibility, for example, of a beneficiary dying before you. There are also various pitfalls to be avoided – some that would invalidate the will and leave your estate subject to the intestacy laws and others which would not invalidate the will but would interfere with the intentions expressed in it. For example, a valid will must be signed by two or more witnesses, who may not also be beneficiaries (or the husbands, wives or civil partners of beneficiaries) under the will; so, if you are leaving anything to your husband, wife or civil partner, say, do not ask him or her to be a witness – the will would be valid but your spouse or civil partner would not be allowed to inherit under it.

If your affairs are complicated – e.g. you run your own business, you have been divorced or you have step-children – or you do not feel confident about your knowledge of the law relating to wills, you would be wise to employ a professional rather than trying to draw up a will yourself. Lawyers claim to make more money from sorting out defective DIY wills than from writing wills themselves.

The traditional source of help drawing up a will is a solicitor. Most high street firms can draw up a simple will – leaving, say, everything to your husband, wife or civil partner – and charges often start as low as £50. If you and your spouse or civil partner draw up similar wills at the same time (often called 'reciprocal wills', 'mirror wills' or 'back-to-back wills'), you might get a special rate of, say, £70 or £80 the pair. But prices vary greatly and, even for a simple will, some solicitors charge in the region of £100 to £150. If your affairs are complicated, the charge will depend on the time the solicitor needs to devote to your case and so you should expect to pay more. Always check the expected price before going ahead.

Solicitors must pass exams, go through rigorous post-graduate training and continue to update their skills through continuous professional development. But dealing with estates is a specialist area, so you may prefer to choose a member of the Society of Trust and Estate Practitioners (STEP).★ Solicitors must belong to a professional body – one of the Law Societies★ – that lays down strict rules of business conduct backed up by disciplinary procedures and ensures that you have access to the Law Society Consumer Complaints Service★ (which is monitored by an independent commissioner) if things go wrong.

Will-writing services are an alternative to a solicitor. These are often small firms working under a franchise or as agents of a larger company. Most work by gathering the necessary details from you and feeding these into a computer which produces your will. Unlike solicitors, people running, or working for, will-writing firms are not required to have any formal legal qualifications, though they will probably have received some initial training and the computer software they are using will have been developed using legal experts; these firms may also use a solicitor to draw up complex wills. In the past, problems have arisen with some of these services: a number of firms have gone bust and, in one case, it was found that a potentially large number of the wills written contained a flaw and might not be valid. However, the will-writers' industry has been developing over the years and now many practitioners voluntarily belong to one of the trade/regulatory bodies operating in this area. The Society of Will Writers (SWW)★ and the Institute of Professional Willwriters (IPW)★ aim to promote the professionalism of their members in the following ways:

- **training** Members of the SWW who have passed examinations relevant to will writing or can display competence in some other way can become fellows of the society and be able to use the initials FSWW. But other members (using the initials ASWW or MSWW) will not normally have the relevant training. All members of the IPW must have passed an exam before being admitted to membership

- **code of conduct** Members of both the SWW and IPW are required to follow the *Code of Conduct and Practice for the Will Writing Profession*. The code sets out rules of good business practice, including: disclosing fees and charges to customers before taking on their business, not taking on work beyond the member's competence, advising customers to seek legal advice if their affairs are beyond the will-writer's competence, having professional indemnity insurance and operating a proper written complaints system.

In the event of a complaint, you should first take the matter to the will-writing firm but, if not satisfied with the response, you can take the complaint to the SWW's or IPW's conciliation service. If conciliation fails, the case can be referred to arbitration. Though there is a fee for this, it is refundable if you win the case. As an alternative to conciliation and arbitration, you could take a complaint to any other relevant body, such as your local Trading Standards Office,* or you could take court action.

Will-writers generally charge a flat fee – say, £45 to £50 for a single will or £70 to £80 for mirror wills. Not surprisingly, their wills tend to have a standardised format – if your affairs are complex, a solicitor will normally be the better choice.

A third source of will-writing is banks, building societies and life insurance companies. These offer a will-preparation service but some insist that you agree to them also acting as executors of the will (which is not generally a good idea – see below). You have an interview with the bank, society or company either at their offices or in your home. The interviewer you meet is not usually the person who actually draws up the will. If a bank or building society writes the will and you have a complaint, you can go to the Financial Ombudsman Service (FOS).* The FOS does not cover insurance companies drafting wills.

Many charities also offer will-writing services. It is essential that you make sure that the solicitor or other will-writer is acting for you alone and that you do not feel under any pressure to make a bequest to the charity in your will.

In addition to writing your will, a solicitor or other will-writing service might offer extras, such as storing your will, drawing up a 'living will' (also called an 'advance directive') or severing a joint tenancy to create a tenancy in common (see page 93). Do not feel pressurised into taking up any of these services unless you want to. Bear the following points in mind:

- **will storage** Most important is that your executors will be able to find your will and can be confident that it is your most recent will. If you are known to have a family solicitor, storing your will with the firm could be a good idea. You do not necessarily have to pay anything for this – some firms will store your will free of charge (because they hope to be employed later in executing your will). If you do not have an ongoing relationship with a solicitor, that might not be the best place to store your will. Other options include a bank safe-deposit box or a safe or strong box at home. Whatever you decide, it is a good idea to give your executors a sealed copy of the will

- **living will** This typically sets out in advance your wishes regarding healthcare – especially refusal of medical treatment – if you become incapacitated by a terminal illness or degenerative disease. In general, medical practitioners are required to give whatever treatment they deem necessary but a patient has the right to refuse treatment. Clearly an unconscious patient cannot do this but refusal can still be effective even if it was given in advance of becoming unconscious. There has been much debate about the legal status in the UK of living wills, but it seems that, provided the document states your intentions clearly and reflects your *informed* decision, a living will is likely to be legally binding. A good place to store a living will would be with your medical records

- **severance of joint tenancy** As discussed on page 93, if you want to transfer ownership of something – such as your home – from a joint tenancy to a tenancy in common, you do not need a formal deed drawn up by a solicitor. Notice in writing from one owner to the other is all that is required. Of course, your notice should clearly identify the property concerned, the action you are taking and the date from which it is effective. If you do not feel confident about getting the detail right, you might prefer a solicitor to draw up a notice for you.

Appointing executors

You have a choice when it comes to deciding who will sort out your affairs for you in accordance with your will: you can appoint a professional as your executor – e.g. a solicitor or your bank – or you can appoint friends or relatives. In general, professionals often charge more and if problems arise, such as long delays, the beneficiaries can do little because they do not themselves have a contract with the executor, so have little access to information and limited power to challenge the executor's actions. If, instead, you appoint relatives or friends, they always have the option of employing a solicitor direct if they need help.

You can choose anyone you like to act as executor (provided they are aged 18 or over when they apply for probate) and it is common to appoint the main beneficiary. Normally, you should appoint at least two executors, just in case one dies before you or refuses to act. Make sure you ask the people concerned whether they would be willing to take on the role.

Bear in mind that being an executor is a demanding task. Your executors will need to locate your will and personal papers, track all your assets and establish their value, establish what gifts you have made during the last seven years, deal with debts and funeral expenses, trace and contact beneficiaries, handle paperwork, deliver an account to the HMRC and ensure any tax is paid. As tax will depend not just on the estate you leave but also on gifts made within the seven years up to death, your executors will be expected actively to try to trace gifts. This may mean trawling through old bank and building society statements and making enquiries among family members. Make sure you choose someone who has the time, energy and confidence to deal with officials and form-filling.

You can make your executors' lives easier if you lodge a record of your assets, their location and any gifts you have made along with your will or personal papers.

Reviewing your will

You should not view making a will as a task once done to be forgotten. As your circumstances alter, so your will needs to be updated. In some situations – for example, if you marry, remarry or form a civil partnership – any will made before the marriage or civil partnership will automatically be invalidated (unless it was a will made specifically in contemplation of the marriage or civil partnership). All bequests and references to your ex-husband, ex-wife or ex-civil partner are automatically revoked by divorce or the dissolution of a civil partnership and the appointment of your 'ex' as guardian of any children will be revoked, unless you have made clear that this is still your intention. In other respects, the rest of your will stands. The same is not true of separation – the whole will including bequests to your spouse or civil partner is still valid; in that situation, you should review the terms of your will.

Other circumstances in which you might want to revise your will are the birth or adoption of a child or if you decide that you would like to leave a legacy to a charity. It is wise to read through your will every two years, say, as a matter of course, to check that it reflects your current wishes.

If you do decide to alter a will – even slightly – it is better to draw up a new will containing the revisions than to add an amendment (a 'codicil'). The trouble with codicils is that they can easily become detached from the will and lost. Beware of stapling, clipping or pinning anything other than a codicil to a will. It is quite likely that any other note or document would be detached before the will was sent for probate and the marks left on the will might then raise doubts about whether there had been a codicil attached that has become lost. Enquiries into the non-existent codicil could delay proceedings.

A new will should always start with a clause revoking any previous wills; this automatically invalidates any earlier wills. (Interestingly, if a will is not automatically revoked – by, say, a later will or marriage – the law requires that you *physically* destroy your will if it is to be revoked. Simply putting a cross through it and scribbling 'cancelled' or 'revoked' across it is not enough.)

Making gifts in your will

In your will, you can give away anything you own. There are different types of gift. The distinction between them is important both for tax reasons (see Chapter 11) and because of the order in which they can be redirected to meet expenses and settle debts that you leave at the time of your death. The main types of gift are described as follows.

Specific gift

This can be a named or identifiable possession such as a piece of furniture, an item of jewellery or a particular car. It may be a specific possession that you own *at the time you write the will*. If you later sell the item the beneficiary who was to have received it will get nothing after all.

Alternatively, you might leave a more general type of specific gift. This would be the gift of a possession but not restricted to a specific item that you own at the time of drawing up the will. For example, you might give away 'the car I own at the time of my death', which would take into account the possibility that you might change your car from time to time.

A specific gift might be even more widely defined: for example, simply 'a car'. In this latter case, the executors of your will would have a duty to make sure that the beneficiary received a car – either one that you owned at the time of death or, if you had none, one bought specifically to fulfil the terms of the will – or, alternatively, the trustees would have to pay over an equivalent sum of money.

Legacies

A 'pecuniary legacy' is a particular type of specific gift which is a straightforward gift of money: for example, '£1,000 to my niece, Claire'.

A 'demonstrative legacy' can be either a general gift or a pecuniary legacy which is to be paid from a specific fund: for example, 'a violin to be paid for out of my account with Barclays Bank' or '£1,000 from my account with the Nationwide'. If there was not enough money in the account, the shortfall would have to be met by using other assets in the estate.

On the whole, it is best to keep bequests of particular items or demonstrative gifts to a minimum. Particularly where your will is made a long time before death, there can be many changes to your possessions and the accounts and investments you hold.

Your personal representative(s) have wide powers (called the power of appropriation) to use any part of your estate to satisfy legacies. For example, if you leave £1,000 to your niece, the executors could give, say, shares worth £1,000 rather than selling the shares and giving her the proceeds from the sale.

Residuary gift

A will which assigned every part of your estate as a particular gift or legacy would be out of date almost immediately, because the value of your estate fluctuates even in the course of your daily transactions and will alter more widely during the course of time. Therefore, it is usual to leave whatever remains of your estate, after all your debts, expenses and various gifts as listed above have been paid, as a 'residuary gift' or 'residue'. You may intend your residue to be a substantial gift or it may be a small amount with, say, the bulk of your estate given away through pecuniary gifts.

To meet debts and expenses, any intestate part of your estate will be used up first, followed by the residue.

EXAMPLE 10.4
Daisy died at the ripe old age of 92. Her sole survivor, Albert, had expected to inherit a sizeable sum. However, Daisy had already given the family home to Albert during her lifetime and clearly considered that was enough, because out of the £750,000 estate that she left, she gave £600,000 to a spread of charities. After deducting outstanding debts, funeral expenses and a small tax bill, Albert inherited the residue of only £20,000.

Gifts you do not want to make

By omission, your will can also express your intention not to leave anything (or only very little) to people who might have expected to inherit from you. However, if these people were dependent on you (or you had a partner who had lived with you for at least two years as husband, wife or civil partner without necessarily being dependent), they have the right to make a claim through the courts under the Inheritance (Provision for Family and Dependants) Act 1975 for reasonable provision out of your estate. The main people who are entitled to make such a claim are as follows:

- your husband, wife or civil partner
- a former husband, wife or civil partner, provided he or she has not remarried (and is not precluded from making a claim under the divorce or dissolution settlement)
- a child of yours (whether legitimate, illegitimate or adopted)
- a child of your family (i.e. a stepchild or foster child)
- an unmarried partner.

An application under the Act must usually be made within six months of the personal representatives being given permission to dispose of the estate, though the court can extend this time limit. The court decides whether or not the applicant is entitled to financial support from the estate and, if it decides in favour of the applicant, it can order the payment of either a lump sum or income (or both).

You might seek to anticipate and thwart such a claim by giving away as much of your estate as possible but this strategy will not work. The court has the power to revoke such gifts in order to ensure that enough funds are available to meet the needs of your surviving dependants.

You can include in your will a statement setting out your reasons for excluding your dependants and the court will take this into account. It would be worth seeking advice from a solicitor about the most effective wording to use.

In Scotland, you cannot disinherit your husband, wife, civil partner or children, who can claim their 'legal rights' to part of your estate. For more information see *Wills and Probate* available from Which? Books.*

Chapter 11

Tax at the time of death

NOT JUST A RICH MAN'S TAX

'When I die, my will is very simple,' said Percy, draining his glass. 'I haven't so very much to leave behind, but I'll give my son a bit to help him with his business. Then, I'll just split what's left between the wife and Rose.'

'You should watch out,' replied his friend as he got up to buy another round. 'If there is any tax to pay, it will probably come out of Rose's share – she might end up with a lot less than you expect.'

When you die, you are deemed to make a gift of all your possessions just before death. There is no capital gains tax (CGT) on your estate, but there might be inheritance tax (IHT) on the estate and there could be extra tax due on gifts which you had made in the seven years before death.

Tax on gifts made before death

Chapter 4 looked at the immediate tax position of gifts made during your lifetime. In the case of potentially exempt transfers (PETs) there was no tax to pay at the time of the gift but, if you die within seven years of making a PET, the gift becomes a 'chargeable transfer' and tax is due. The effective rate of tax ranges from 8 per cent up to 40 per cent, depending on the time that has elapsed since you originally made the gift (see page 70).

Similarly, a chargeable transfer – on which tax may have been paid at the time of the gift but at the lower lifetime IHT rate of 20 per cent – will be reassessed and there may be further tax to pay if you die within seven years of making the gift (see page 68).

The reassessment of these earlier gifts and the payment of any tax which becomes due on them is entirely separate from the calculation of tax on your estate. However, if you made PETs within seven years of dying, the fact that they have been reassessed as chargeable gifts will increase your running total up to the time of death and that could create an IHT bill, or increase the amount of IHT payable, on your estate. What is more, there is no 'taper relief' (see page 71) on any extra tax payable on the estate due to the reassessment of PETs. This is a constant source of confusion but taper relief can apply only to tax on the reassessed PETs themselves; taper relief has no impact whatsoever on extra tax on the estate.

Tax on your estate

On your death, IHT is due on the value of your estate plus your running total of gifts made in the seven years before death if they come to more than the tax-free slice. The tax-free slice for 2005–6 is £275,000. See Chapter 4 for previous years' figures. This may seem a large sum but £275,000 can soon be swallowed up, especially if you own your own home. Your estate is made up of:

- the value of all your possessions at the time of death, including your home, car, personal belongings, cash and investments
- *plus* any gifts with reservation (see page 74) that you made and any assets which you elected to be treated as if they were gifts with reservation in order to escape the pre-owned asset tax (see page 88)
- *plus* the proceeds of any insurance policies which are paid to your estate
- *less* your debts
- *less* reasonable funeral expenses.

This total is called your 'free estate' and it is the amount that is available for giving away. For the purpose of calculating any IHT, you can deduct from the free estate any gifts made in your will that count as tax-free gifts (see below). But you must *add* all the PETs and other taxable gifts which you made in the seven years before death to find the relevant running total. If the running total comes to more than the tax-free slice, inheritance tax at a rate of 40 per cent is payable.

Gifts under your will

If the value of your estate plus taxable gifts in the seven years before death comes to less than the tax-free slice, making gifts under your will is fairly straightforward. Assuming that the estate is sufficiently large (after paying off debts and expenses), the recipients will receive the amounts that you specify in your will.

However, if there is inheritance tax due on the estate, matters are not always so simple. To work out how much the recipients will actually receive, you need to know how tax will be allocated between the various gifts. For IHT purposes, there are three types of gift which you can leave in a will:

- **tax-free gifts** (see above and Chapter 2) There is no tax at all on these
- **free-of-tax gifts** (not to be confused with tax-free gifts) The recipient gets the amount you specify and any tax due is paid out of the residue of the estate
- **gifts which bear their own tax** With these, the amount you give is treated as a gross gift *out of which* the recipient must pay any tax due.

In general, a specific gift under your will is automatically treated as a free-of-tax gift unless it is tax-free or you have explicitly stated that the gift should bear its own tax. But, to avoid confusion, it is a good idea to state for every gift whether it is 'free-of-tax' or 'to bear its own tax'. Beware of specifying that a gift of a thing – for example, a piece of jewellery, furniture, painting or other heirloom – should bear its own tax, unless you are confident that the recipient has other resources from which to pay the tax. Otherwise, the gift you have made may need to be sold in order to pay the tax due.

Whatever is left of your estate after deducting specific gifts is called the 'residue' or 'residuary gift'. The residue can be either a tax-free gift or taxable, in which case it bears its own tax. The residue may be split, with part counting as a tax-free gift and part as a taxable one.

The fun starts when you try to calculate how much tax will be deducted either from the residue of the estate or from the specific gifts. The calculations vary depending on the mix of gifts which you are making. The following sections describe the main possibilities.

If you find the calculations that follow daunting, do not despair – you can ask your solicitor or accountant to work out for you the tax position of various gifts that you are considering as part of your will. The most important point is that you should be aware that tax can affect the gifts in different ways.

If all your gifts are tax-free

This is the simplest case. As with lifetime gifts, some gifts from your estate are free of IHT, in particular: gifts of any amount to your husband or wife, gifts to charities, gifts of national heritage property, gifts to political parties and gifts to Housing Associations (see Chapter 2 for more details).

So, for example, you might make a gift to charity and leave the residue to your husband or wife. Since both types of gift are tax-free, there is no inheritance tax at all.

EXAMPLE 11.1

When Connie dies in October 2005, she leaves an estate made up as follows:

Cottage	£65,000
Personal possessions	£21,500
Cash in bank	£496
Investments	£331,204
Gross value of estate	£418,200
less various small debts	£500
less funeral expenses, administration costs, etc.	£2,700
Net value of 'free estate'	£415,000

Connie had made no gifts during the previous seven years. Since the value of the estate exceeds the tax-free slice, you might expect IHT to have been payable. In fact, it was not because Connie used the whole of the 'free estate' to make tax-free gifts. She left a legacy of £100,000 to charity and the residue to her husband.

If all your specific gifts bear their own tax

Again, this is a relatively simple case. The amount of tax on each gift is in proportion to the values of chargeable gifts. This is done by working out the tax due on the whole of the chargeable estate and then expressing this as a percentage of the chargeable estate – this gives you an 'effective' IHT rate. The effective rate is then applied to each gift that is to bear its own tax to find out the amount of tax due on the gift. Example 11.2 should make this clear.

EXAMPLE 11.2

Jim dies in July 2005 leaving an estate of £550,000. He makes two specific gifts bearing their own tax: £150,000 to his friend Ben and £180,000 to his cousin Gerald. He leaves the residue to his wife. Jim made no PETs or chargeable transfers in the seven years before he died. The tax position is worked out as follows:

TAX POSITION OF THE ESTATE

Value of free estate	£550,000
less tax-free gifts (i.e. residue to his wife)	£220,000
Chargeable part of estate	£330,000
less tax-free slice	£275,000
	£55,000
Tax on £55,000 @ 40%	£22,000
Effective tax rate ([£22,000 ÷ £330,000] × 100)	6.667%

WHO GETS WHAT

Tax on Ben's gift @ 6.667%	£10,000
Net amount Ben receives	£140,000
Tax on Gerald's gift @ 3.571%	£12,000
Net amount Gerald receives	£168,000
Amount left to wife	£220,000

If all your specific gifts are free of tax

The main complication in this situation is that, when the estate pays the tax due (out of the residue), it is deemed to be making a gift of the tax as well. To take account of this, all the free–of–tax gifts must be 'grossed up', which simply means that you find the total that equals the amount of the actual gifts plus the tax on them. The tax is then deducted from the residue.

EXAMPLE 11.3

Alec also dies in July 2005 leaving an estate of £550,000. He makes two specific gifts which are free of tax: £150,000 to his friend Douglas and £180,000 to his friend Annette. He leaves the residue to his wife. Alec made no PETs or chargeable transfers in the seven years before he died. The tax position is worked out as follows:

STEP 1: GROSSING UP THE GIFTS

[1]*Add together* all free-of-tax gifts (£150,000 + £180,000)	£330,000
[2]*less* tax-free slice	£275,000
	£55,000

[3]gross up £55,000 at the 40% tax rate
(i.e. divide by 1 – 0.4 = 0.6)   £91,667

The grossed-up value of the gifts is   _____
£91,667 + £275,000   £366,667

STEP 2: TAX POSITION OF THE ESTATE

[4]Value of estate   £550,000
less tax-free part of the estate
(£550,000 – £366,667)   £183,333

[5]Chargeable estate   £366,667
less tax-free slice   £275,000
                                                                                    _____
                                                                                    £91,667

[6]Tax on £91,667 @ 40%   £36,667

STEP 3: WHO GETS WHAT

Net amount Douglas receives   £150,000
Net amount Annette receives   £180,000

Amount left to wife
[7](£550,000 – £150,000 – £180,000 – £36,667)   £183,333

Notes
1 The free-of-tax gifts are added together. This is not their taxable value, because they need first to be grossed up. Note that, at this stage, we do not know what part of the estate is tax-free, because we do not know yet how much tax must be deducted before the residue passes to Alec's wife.
2 We do not gross up the whole of the free-of-tax gifts, because some fall within the tax-free slice. Therefore, at this step, we deduct the tax-free slice to leave just the (net) value of the gifts which are to be taxed.
3 The gifts are grossed up at the death rate and the tax-free slice is added back to give the full grossed-up value of the free-of-tax gifts.
4 We now have the information to find the tax-free part of the estate. (The arithmetic seems circular in this example, but using this method allows us to deal with more complicated examples later on.)
5 The value of the estate less the tax-free part leaves the chargeable estate.
6 Tax is due on the chargeable estate less the tax-free slice at the death rate of 40 per cent.
7 There is, of course, no tax deducted from the free-of-tax gifts. All the tax is paid out of the residue, so the amount left to Alec's wife is the value of his estate less the gifts to other people less the tax bill.

If you leave a mixture of free-of-tax gifts and other types of taxable gift

This is the most complex situation and is illustrated in Example 11.4. Problems arise because the free-of-tax gifts must be grossed up by the IHT rate. The snag is that we do not know what IHT rate to use. The correct IHT rate will depend on the amount of tax due on the whole chargeable estate which is made up of the gifts bearing their own tax as well as the free-of-tax gifts. But we cannot work out tax on the whole estate until we know the grossed up value of the free-of-tax gifts…As you can see, we are in a circular trap. The way out of the trap is to use a process called 'iteration'. Using iteration, you start with an estimate of the IHT rate – initially the death rate of 40 per cent – and repeat the calculation, each time using an improved estimate. You could go through the calculation several times until you were using the correct IHT rate. In practice, the tax authorities let you stop after two rounds by which stage the IHT rate you are using is not perfect but ensures most of the tax due is collected. The note on page 178 following Example 11.5 shows how the calculation works.

You will need to do the same sort of calculation if, in addition to leaving free-of-tax gifts, you also divide the residue so that part is tax-free and part is taxable – this would be the position, for example, if you divided the residue between your children and your husband or wife. The taxable part of the residue is treated as if it is a gross gift bearing its own tax, so it does not need to be grossed up. See Example 11.5.

EXAMPLE 11.4

Suppose, in Example 11.3, Alec left £150,000 free of tax to Douglas and £180,000 free of tax to Annette, as before, but also left a gift of £10,000 to bear its own tax to his daughter Judy. He leaves the residue to his wife. The tax position is as follows:

ROUND 1
STEP 1: GROSSING UP THE GIFTS

[1]*Add together* all free-of-tax gifts (£150,000 + £180,000)	£330,000
[2]*less* tax-free slice	£275,000
	£55,000
[3]gross up at the 40% tax rate (i.e. divide by 0.6)	£91,667
The grossed-up value of the gifts is £91,667 + £275,000	£366,667

STEP 2: TAX POSITION OF THE ESTATE

[4]Value of estate	£550,000
less tax-free part of estate (£550,000 – £366,667 – £10,000)	£173,333
[5]Chargeable estate	£376,667
less tax-free slice	£275,000
	£101,667
[6]Tax on £101,667 @ 40%	£40,667
[7]Notional rate of IHT ([£40,667 ÷ £376,667] × 100)	10.796%

ROUND 2
STEP 1: [8]RE-GROSSING UP THE GIFTS USING A BETTER ESTIMATE

Total free-of-tax gifts	£330,000
gross up at the notional IHT rate (i.e. divide by 1 – 0.10796 = 0.892)	
Re-grossed-up value of free-of-tax gifts	£369,955

STEP 2: REVISED TAX POSITION OF THE ESTATE

[9]Value of estate	£550,000
less tax-free part of estate	
(£550,000 – £369,955 – £10,000)	£170,045
New total for chargeable estate	£379,955
less tax-free slice	£275,000
	£104,955
[10]Tax @ 40% on £104,955	£41,982
Final estate rate ([£41,982 ÷ £379,955] × 100)	11.049%

STEP 3: WHO GETS WHAT

[11]Tax on Judy's gift @ 11.049%	£1,105
Net amount Judy receives	£8,895
[12]Net amount Douglas receives	£150,000
Net amount Annette receives	£180,000
[13]Tax to be deducted from residue (£41,982 – £1,105)	£40,877
[14]Amount left to wife (£550,000 – £150,000	
– £180,000 – £10,000 – £40,877)	£169,123

Notes
1   The free-of-tax gifts are added together. This is not their taxable value, because they need to be grossed up.
2   We do not gross up the whole of the free-of-tax gifts, because some fall within the tax-free slice. Therefore, at this step, we deduct the tax-free slice to leave just the (net) value of the gifts which are to be taxed. In reality, there is another taxable gift that should also benefit from the tax-free slice, but the tax rules simplify the procedure by ignoring that gift for now.
3   The free-of-tax gifts are grossed up at the death rate (40%) and the tax-free slice is added back to give the full grossed-up value of the free-of-tax gifts. This is a first approximation, because we have yet to take account of the other taxable gift which will derive some benefit from the tax-free slice.
4   We now have the information to make a first approximation of the tax-free part of the estate. This is the value of the estate less the grossed-up free-of-tax gifts less the gift bearing its own tax.
5   The value of the estate less the tax-free part leaves our estimate of the chargeable estate.
6   Tax is worked out on this first approximation of the chargeable estate at the death rate of 40 per cent after deducting the tax-free slice.

7 Dividing the amount of tax by the value of the chargeable estate gives us the rate of IHT on the chargeable estate, called the 'notional rate'.

8 We can now get a more accurate figure for the gross value of the free-of-tax gifts by grossing them up at the notional rate of IHT.

9 The estate can now more accurately be divided into its elements: the tax-free part and the chargeable part.

10 Tax at the death rate can now be calculated on the chargeable part. This gives the actual tax bill to be divided between the various bequests. The rate of tax to be applied to each gift is found by dividing the tax bill by the value of the chargeable estate.

11 Judy's gift bears its own tax, so the amount she receives is reduced by the tax due.

12 The free-of-tax gifts are intact with tax on them being borne by the residue.

13 Tax to be deducted from the residue is the total tax bill less any tax being borne by particular bequests.

14 The residue is the value of the estate less the value of the bequests less the tax on the free-of-tax gifts. There is, of course, no tax deducted from the free-of-tax gifts. All the tax is paid out of the residue, so the amount left to the wife is the value of the estate less the gifts to other people less the tax bill.

EXAMPLE 11.5

Percy dies in October 2005 leaving an estate of £800,000. He makes a specific free-of-tax gift of £350,000 to his son, Harold, and leaves the residue equally to his wife and his daughter, Rose. Percy made no PETs or chargeable transfers in the seven years before he died. The tax position is worked out as follows:

ROUND 1

STEP 1: GROSSING UP THE GIFTS

[1]*Add together* all free-of-tax gifts	£350,000
[2]*less* tax-free slice	£275,000
	£75,000
[3]gross up at 40% tax rate (i.e. divide by $1 - 0.4 = 0.6$)	£125,000
The grossed-up value of the gift is £125,000 + £275,000	£400,000

STEP 2: TAX POSITION OF THE ESTATE

[4]Value of estate	£800,000
less tax-free part of the estate (£800,000 – £400,000 – [residue ÷ 2])	£200,000
[5]Chargeable estate	£600,000
less tax-free slice	£275,000
	£325,000
[6]Tax on £325,000 @ 40%	£130,000
[7]Notional rate of IHT ([£130,000 ÷ £600,000] × 100)	21.667%

ROUND 2
[8]STEP 1: RE-GROSSING UP THE GIFTS

Free-of-tax gift	£350,000
gross up at the notional IHT rate (i.e. divide by [1 – 0.21667] = 0.78333)	
Re-grossed up value of free-of-tax gift	£446,809

STEP 2: REVISED TAX POSITION OF THE ESTATE

[9]Value of estate	£800,000
less tax-free part of estate (£800,000 – £446,809 – [residue ÷ 2])	£176,596
New total for chargeable estate	£623,404
less tax-free slice	£275,000
	£348,404

[10]Tax @ 40% on £348,404   £139,362

Final estate rate ([£139,362 ÷ £623,404] × 100)   22.355%

STEP 3: WHO GETS WHAT

[11]Harold receives   £350,000

Tax on Harold's legacy @ 22.355% of £446,809
(to be borne by estate)   £99,884

[12]Residue (£800,000 – £350,000 – £99,884)   £350,116

[13]Wife receives (½ × £350,116)   £175,058

[14]Tax on Rose's share of the residue
@ 22.355% × £175,058   £39,134

Rose receives (£175,058 – £39,134)   £135,924

Notes
1   The free-of-tax gifts are added together. This is not their taxable value, because they need to be grossed up.
2   We do not gross up the whole of the free-of-tax gifts, because some fall within the tax-free slice. Therefore, at this step, we deduct the tax-free slice to leave just the (net) value of the gifts which are to be taxed. In reality, there is another taxable gift (half the residue) that should also benefit from the tax-free slice, but the tax rules simplify the procedure by ignoring that gift for now.
3   The free-of-tax gifts are grossed up at the death rate and the tax-free slice is added back to give the full grossed-up value of the free-of-tax gifts. This is a first approximation, because we have yet to take account of the other taxable gift which will derive some benefit from the tax-free slice.
4   We now have the information to make a first approximation of the tax-free part of the estate. This is the value of the estate less the grossed-up free-of-tax gift (£400,000) less half of what remains ([£800,000 – £400,000] ÷ 2), which will be a gift bearing its own tax.
5   The value of the estate less the tax-free part leaves our estimate of the chargeable estate.
6   Tax is worked out on this first approximation of the chargeable estate at the death rate of 40 per cent after deducting the tax-free slice.
7   Dividing the amount of tax by the value of the chargeable estate gives us the rate of IHT on the chargeable estate, called the 'notional rate'.
8   We can now get a more accurate figure for the gross value of the free-of-tax gifts by grossing them up at the notional rate of IHT.
9   The estate can now more accurately be divided into its elements: the tax-free part and the chargeable part. This latter comprises the re-grossed up gifts (£446,809) plus the taxable part of the residue ([£800,000 – £446,809] ÷ 2).
10 Tax at the death rate can now be calculated on the chargeable part. This gives the actual tax bill to be divided between the various bequests. The rate of tax to be applied to each gift is found by dividing the tax bill by the value of the chargeable estate.
11 The free-of-tax gift to Harold is intact with tax on it being borne by the residue.
12 The residue is the value of the estate less the value of the free-of-tax bequest less the tax on the free-of-tax gift (calculated at the final estate rate).
13 The wife receives half the residue as specified in the will.
14 The remaining half of the residue goes to Rose, but this is a taxable bequest. Tax is found by multiplying her half of the residue by the final estate rate. This substantially reduces Rose's share of the residue.

For enthusiasts: how the tax due in Example 11.5 was estimated

Each round of the calculation involved grossing-up the free-of-tax gift. We started by using an estimated rate and each time arrived at a new notional tax rate. We could make the calculation more accurate by repeating the calculation through several rounds and in the end we would have a calculation where the rate used at the start to gross up the free-of-tax gift would be as near as makes no difference the rate we arrived at by the end of the calculation. At that stage, the sum of tax on the individual gifts under 'Who gets what' would equal the total tax bill found in the last 'Revised tax position of the estate'. If we stop the calculation before then, the sum of tax collected does not quite equal the total tax bill – ie there is a 'calculation error'. The table below shows how the calculation error (£344 at Round 2) declines each time we refine the calculation. Since reducing the error to zero involves a lot of work for only a small increase in the amount of tax collected, the tax legislation instructs that we stop the iteration after two rounds.

	EXAMPLE OF THE ITERATIVE PROCESS				
	Round 1	Round 2	Round 3	Round 4	Round 5
STEP 1: GROSSING UP THE GIFTS					
Free-of-tax gift	£350,000	£350,000	£350,000	£350,000	£350,000
Tax-free slice	£275,000				
Taxable part of free-of-tax gift	£75,000				
Grossing-up rate	40%	21.667%	22.355%	22.411%	22.415%
Grossed-up value of free-of-tax gift	£400,000	£446,809	£450,769	£451,094	£451,120
STEP 2: TAX POSITION OF THE ESTATE					
Value of estate	£800,000	£800,000	£800,000	£800,000	£800,000
Tax-free part of estate	£200,000	£176,596	£174,615	£174,453	£174,440
Chargeable estate	£600,000	£623,404	£625,385	£625,547	£625,560
Tax-free slice	£275,000	£275,000	£275,000	£275,000	£275,000
Taxable part of estate	£325,000	£348,404	£350,385	£350,547	£350,560
IHT death rate	40%	40%	40%	40%	40%
Estimated tax on estate	£130,000	£139,362	£140,154	£140,219	£140,224
Notional rate of IHT	21.667%	22.355%	22.411%	22.415%	22.416%
STEP 3: WHO GETS WHAT					
Tax on free-of-tax gift	£86,667	£99,884	£101,021	£101,114	£101,122
Tax on half residue	£39,361	£39,134	£39,105	£39,102	£39,102
Calculation error	£3,972	£344	£28	£2	£0

Quick-succession relief

If you left a substantial gift in your will to someone – for example, a son or daughter – who then died shortly after you, there could be two IHT bills on the same assets in a short space of time. To guard against this, a claim can be made for 'quick-succession relief'. This is available where the person inheriting the assets dies within five years of the assets becoming part of that person's estate (even if the assets are then sold or given away before the recipient's death). The relief is tapered: full relief is given if the recipient's death occurs within one year of the gift; a reduced rate applies if a longer time elapses (see Table 11.1).

Quick-succession relief is also available where the original gift was a lifetime gift and the recipient dies within five years. However, the amount of tax due, if any, on the original gift will not be known until seven years have passed since the gift was made, so there will be a delay before the amount of any relief can be calculated.

Table 11.1 Quick-succession relief

Years between first and second death	Tax relief on second death as a percentage of tax applicable to the original gift[†]
Up to 1	100
More than 1 and up to 2	80
More than 2 and up to 3	60
More than 3 and up to 4	40
More than 4 and up to 5	20
More than 5	no tax relief

[†]The percentage is multiplied by the formula:

$$\frac{G - T}{G} \times T$$

where G = the gross amount of the original gift

T = the tax paid on the original gift.

EXAMPLE 11.6

In February 2002 Ahmed gives his nephew, Jagdish, £30,000. The gift is a PET but sadly Ahmed dies two years later. The PET is reassessed as a chargeable gift (see page 71) and Jagdish pays £9,600 tax that then becomes due.

Tragically, Jagdish is killed in a car crash in November 2005. His estate of £450,000 passes to his partner. They were not married and IHT of

£70,000 is charged on the estate. However, this is reduced by quick-succession relief in respect of the gift from Ahmed. The gift was made more than three but less than four years before Jagdish's death so the quick-succession relief percentage is 40 per cent. The relief is worked out as follows:

$$40\% \times [(£30,000 - £9,600) / £30,000] \times £9,600 = £2,612$$

Tax on Jagdish's estate becomes £70,000 − £2,612 = £67,388.

Passing on your business

Handing on your business is a complex matter. There are many different ways of arranging the transfer, and which is appropriate for you will depend very much on your particular circumstances. You would be unwise to make plans without seeking professional advice from your accountant and a solicitor. Business planning is outside the scope of this book but it is worth pointing out here the important reliefs against IHT that may be available to you and your heirs.

Business property relief

If, on death, your business passes to someone else, your personal representatives may be able to claim 'business property relief' which will reduce the value of the transfer of the business for IHT purposes and thus reduce or eliminate any IHT otherwise payable. To be eligible, you must have been in business for at least two years. Only 'qualifying' business assets attract relief; these are assets which are either

- used wholly or mainly for the purpose of your business, or
- are required for future use by the business.

Assuming you operate your business as a sole trader or as a partner in a partnership, business property relief will be given at the higher rate of 100 per cent – that is, it could completely eliminate an IHT charge.

EXAMPLE 11.7

Gerald dies leaving a greengrocery valued at £500,000 which he has run for the last ten years. In his will, he hands the business to his son, Paul. He also leaves £250,000 to his wife. The IHT position is as follows:

Value of free estate	£750,000
less tax-free gift to wife	£250,000
Value of grocery business	£500,000
less 100% business property relief	£500,000
Chargeable part of the estate	£0

Relief of 100 per cent is also available if you pass on a holding of shares in an unquoted company – which includes shares traded on the Alternative Investment Market (AIM).

A lower rate of business property relief – set at 50 per cent – is available to set against transfers of a *controlling* holding (i.e. 5 per cent or more) in a fully quoted company.

Business property relief is intended to take most hand-overs of family companies outside the IHT net. However, even 100 per cent relief will not necessarily entirely mitigate an IHT bill. In particular, you should note that, if the business property is subject to a binding contract for sale, relief will not normally be given. This might be the case where, say, a partnership has arranged that the surviving partners will buy out the share of a partner who dies; the deceased partner's share of the business would not qualify for relief in this situation. This sort of problem can be avoided with some advance planning – for example, by giving surviving partners the option but not the obligation to buy – so it is very important that you get advice from an accountant★ or other tax adviser★ at the time you draw up the partnership agreement.

Most types of business can qualify for business property relief. The only exception is businesses whose sole or main activity is dealing in stocks, shares, land or various other investments. Letting out property does not normally count as a business and so does not usually qualify for business property relief.

Any IHT due after business property relief has been given can be paid by interest-free instalments over a period of ten years.

Agricultural property relief

Agricultural property relief – which is similar to business property relief – is available when a farm is handed on. The relief, which is given automatically and does not have to be claimed, is given against the agricultural value of the land and buildings. The equipment and stock do not qualify for agricultural property relief but they may qualify for business property relief (see above). Note that the agricultural value of the farm may be lower than the market value if, say, the land has development value – the excess will not qualify for agricultural property relief, though it may be eligible for business property relief.

To qualify for agricultural property relief, you must either have occupied the farm, or a share of it, for the purpose of farming for at least two years, or you must have owned the farm, or a share in it, for at least seven years. If you farmed the land yourself, relief is given at the higher rate of 100 per cent. If you let the land to someone else to farm, relief is restricted to the lower rate of 50 per cent.

As with business property relief, agricultural property relief is also not available if the farm is subject to a binding contract for sale (see above).

Any IHT due after relief has been given can be paid by interest-free instalments over a period of ten years.

Telling the taxman

When you die, your personal representatives will be responsible for sorting out your estate. Before they can distribute any of your assets to your heirs, they must obtain probate (in England, Wales or Northern Ireland) or confirmation (Scotland) which is proof of their right to dispose of the assets. Probate or confirmation is granted only after any inheritance tax due has been paid (or in some cases partly paid) or your representatives have shown that no tax is due.

If no inheritance tax is due and the estate counts as an 'excepted estate', your representatives will normally deliver a simplified account of the assets in your estate to the Probate Registry★ on form IHT205 (England or Wales), the Probate and Matrimonial Office★ on form IHT205 (Northern Ireland) or Sheriff's Court★ on form C1

(Scotland). The relevant form will be included in the pack your representatives are sent on contacting the relevant registry, office or court or they can download it from the HMRC* website.

For deaths on or after 6 April 2004, an excepted estate is one where all the following conditions are met:

- the person who died had their permanent home in the UK
- the estate involves either no trusts or only one trust in which the deceased person had an interest in possession
- no more than £100,000 of the estate is trust property
- no more than £75,000 of the estate property is situated outside the UK
- any gifts in the seven years before death were of cash, chattels, quoted shares or securities, land or buildings and came to no more than £100,000. Gifts covered by the small gifts exemption, yearly tax-free slice, wedding gifts and normal expenditure out of income can be ignored but other tax-free gifts must be included
- any gifts of and buildings within the seven years before death were outright gifts to another person (eg not gifts into a trust)
- the person who died had not made any gifts with reservation (see page 74) or elected to have any transfers treated as if they had been gifts with reservation in order to escape the pre-owned assets tax (see page 88)

AND THE ESTATE IS EITHER

- **small** The gross value of the estate and gifts in the seven years before death does not exceed the inheritance tax-free slice

OR

- **exempt** The gross value of the estate and gifts in the seven years before death does not exceed £1 million and the value of the estate, excluding amounts passing tax-free to a spouse, civil partner or charity, comes to no more than the tax-free slice.

The relevant tax-free slice is normally the amount for the year in which death occurs but is the amount for the previous tax year if the death occurred between 6 April and 5 August inclusive and the representatives apply for probate by 5 August.

If the estate is not an excepted estate or if inheritance tax is due, the personal representatives must complete a detailed account on form

IHT200 which they can obtain from the HMRC★ and which is sent to the relevant Capital Taxes Office★. The time limit for sending in form IHT200 is 12 months from the end of the month in which death occurred or, if later, within three months of the personal representatives starting to act.

For detailed information about the personal representatives role and how to complete the forms involved, see *Wills and Probate* available from Which? Books★.

Paying the tax

The time limit for paying inheritance tax is within six months of the end of the month in which death occurred or, if sooner, before probate/confirmation can be granted. This is generally earlier than the time limit for delivering the IHT200 and your personal representatives may find initially they have to base the tax bill on an estimated account. Once the account is finalised, they pay any extra tax due or claim a refund of any overpayment. Interest is charged on tax paid late and added to refunds.

Having to pay the tax before the grant of probate/confirmation throws up another problem. The personal representatives will not necessarily have any ready cash with which to pay the bill. Although in general assets cannot be released to the representatives before probate/confirmation, there is an exception which allows some types of asset to be released early specifically to pay the inheritance tax under a scheme whereby the money due is transferred direct to the HMRC. These assets are: most National Savings & Investments products, gilts and, where banks and building societies have signed up to the scheme, money held in bank and building society accounts. If there are no such assets available or they fall short of the amount of tax due, the personal representatives may need to take out a temporary loan to pay the tax.

Where tax is due in respect of land, buildings, shares that gave the deceased a controlling interest in a company (whether listed or unlisted) or certain unquoted shares, the personal representatives can apply to pay the tax in ten equal yearly instalments. Interest is charged on the amount outstanding.

The HMRC can agree to accept heritage property in lieu of some or all of the IHT due. Eligible property includes pictures, prints, books, manuscripts, works of art and scientific objects, provided they are 'pre-eminent' for their national, scientific, historic or artistic interest. Buildings and land of outstanding scenic, historic or scientific interest and items associated with them are also eligible.

Personal representatives may find the following HMRC leaflets, available from Capital Taxes Offices,* particularly helpful:

- IHT3 *Inheritance tax. An introduction*
- IHT4 *Notes on informal calculation of inheritance tax*
- IHT11 (or IHT11(S) for Scotland) *Payment of inheritance tax from National Savings or from British Government Stock on the Bank of England Register*
- IHT12 (or IHT12(S) for Scotland) *When does an estate qualify as an excepted estate?*
- IHT14 *Inheritance tax. The personal representatives' responsibilities*
- IHT15 *Inheritance tax. How to calculate the liability*
- IHT17 *Inheritance tax. Businesses, farms and woodlands*
- IHT210 *How to fill in form IHT200.*

Chapter 12

Receiving an inheritance

IT'S NEVER TOO LATE, BUT . . .

'So you mean that we can, in effect, rewrite Dad's will to swap the gifts around and cut the tax bill?'

'Precisely, Miss Cale. The law does currently allow this,' said the solicitor, somewhat ponderously. 'However, I should point out that matters would have been a great deal simpler and cheaper had Mr Cale made satisfactory arrangements *before* his death. There would have been considerably greater scope for minimising – or even eliminating – the inheritance tax bill had he done so.'

Your rights as a beneficiary

Finding out about an inheritance

One of the jobs of the personal representatives appointed to sort out a will is to trace the beneficiaries named in the will. In many cases, the personal representatives are also the beneficiaries or close relatives of them, so there is no problem letting the beneficiaries know about their inheritance.

If you are named in a will but the personal representatives don't know how to contact you, they must make reasonable searches to try to find you. This might include, for example, checking the deceased's address books, questioning relatives and friends of the deceased, and employing a specialist tracing agency.

In other cases, the will might not name you specifically but perhaps you are one of a class of beneficiaries and the personal representatives might not be aware that you exist. In general, if you were to turn up after the estate had been distributed with a valid claim to an inheritance, the personal representatives would be personally liable to meet your claim. But the representatives can protect themselves by publishing appropriate notices calling for beneficiaries and creditors of the estate to make themselves known. The notices must appear in *The London Gazette*, a newspaper local to the area where any land in the estate is situated, and any other local or national newspapers that are appropriate given the circumstances. They must give a period of at least two months during which you should get in touch – the notice will give contact details of the personal representatives or their solicitors.

If you have not come forward within the notice period, you no longer have a claim against the personal representatives. However, you do still have the right to pursue your claim to the inheritance and, if it is valid, have the right to try to recover the assets or money involved from the other beneficiaries. If they are sympathetic, they might agree to share the estate with you. If not, you would need to pursue your case through the courts. Even if your claim is established, it might not be possible for you to inherit if the assets or money has already been dissipated and can no longer be traced. This is a complex area and you will need the help of a solicitor*.

Problems with executors

While an estate is in administration, the money and property belong to the personal representatives, not the beneficiaries. The personal representatives are not even holding the estate property on trust for the beneficiaries, because until the estate is sorted out the representatives cannot know how much of the property will have to used to meet bills and pay off other creditors. In the worst event, after all the expenses and debts, there might not be anything left to share out amongst the beneficiaries. So, even if you have been left a specific item in a will – 'the ormolu clock', 'my ruby necklace', 'my stamp collection' – you have no right to it until the representatives release it. However, beneficiaries could object if the personal representatives sold an asset unnecessarily.

Personal representatives are allowed a period of at least a year in which to sort out the estate. Some estates are complex and will take much longer – sometimes many years. But at some point, you might feel the representatives are dragging their heels and should speed up.

Other problems might be the impression that representatives are taking too much from the estate in expenses or charges, selling assets at less than their full value, or worse.

In general, your only course of action is to apply to a court for help. A court has a range of possible remedies, for example, requiring personal representatives to seek court approval before selling or distributing assets and replacing or removing personal representatives. You could take out a personal action against a representative for redress or against people you believe have wrongly received assets from the estate. Again, you are in a complex area and should get help from a solicitor*.

Tax and your inheritance

Inheritance tax

There is no inheritance tax as such on anything you receive under a will. But the estate may have had to pay tax and, depending on the type of bequest you receive, this tax may have reduced the amount you received as described in Chapter 11. If you have been left a bequest that bears its own tax (see page 167), a share of the estate tax bill will have been deducted from any cash sum before it is handed over to you. Such gifts are more problematic if you are left an asset rather than money. In that case, you will have to find cash from elsewhere to pay the tax or alternatively sell the asset in order to raise the cash to pay the tax.

Even if there is a delay before the estate is distributed, if you inherit an asset (rather than cash), you are treated as having acquired it on the date of death of the deceased at the open market value of the item on that date. This will be the same as the value of the asset as shown in the estate accounts.

Capital gains tax

For capital gains tax (CGT) purposes, you are also treated as having acquired an asset that you inherit on the date of death of the deceased at its open market value on that date.

If the personal representatives sell assets and pay out cash to the beneficiaries, it is the estate not the beneficiaries that is liable for any CGT on the sale due to an increase in value since the date of death.

Of course, any tax paid by the estate reduces the amount left to be distributed to the beneficiaries. Usually tax bills will reduce the residue of the estate but if the residue has been used up other bequests could be affected.

Income tax

There is no income tax on the actual inheritance you get but there could be tax on any income earned by the estate after the date of death and before the estate is wound up.

The personal representatives are responsible for income tax on any income received by the estate during administration. They pay tax at the basic rate, savings rate or 10 per cent dividend rate, depending on the type of income.

If any of the income is paid out to you either during administration or when the estate is finally distributed, it counts as part of your income for the year in which you receive it. With the income from a UK estate, you get a tax credit for the tax already paid at the basic, savings or dividend rate. If you are a non-taxpayer or pay tax at the starting rate, you can reclaim all or part of the basic rate or savings rate tax credit. You cannot reclaim any of the tax credit with dividends. If you are a higher rate taxpayer, you have extra tax to pay on the grossed-up amount of the income. (Grossing up means you add the tax credit to the income you received to find the before-tax amount.)

The personal representatives should give you a completed certificate R185 (Estate income) setting out the amount of each type of income, the amount of each tax credit and whether it is reclaimable.

The position is more complicated if you receive income from a foreign estate. In that case, there might be UK income tax to pay. You will need to fill in a tax return including the supplement headed 'Trusts etc'. The notes accompanying the supplement give details of what tax might be due and what to enter on the return.

If you were left cash in the will and there is a delay before the cash is paid out to you, you might receive interest from the personal representatives in recognition of the delay. Usually, you will receive the interest without any tax deducted and, if you are a taxpayer, you must declare this income and pay any tax due.

EXAMPLE 12.1

Sanjay's uncle died in December 2004 and his cousin, Rajiv, is dealing with the estate. In 2005–6, Rajiv paid out some of the cash from the estate which included interest which had been earned since the date of death. Sanjay received interest of £80 together with a tax credit of £20 representing tax at the savings rate of 20 per cent which had already been deducted. Sanjay is a higher rate taxpayer, so he has extra tax to pay. The grossed-up interest is £80 + £20 = £100. Tax at the higher rate would be 40% × £100 = £40 but Sanjay can set the tax credit against this leaving £20 tax to pay.

Cash or assets?

Your options

Typically an estate will be made up of a mix of cash (bank accounts, savings accounts and so on) and assets (for example, property, furniture, other personal possessions, shares). Unless you have been left specific items, the personal representatives might offer you the choice of taking your inheritance in the form of cash or some of the assets in the estate. Substituting assets instead is an example of 'appropriation' (see page 162). The choice has tax implications:

- **cash** The personal representatives sell assets in order to pay you cash. They are liable for any CGT on an increase in the value of the assets since the date of death and the tax is a bill paid using the estate's funds. The personal representatives are liable for CGT at a single 40 per cent rate but have a tax-free allowance set at half the rate an individual gets (£4,250 in 2005–6). If the asset has fallen in price since death, the representatives could set the loss against other gains made by the estate or alternatively use the lower value to adjust the inheritance tax bill due on the estate, in either case saving tax at 40 per cent. You, as beneficiary, have no personal CGT liability and cannot make use of any losses, because you receive cash
- **assets** The personal representatives pass the assets direct to you. You are treated as having acquired the assets on the date of death. Therefore you become liable for any CGT on any increase in value

since the date of death, but only when you eventually sell the assets. You may be liable for CGT at 10, 20 or 40 per cent, depending on your personal tax position and have an annual tax-free allowance of £8,500 in 2005–6 (see Chapter 3). If the assets fall in value, you can use the loss in the normal way as set out in Chapter 3.

Often the residue of an estate is to be divided among several beneficiaries. If some of the beneficiaries opt for cash and others for assets, the personal representatives need to value the assets in order to ensure that each beneficiary gets a correct share. If the price of the assets changes frequently – as in the case of, say, shares – the personal representatives will need to set a fixed day on which the valuation will take place.

Deciding what to do

Taking cash
Opting for cash could be worthwhile if you want to spend some of your inheritance straight away, maybe pay off your mortgage or other debts.

If you would want to invest your inheritance, taking cash might still be sensible if you expect asset prices to fall or the assets are not the sort you would want to invest in.

Taking the assets to sell immediately
Weigh up the tax position. Would the CGT you would have to pay be less than the amount the personal representatives would pay? Or, if the assets are standing at a loss, could you claim more tax relief than the representatives?

Also consider the sale price and any selling costs. Could the personal representatives get a better deal than you? This might be the case if, say, the assets are shares and the personal representatives would be selling in bulk.

Would you benefit from any tax or cost savings made by the personal representatives (because you get a share of the residue) or would the benefit go to other beneficiaries under the will?

Taking the assets to keep
This could be a good idea if the assets are suitable for you and the type you would choose to hang on to. If the assets are investments, you

need to consider how they fit in with your overall financial planning and whether they match the level of risk you are comfortable taking. To explore this aspect, see *Be Your Own Financial Adviser* from Which? Books*.

Renouncing your inheritance

You cannot be forced to accept an inheritance if you don't want to. One option is to 'disclaim' it.

A disclaimer must cover the whole of the item concerned, not part of it. For example, if you were left 'the money in my current account' you could not give up just half of it and take the rest. But where you have been left more than one distinct item, you could disclaim one but accept another. You cannot disclaim an inheritance if you have already accepted it or started to benefit from it (by, for example, receiving interest from it).

The inheritance effect of the disclaimer is as if your right to inherit had not existed. So, if you disclaim part of the residue of an estate, the intestacy rules take over for the part you disclaimed. In other cases, whatever you disclaim becomes part of the residue and is passed on in accordance with the rest of the will or, if there was no will, the intestacy provisions.

As far as inheritance tax and CGT go, the disclaimer is treated as if it had been made by the deceased person provided certain conditions are met in which case there are no tax implications for you. (There could be inheritance tax implications for the estate if, say, the bequest to you was a tax-free gift but will now pass as a taxable gift to someone else.) The conditions are that the disclaimer is made within two years of the date of death, made in writing and you do not receive anything in return for making the disclaimer. If you do not meet these conditions, you are treated as having made a lifetime gift (usually a potentially exempt transfer) to whoever gets the item instead (see Chapter 4) and as having made a disposal for CGT purposes (see Chapter 3).

The special tax treatment does not extend to income tax. This does not normally cause a problem, but if the effect of your disclaimer is that the bequest passes instead to your unmarried child under age 18 the HMRC is likely to argue that the anti-avoidance settlements legislation applies (see page 96). This would mean that any income – and from a future date possible any capital gain (see page 97) – produced by the item is taxed as yours.

Changing your inheritance

Another way of changing your inheritance is to draw up a 'variation'. In effect, this is like re-writing the will of the person who died, though technically you are not varying the will itself just the gifts made under it.

Unlike a disclaimer, with a variation you decide how the inheritance should be redirected. It can be used not simply to renounce an inheritance (say, in favour of your grandchildren instead of you) but to alter its form (for example, changing an outright gift to a life interest) or save tax (for example, ensuring that the deceased person's tax-free slice is used).

Other differences from a disclaimer are that a variation can be made even if you have already started to benefit and it can affect just part of the inheritance if that's what you want.

A variation must be agreed by all the original beneficiaries affected by the will or that part of it which is to be varied. These beneficiaries must be aged at least 18 and of sound mind. If one or more of the beneficiaries is a child, it may still be possible to vary the will but the consent of a court will be required. A variation cannot be revoked or changed again. But you could vary a will more than once if each variation dealt with different assets under the will.

Provided certain conditions are met, the variation is treated for inheritance tax and CGT purposes as if the new pattern of bequests had been made by the deceased person. This means there are no inheritance tax or CGT implications for you, but there could be inheritance tax implications for the estate (and this might be a reason for making the variation). The conditions are that the variation is made within two years of the death, in writing including specific wording to state that the variation is to be effective for inheritance tax and CGT, you do not receive anything in return for making the variation, and if extra tax is due the personal representatives must send a copy of the variation to the HMRC.

A variation that does not meet the conditions would result in the new 'bequests' being treated as lifetime gifts (usually potentially exempt transfers) from the original beneficiaries to the new ones with the normal inheritance tax (see Chapter 4) and CGT (see Chapter 3) implications.

The special tax treatment does not extend to income tax. Therefore a parent who makes a variation in favour of their unmarried child under age 18 would be caught by the anti-avoidance settlements legislation (see page 96). This means that any income – and from a future date possibly capital gains too (see page 97) – produced by the assets concerned would be taxed as that of the parent.

EXAMPLE 12.2

When Fred died, his will revealed that he had left £600,000 to his wife, Betty, and the residue of his estate to his daughter, Linda. His daughter's share was £50,000 on which no tax was due, because Fred's taxable estate plus a couple of PETs made in the last seven years came to a running total of only £60,000.

Betty intends, when she dies, to leave everything to Linda but this will mean a large IHT bill on an estate made up of Betty's own £20,000 and the £600,000 left to her by Fred. Assuming she had made no chargeable gifts in the seven years before death, tax of [£620,000 – £275,000 = £345,000] × 40% = £138,000 would be payable (based on 2005–6 rates). But this bill could be reduced if some changes are made to Fred's will.

Betty does not need the whole £600,000, so she and Linda make a deed of variation directing that Fred's estate of £650,000 be split as follows: £265,000 to Linda – which, with the earlier PETs, uses up the whole of Fred's tax-free slice – and the residue of £385,000 to his wife. There is still no IHT to pay on Fred's estate and the potential bill when Betty dies is reduced to [£385,000 + £20,000 – £275,000 = £130,000] × 40% = £52,000. This is a saving of £86,000.

Claiming support from an estate

You might not have been left anything in a will or under the intestacy rules but nevertheless feel that you are entitled to claim something from the deceased person's estate.

In England and Wales, you may have a valid claim under the Inheritance (Provision for Family and Dependants) Act 1975. Similar legislation applies in Northern Ireland, but not in Scotland (where however some dependants have 'legal rights' – see page 154). The rules described here are those for England and Wales.

You are eligible to make a claim to the court for support from the deceased person's estate if you are:

- the deceased person's husband, wife or civil partner
- their former husband, wife or civil partner. (However, the divorce or dissolution settlement might specifically preclude any claim or be such that a claim for further support out of the estate is unlikely to succeed)
- someone who was in a relationship with and lived with the deceased continuously during at least the last two years before death
- a child of the deceased
- any other person who was partly or wholly maintained by the deceased.

You must normally make your claim within six months of the personal representatives getting probate, although the courts do have discretion to accept a later claim.

You have no automatic rights. The court decides whether or not your claim succeeds, based on the facts of the case, including for example what resources of your own you have, how large the estate is, what other obligations must be met out of the estate, and so on. If you are successful, you could be awarded an income from the estate, a lump sum, or specific assets (such as a house) either from the estate or bought with money from the estate.

Chapter 13
Inheritance planning

COVERED

'Mum, this is awkward to talk about, but what happens to me if you die one day? It works brilliantly us sharing the house like this and I know you intend to leave everything to me. But I doubt I could stay here without you. There would a big inheritance tax bill and I'd have to sell the house to pay it.'

Gilly put her arm round Samantha. 'Don't worry. All sorted. I'm paying premiums for an insurance policy that should pay you enough to cover any tax bill. So hopefully you would be able to stay on.'

This chapter draws together a number of points discussed in earlier chapters and introduces some new ones to show what you can do to plan your giving through inheritance more precisely and tax-efficiently.

The particular strategies you adopt will depend largely on your personal intentions and circumstances. Although many of the points given below can be applied simply and with a minimum of paperwork, others are not so straightforward and may hide potential pitfalls that you should take into account. Always seek advice from, for example, a solicitor★ or accountant★ if you are in any doubt about a proposed course of action. And, if you are giving away large sums, get advice first.

There are two main aims to planning inheritance:

- to make sure that your estate is divided as you had wished
- to minimise the amount of tax to be paid on the estate.

Clearly, the two aims are interlinked since a lower inheritance tax (IHT) bill means that more of your estate is left to give to your family and friends. Strategies to meet either or both aims are discussed below.

Many more complex tax saving schemes aim to minimise tax on your estate at death by taking valuable assets out of your estate while still enabling you to use the assets during your lifetime without triggering the gift with reservation rules (see page 74). The scope for this type of planning has been severely reduced by the introduction of the pre-owned assets tax (see Chapter 5) and the government's threat to introduced further 'retroactive' measures to counter successful tax avoidance schemes (see page 84). Broadly, you would appear to be safe using tax saving opportunities which are specifically allowed in the tax legislation (for example, making tax-free gifts, using your tax-free slice). But if you contemplate anything more complex, you should get professional advice and be aware that any tax savings could disappear if the scheme becomes the target of a change in tax law.

Gifts when you die

Make tax-free gifts in your will

Some gifts you make on death are always free of IHT, for example, bequests to charity and whatever you leave to your husband, wife or civil partner (provided they are UK-domiciled – otherwise there is a limit of £55,000). In addition to these and other gifts that are always tax-free whether made on death or during your lifetime (see Chapter 2), there are a few gifts that are specifically tax-free on death only:

- lump sum from a pension scheme, provided the trustees had discretion to decide who would receive it (though in practice they generally follow any nomination made by you). The lump sum by-passes your estate altogether and goes straight from the scheme to the recipient
- similarly the proceeds of a life insurance policy that was written in trust for the recipient. The proceeds by-pass the estate, going straight from the life insurance company to the recipient
- the whole estate if the person died from a wound, accident or disease acquired or exacerbated while on active service against an enemy. To claim this exemption, the personal representatives need a certificate from the Ministry of Defence
- £10,000 received by the deceased as an ex-gratia payment to the survivors (or spouses of survivors) who were prisoners of war held by the Japanese during the Second World War

- amounts received by the victim (or his or her spouse) from specified schemes that provide compensation to people (such as Holocaust victims) for wrongs suffered during the Second World War.

Use your tax-free slice

Try to make use of your tax-free slice (which covers the first £275,000 of chargeable transfers in the 2005–6 tax year), and bear in mind that some gifts – for example, to your husband, wife or civil partner or to charity – are always tax-free.

It may be tempting simply to leave everything tax-free to your spouse or civil partner but this can mean an unnecessarily large tax bill when he or she dies (see Example 13.1). Planning instead to use your tax-free slice can save as much as 40% × £275,000 = £110,000 in tax in 2005–6.

EXAMPLE 13.1

Sam dies and leaves his whole estate of £200,000 to his wife, Harriet. Since this is a tax-free gift, there is no IHT to pay. When Harriet dies her free estate is valued at £300,000 and is left completely to their only child, Phyllis. There is IHT to pay on the estate calculated as follows:

Value of free estate	£300,000
less tax-free slice	£275,000
	£25,000
Tax on £25,000 @ 40%	£10,000

However, suppose instead that Sam had left £50,000 to Phyllis (on which no IHT would be payable because it would be covered by the tax-free slice) and the remaining £150,000 to Harriet. On Harriet's death, her estate would have been valued at £250,000. Giving this to Phyllis would have been completely covered by Harriet's tax-free slice, so no IHT would be payable. Straightforward planning to make use of Sam's tax-free slice would save £10,000 in tax.

If you and your husband or wife intend to leave something to your children, it may be best to draw up your wills so that whoever dies first leaves part of the estate directly to the children. This will ensure that at least some use is made of the available tax-free slice. The remainder of the estate can be left to the surviving spouse. If you can, arrange the wills so that both of you can make maximum use of your tax-free slices but take care to ensure that the surviving spouse will have enough to meet financial needs.

Be aware of how gifts are taxed

Examples 11.2 and 11.3 in Chapter 11 are intentionally identical, except that in one the gifts bear their own tax and in the other the gifts are free-of-tax. The outcomes highlight two important points which you should bear in mind when planning gifts under your will:

- a gift which bears its own tax will generally be smaller than a gift of the same size which is free of tax
- leaving free-of-tax gifts reduces the size of the residue. If you leave a lot of free-of-tax gifts, the residue may be reduced to a trivial amount (or nothing at all).

Consider will trusts

There are several situations in which setting up a trust in your will can be particularly useful. The first is where you want to give some of your assets to the next generation but your wife or husband will carry on needing the income from, or use of, those assets. One way around this is to leave the assets in trust, giving your spouse an interest in possession during his or her lifetime, with your children (or perhaps their children) holding the reversionary interest (see page 111). But note that, while this ensures that your assets are used largely as you would wish, it does not have any IHT advantage. This is because, under IHT, a person with an interest in possession is deemed to own the underlying trust assets and to give them away when the interest ends. So there could be a large IHT bill at the time of the second death. You could avoid this problem by using a discretionary trust instead, with both your spouse and your children named as beneficiaries. This would be tax-efficient provided the transfer of assets into the trust was covered by your tax-free slice or one of the other exemptions.

However, an interest-in-possession trust can be useful for IHT planning if assets are being passed to subsequent generations. This is because a reversionary interest does not count as part of a person's estate and so there is no IHT liability if it is transferred to someone else. If your children held the reversionary interest in a trust, they could easily transfer this interest to their own children if they wished to do so, without incurring any IHT liability.

Under IHT law, you can use your will to set up a discretionary trust and, provided the trust property is distributed within two years of your death, the gifts from the trust are treated for IHT purposes as if they had been bequests under your will. This can be a useful device if, say, you hope to use your tax-free slice as described on page 199 but you are not sure at present whether your husband or wife would be able to manage without the assets. Your will could direct that an amount up to the tax-fee slice be left in trust with, say, your children and surviving spouse as potential beneficiaries. The trustees could then distribute the trust property taking into account the needs of your spouse at that time.

Another important planning use of will trusts is where you are passing on your business. Rather than pass total control to, for example, a relatively inexperienced son or daughter, or to a spouse who is not involved in the business, it may make sense to put the land or property used by the business into trust. Provided the owner qualifies for business property relief or agricultural property relief, the trust will also qualify (see page 180). This is a complex area and you should seek the advice of your accountant* and/or solicitor.*

A trust set up under your will is deemed to start on the date of death.

Using lifetime gifts

One way to reduce the IHT payable on your death is to reduce the size of your estate by making gifts during your lifetime. However, before going down this road, you must consider your own financial needs. Any IHT payable on your estate is not really your problem; it will simply reduce the amount by which others benefit from your estate. It is not worth jeopardising your financial security in order to reduce the IHT bill of your heirs. So the first planning point is: do not give away more than you can afford to do without.

Assuming that you can afford to make a number of gifts during your lifetime, you will obviously want to ensure that they do not themselves give rise to a large tax bill. Chapter 2 lists the gifts which you can make during your lifetime which are tax-free.

It is not enough to look only at the IHT position of lifetime gifts. You must also consider the capital gains tax (CGT) position (see Chapters 2, 3 and 9). Taking the two taxes together, the 'best' gifts to make will tend to be the following:

- cash gifts (always free of CGT) that qualify for an IHT exemption
- cash gifts that count as PETs (see page 69) for IHT purposes
- business assets that qualify for hold-over relief from CGT (see page 53) and count as PETs for IHT or qualify for business property relief
- other gifts that are exempt from IHT or that count as PETs and for which the CGT bill is relatively small due to unused CGT allowance, indexation allowance or CGT taper relief (see Chapter 3).

Anti-avoidance rules

In an ideal world, you would be able to make tax-efficient lifetime gifts to reduce the eventual tax on death but in the meantime continue either to have the use of the assets you give away or to get an income from them. Not surprisingly, the tax authorities do not recognise this as a genuine gift. As described in Chapter 4, if you give something away but continue to benefit from it, you fall foul of the IHT gift with reservation rule. This works by continuing to include the value of the gift as part of your estate either until you cease to benefit or until you die, whichever happens first. A variety of complicated schemes have been marketed which aim to exploit legitimate loopholes in the legislation to let you both reduce the size of your estate and continue to receive an income from the gifted assets – see page 208–213 for an outline of some of the more common schemes. Some continue to be effective. Others are now caught by the pre-owned asset tax (see Chapter 5).

If you are attracted to complicated tax planning, always get professional advice and bear in mind the following points:

- arranging your tax affairs within the rules so as to pay as little tax as possible is usually legitimate tax avoidance. But going against the rules is illegal tax evasion for which there are heavy penalties including the possibility of a prison term

- the courts are wise to 'shams' – in other words, attempts to dress up illegal tax arrangements to look like legal ones
- even where an arrangement seems to be within the law it may fall foul of the 'associated operations' rules. These have built up through case law and mean that a series of transactions can be looked at as a whole. If they do not have a bona fide commercial motive and have been devised primarily as a way of saving tax, they can be deemed to be an artificial tax-avoidance scheme and the tax-saving effects nullified
- the HMRC takes an aggressive approach towards tax-avoidance schemes. It is prepared to challenge schemes through the HMRC Commissioners and subsequently the courts, so there is no guarantee that a complicated scheme that you thought would save tax actually will do so at the end of the day. In addition, you may run the risk of becoming involved in lengthy and costly legal disputes
- even if the taxpayer wins a case against the HMRC, the government can change the law to close loopholes and ban schemes. Although such changes are seldom retrospective in the strict sense of the word, the HMRC has moved the goal posts by showing its willingness to introduce 'retroactive' measures. A retroactive change does not impose a tax bill for past tax years but does impose a tax bill now on actions you took in the past. So any action you take now which seems to save tax could give rise to a future tax bill if the law is changed.

Make tax-free lifetime gifts

Particularly important for IHT purposes is your yearly tax-free exemption (see page 29), which lets you give away up to £3,000 each year without incurring any IHT liability. If you choose cash gifts, there will be no CGT either.

Another very useful gift which is free of IHT is normal expenditure out of income – this can be particularly handy when used in conjunction with an insurance policy (see page 205).

For tax purposes alone, it is not generally worth making, in your lifetime, a gift which would in any case be tax-free on your death: for example, a gift to charity. A safer course would be to retain the assets in case you need to draw on them and make the desired gift in your will.

Give assets whose value will rise

If your aim is to reduce the value of your estate at the time you die, then it makes sense to give away assets whose value you expect to increase. In that way the increase will accrue to the recipient of the gift and will be outside your estate.

Consider lifetime gifts to a trust

Generally, you cannot be a beneficiary or potential beneficiary of a trust you set up without the assets you put into it counting as a gift with reservation. However, your husband or wife can benefit under the trust without triggering these rules *provided* that you yourself in no way benefit from your spouse's interest in the trust. Even in the latter case, however, the income tax and CGT rules may make this type of arrangement unattractive (see page 132).

A further exception to the gift with reservation rules is that if you retain a reversionary interest (see page 111) in a trust to which you have given assets, the gift does not count as one with reservation.

Beware of setting up more than one trust on the same day, if one of them is a discretionary trust. If you do, it may increase the periodic charge on the discretionary trust.

If you yourself inherit money or assets which are surplus to your needs, you might consider putting them into trust straight away to benefit your children or grandchildren – this is a practice known as 'generation-skipping'. The transfer can often be made tax-efficiently through a 'deed of variation' (see page 194) or possibly a 'disclaimer' (see page 193).

Make loans

One way to 'freeze' the value of part of your estate is to make an interest-free loan to someone and leave him or her to keep the proceeds from investing the loan. A condition of the loan would normally be that it is repayable on demand. From your point of view, this is more secure than making an outright gift and can be a useful arrangement if you are unsure whether or not you will need the money back at some time in the future.

Of course, there is little point demanding repayment of a loan if the borrower simply does not have the money available to repay you. An even more secure route would be to make the loan to a discretionary trust and to name the intended recipient as a potential beneficiary under the trust.

Using life insurance

There are three straightforward ways in which life insurance can be a useful inheritance planning tool:

- covering the potential tax bill on a PET
- making a gift which builds up outside your estate
- covering an expected tax bill on your estate.

These are discussed in turn below. All rely on making use of two factors:

- **Tax-free gifts** Taking out insurance for the benefit of someone else means that the premiums count as gifts. You can ensure that there is no possibility of IHT on these premiums if you make sure they count as tax-free gifts. The most commonly used exemptions are to make the premiums as normal expenditure out of your income or to ensure that they fall within your yearly tax-free exemption of £3,000.
- **Trust status** If the proceeds of an insurance policy are payable to you, the payout will be added to your estate when you die, which will increase the size of your estate and will cause delay before your beneficiaries have access to the payout. Therefore, it is important that the policy proceeds are paid direct to the intended beneficiary. You make sure this happens by 'writing' the insurance policy 'in trust', which means that the policy is held in trust for the benefit of whomever you name and the proceeds are the property of that person rather than of you or your estate. Insurance companies will generally write a policy in trust for you at no extra charge (since they are able, in most cases, to use standard documents).

The cost of insurance increases with the likelihood of the insurance company having to pay out. So, if you are in poor health, or very old, buying life insurance may be very expensive.

PETs and insurance

If you make a gift which counts as a PET, you may want to be absolutely sure that any IHT bill which subsequently arises could be paid. (Similarly, you might want to ensure that any extra tax on a chargeable gift arising on death could be paid.) One way of ensuring this would be to take out a 'term insurance' policy. Term insurance pays out if you die within a specified time – in this case, seven years; should you survive the specified period, it pays out nothing. Since the liability for IHT on a PET decreases as the years go by, the cover you need can also reduce – in other words, you want 'decreasing term insurance'. See Example 13.2.

EXAMPLE 13.2

In 2005–6 Jeremy gives his niece, Penny, a gift of £10,000. It counts as a PET, so there is no tax to pay at the time of the gift. However, Jeremy's running total exceeds £275,000 and, if he were to die within seven years of making the gift, Penny would face a demand for tax on the gift. The potential tax liability would be as follows:

Years between gift and death	% Rate of tax on the gift (at 2005–6 tax rates)	Potential tax bill (£s)
Up to 3	40	4,000
More than 3 and up to 4	32	3,200
More than 4 and up to 5	24	2,400
More than 5 and up to 6	16	1,600
More than 6 up to 7	8	800
More than 7	no tax	0

Jeremy takes out a seven-year term insurance which would pay Penny £4,000 if he died within the first three years and a reducing sum thereafter to cover the tax bill which would arise.

Reducing the size of your estate

You could use life insurance to build up a gift which does not count as part of your estate. For example, you might use the full £3,000 yearly tax-free exemption to pay the premiums for an investment-type life insurance policy (see box on page 208) that will pay out to the recipient either after some specified period (in which case, you need an 'endowment policy') or when you die (in which case, you need a 'whole-life policy').

In choosing this strategy, you will need to weigh it against alternative strategies: for example, setting up a trust which could invest in a wide range of assets. The 'up-front' costs of setting up your own trust will be higher but the ongoing costs could work out to be less than for a life insurance policy. If you have relatively small sums to give, the insurance route would be more appropriate.

Since April 2001, you can use personal stakeholder pension schemes in a similar way by making regular contributions to a scheme for someone else (see example on page 28). The charges for stakeholder schemes are capped at 1.5 per cent of the amount in the pension fund for the first ten years and 1 per cent thereafter.

Paying IHT when you die

You could take out a whole-life policy (which pays out *whenever* you die) to provide a lump sum to meet an expected IHT bill on your estate. In essence, this is no different from using insurance as a way of making a gift on death as already discussed but the factors to consider are slightly different: you could save in your own investment fund (either within your estate or within a trust) to meet a potential IHT bill but it would take time to build up the full amount needed. If you died in the meantime, your investment would be insufficient to cover the IHT. Taking out a whole-life insurance policy removes that risk because (provided you have bought the appropriate level of cover) it would pay out the full amount needed whether you die sooner or later.

If you have made a PET and die within seven years, the PET will use up some of the tax-free slice available at the time of death. This could cause extra tax to be due on the estate. Therefore, in addition to a whole-life policy to cover the main tax on the estate, it may be worth taking out a seven-year level term insurance policy to cover the extra tax bill on the estate if you die within seven years of making a PET. This is quite separate from a decreasing term insurance policy to cover possible tax on the PET itself (see above).

More complicated IHT planning

Life insurance has been at the heart of many schemes that aim to let you reduce your estate through lifetime gifts yet retain an income from the gifted assets without triggering the gift with reservation rules. There are two reasons why life insurance is particularly suitable for these schemes:

- policies can easily be written in trust
- special tax rules allow you to make regular withdrawals of capital from an insurance policy – see box below – which can be used to provide an 'income' stream.

A very brief outline of some of the main schemes is given here, but you should always get advice either from the life insurance company concerned or an independent professional before deciding to use such a scheme. Each basic scheme often varies in detail from one company to another and may be given a variety of names, so make sure you understand what type of scheme you are being offered and how it fits with your planning objectives. Bear in mind that tax-saving schemes may be challenged by the HMRC (see page 202).

SPECIAL TAX RULES FOR LIFE INSURANCE

There are two types of life insurance: term insurance which provides protection only by paying out if you die within a specified period but lapsing without any payout if you survive; and investment-type life insurance where your premiums are invested and the policy builds up a cash value. Investment-type life insurance usually also has some protection element (paying out on death either within a specified period or whenever it occurs) though often the amount of protection is small.

With investment-type policies, the insurance company usually pays tax on income and gains from the underlying investments. If the policy is a 'qualifying' one, there is no more tax for you to pay when you receive a payout from the policy.

With a 'non-qualifying policy', when the policy pays out, there may be some income tax for you to pay, but only if you are a higher-rate taxpayer. However, a special facility lets you draw an 'income' each year up to one-twentieth (5 per cent) of the premium(s) you have paid without any tax being due at the time. Tax is deferred – for example, until the policy comes to an end – and is then charged with reference to your tax position at that time.

Gift and loan plans

These are also called 'loan trusts'. You make a small gift to start up a discretionary trust – for example, a gift of £3,000 using your yearly tax-free exemption (see page 29). The beneficiaries are whoever you want eventually to receive your gift.

You then make a much larger interest-free loan to the trust. Under the terms of the loan it will normally be repaid in annual instalments but the whole amount is repayable on demand or in the event of your death. The annual loan repayments provide you with 'income'.

The trust invests the gift and the loan. Any growth-oriented investment could be used but often a single-premium life insurance bond is chosen. Five-per-cent withdrawals can then be made from the bond under the special tax rules for life policies (see box opposite) and these fund the loan repayments.

On your death, the trust repays the loan to your estate and the remaining trust property – which is outside your estate – passes to the beneficiaries. The longer the trust has run, the larger the amount that has built up outside your estate will normally be.

These schemes should not be caught by the gift-with-reservation rules because you as settlor cannot benefit under the trust and the loan repayments are a contractual right not a benefit. Initially, the HMRC argued that these schemes were caught by the pre-owned assets tax (POAT). However, later the HMRC conceded that the schemes were not caught after all and this has now been confirmed in the HMRC guidance notes on POAT.

EXAMPLE 13.3

Adam makes a gift of £3,000 to a trust in favour of his children. Subsequently he lends the trust £97,000 repayable on demand or on death. The trust uses the £100,000 to buy a single-premium insurance bond. It withdraws 5 per cent of the premium – in other words 5% × £100,000 = £5,000 – each year to pay to Adam in part-repayment of the loan. This provides Adam with his income.

Ten years later, Adam dies. The value of the bond stands at £102,500, and 10 × £5,000 = £50,000 of the original loan has been repaid, so the trustees must now repay the remaining £97,000 − £50,000 = £47,000. This leaves £102,500 − £47,000 = £55,500 to pass IHT-free to the children.

Back-to-back plans

You use a lump sum to buy an annuity that pays out an income for the rest of your life. Your estate is immediately reduced by the amount you pay for the annuity. This is because the annuity will automatically stop when you die and therefore has no capital value to be included in your estate.

You also take out a whole-life insurance policy written in trust for the benefit of whoever you want to receive your eventual gift. This is an investment-type insurance that builds up a cash value. The policy has annual premiums and these are funded using part of each annuity payment. The remaining annuity payment provides you with income.

The premiums for the whole-life policy are gifts to the beneficiary but should qualify for the normal expenditure out of income exemption (see page 27).

When you die, the whole-life policy pays out the greater of its cash value or the sum assured to the beneficiaries, by-passing your estate.

There is a risk that a back-to-back plan could be caught by the 'associated operations' rules – see page 79 – in which case you might be treated as making a gift of, say, the whole lump sum put into the plan instead of just the premiums paid for the whole-life policy. This risk is thought to be avoided if you buy the annuity and the whole-life policy from two separate life companies.

Discounted gift plans

These plans also aim to reduce the value of your estate but give you a continuing income from the gifted assets. There are several variations on the theme and one example is described below.

You use a lump sum to buy a series of single-premium endowment policies. These are investment-type insurance policies that pay out if you die within a set period or pay out a lump sum at the end of the period if you survive. The payout both on death and on maturity depends on investment growth.

Each policy is written under an interest-in-possession trust (see Chapter 7), so that if you die, it pays out, by-passing your estate, to the beneficiary you have named, but if the policy reaches maturity the proceeds are paid to you – in other words you have a reversionary interest. There is no IHT charge when property in trust reverts to the original settlor. The reversionary interest is treated as a quite separate asset from the interest the beneficiaries have, and the HMRC has said that the retention by the settlor of the reversionary interest does not trigger the gift with reservation rules.

The policies are designed so that one matures each year up to your reaching, say, age 100. The maturing policies provide you with an income – this will be variable because it depends on investment growth.

At the time you set up the plan, you are treated as having made a PET to the beneficiary which is tax-free provided you survive seven years. The amount of the PET is the original lump sum less the estimated value today of the income you will get from the maturing policies. Because the income is uncertain (you may die before all the policies mature) and accrues in the future (when its buying power may have fallen), the value of the income is discounted (reduced). The amount of discount depends on your age and health. The larger the discount, the more efficient the gift, but the HMRC would challenge an unrealistic valuation.

In its guidance notes on POAT, the HMRC has indicated that, with most discounted gift plans, the separate interest carved out for the settlor is held by the insurance company on bare trust for the settlor. A bare trust does not count as a settlement for the purposes of POAT and so most such schemes should not be caught by the tax.

EXAMPLE 13.4

Haseena, aged 80, invests £100,000 in a discounted gift plan. This buys her 20 single-premium bonds of £5,000 each with one maturing each year until she reaches age 100. The bonds are written in trust, so that on maturity each one pays out to her but if she dies before a bond matures it pays out to her niece, Amanda. The insurance company works out that the discounted value of the plan is £75,000 – this is the value of the PET Haseena has made.

Ten years later, Haseena dies. There is no tax on the PET because Haseena survived seven years. She has received an increasing income each year from the maturing bonds. Ten of the bonds remain in force and the proceeds of these are paid IHT-free to Amanda.

Retained interest trusts

Again, the aim is to give away assets but continue to receive income. This time, you use a lump sum to buy a single-premium insurance bond (an investment-type policy). The bond is split into two separate parts: a 'retained interest' which is yours and the gifted part which is held on trust for the beneficiary you name.

Under the special tax rules for life insurance (see box on page 208), you can take a tax-efficient 'income' up to 5 per cent a year of the premium you paid for the bond. This is 5 per cent of the whole premium regardless of the subsequent split of the bond into two parts. However, the income is actually paid only from the retained part. The retained part does benefit from any investment growth, but nevertheless is progressively eroded as you draw out the income. If you survive long enough to use up the retained part completely, the income has to stop.

Meanwhile, the gifted part of the bond grows outside your estate as investment growth is added and on your death passes IHT-free to the beneficiary.

At the time you set up the trust, you are deemed to have made a PET equal to the premium paid for the bond less the value of the part you have retained.

The interest you retain is carved out as a separate interest and so the gift with reservation rules should not apply. Your interest is likely to be held by the insurance company either on a bare trust and so outside the scope of POAT, or possibly as a separate trust which forms part of your estate and so is exempt under POAT.

Family wealth trusts

This type of arrangement enabled you to reduce the value of your estate but still have the option to recover some or all of your money if circumstances changed later on. It is a type of 'Eversden' scheme (see page 76) and remains effective if set up before 20 June 2003. From that date onwards, such arrangements are caught by the gift with reservation rules and so not effective.

You made a gift to a flexible trust (see page 104) which initially was set up to give your husband or wife a life interest. The trustees later on used their discretion to revoke the life interest in favour of a group of beneficiaries including, say, your children but also you and your husband or wife. Your spouse, who lost the life interest, was treated as making a PET of the trust property to the new beneficiaries, so this gift was free of IHT provided he or she survived seven years.

This type of arrangement is a settlor-interested trust (see page 132) but, in the case of pre-20 June 2003 schemes, the gift with reservation rules do not apply because initially you made a gift of the life interest to your husband or wife. The gift to your spouse was exempt (see page 76), which meant the reservation rules did not bite.

Pre-20 June 2003 schemes are now caught by the POAT (see Chapter 5) because this is a settlement under which any income would be treated as yours because of the anti-avoidance settlement rules. Schemes set up on or after 20 June 2003 are not caught by POAT because instead the inheritance tax gift with reservation rules apply.

Using long-term care insurance

The longer you live, the greater the chance that you may suffer some infirmity in your old age. If you then need a carer to help you with day-to-day living or have to move into a residential or nursing home, this will inevitably be expensive. If your capital comes to less than £20,500 (England and Northern Ireland), £19,500 (Scotland) or £20,000 (Wales) in 2005–6 and your income is low, the state will pay some or all of the costs for you if you need to move into a care home. If your capital is greater than this, you will have to pay out of your own pocket until the stage at which your capital has been run down to less than that limit.

If you had to move into care and your husband or wife or a dependant would be left at home, the value of your house should not be included in the assessment of how much capital you own. But, if you had been living alone, your home would normally count as part of your capital and might have to be sold to cover the care fees.

You could consider long-term care insurance as a way of protecting your capital and, thus, the inheritance you want to pass on to your heirs. In brief, long-term care insurance pays out a regular sum towards the cost of care either in your own home or in a residential or nursing home if you can no longer carry out a given number of specified 'activities of daily living' (ADLs) for yourself.

Long-term care insurance is costly and so buying a policy makes a large dent in your assets. But you can view this as a damage-limitation strategy because the policy will pay out however long you need care. Without this type of protection, a prolonged spell in a nursing or residential home would quickly and progressively eat up your capital. A care home easily charges around £400 to £500 a week – in other words, about £20,000 to £26,000 a year.

For a detailed look at long-term care policies, see *The Which? Guide to Insurance* or *Be Your Own Financial Adviser*, both available from Which? Books.★

Equity release schemes

Equity release schemes are mainly designed to address the problems of older homeowners who are 'asset rich, cash poor' enabling them to raise extra income or a cash sum from the value of their home while retaining the right to live there. But increasingly they are also being seen as a way to mitigate inheritance tax.

Rising house prices during the 1990s and early 2000s have increased the wealth of many homeowners who in most respects would not consider themselves to be wealthy into the reach of inheritance tax. Planning during your lifetime to reduce inheritance tax on your death is very difficult if your only big asset is the home that you live in. As discussed in Chapters 4 and 5, making a lifetime gift of something that you continue to use is either ineffective for inheritance tax because it is caught by the gift with reservation rules (see page 74) or saves inheritance tax only to trigger pre-owned assets tax bills. One of the few planning devices that might help is using an equity release scheme. There are two types:

- **lifetime mortgage**. You take out a loan against the value of your home. You use the loan to provide cash, an income or both. Interest, rather than being paid monthly, is usually added to the outstanding loan and the whole lot paid off either when you die or if you move permanently into care

- **reversion scheme**. You sell part of your home and use the cash raised either as a lump sum, to provide an income or a mixture of both. You retain the right to live in the home either rent-free or for a peppercorn amount until you die or move permanently into care.

In either case, schemes can be taken out for a single person or a couple. In the latter case, the right to remain in the home continues until the second of you dies or moves into care.

These schemes reduce the value of your estate and so reduce any potential inheritance tax bill in two ways. Firstly (but not particularly helpfully), because the lender or reversion company has to wait many years until it gets its money, you do not get full value for the part of your home you mortgage or sell. The precise deal will depend on your age and other factors, but for example you might sell 60 per cent of your home but receive a cash sum equal to only 30 per cent. Or you might borrow £40,000 but after interest has been rolled up end up repaying £90,000. So you get an instant depreciation in the value of your estate. In the case of a lifetime mortgage, the value of the outstanding loan will be deducted from the value of your estate at death (see page 166). With a reversion scheme, the value of the part of the home you have sold ceases immediately to be part of your estate.

Secondly, and more positively, the money released is yours to do with as you will. You could spend the money. You could use it to make lifetime gifts, as described earlier in this chapter. You could use it to buy an annuity which provides you with extra income for life. The annuity ceases to be part of your estate at the time you die because the income stops on death. But if you keep and invest the money raised, it will continue to be part of your estate, in which case the equity release scheme will not be particularly effective in saving inheritance tax.

Before opting for an equity release scheme, consider your options carefully and make sure you are aware of all the conditions and potential pitfalls. Some particular points to consider are:

- you would get better value from your home by selling it and moving somewhere cheaper
- capital and/or income raised from a scheme can reduce your entitlement to pension credit, help with care costs and other means-tested benefits

- income raised from a scheme can result in a higher tax bill if it means you lose age allowance
- some unscrupulous advisers persuade customers to release more capital than they need and to invest the excess usually in stock-market-linked bonds that earn the adviser commission. The recommended investments may be totally unsuitable given your total resources and attitude towards risk. The return from the investments is unlikely to exceed the cost of the money you have borrowed or the effective cost of selling part of your home. And retaining as investments the money released does not reduce the value or your estate for inheritance tax purposes.

Equity release schemes which you take out at arm's length with a commercial company are outside the scope of POAT (see Chapter 5). But if, on or after 7 March 2005, you arrange your own scheme with, say, a relative or friend, you might be caught. However, bear in mind that a yearly benefit of less than £5,000 does not trigger a POAT bill.

Gifts from the deathbed

If, say, you are seriously ill and do not expect to live for long, you might make a gift in contemplation of your death – known as a *donatio mortis causa*. Such a gift does not take effect until your death and it lapses completely if you do not die after all (or if the recipient dies before you).

In a situation as described above, should your intention be to make an outright gift to someone that is not conditional on your dying, it would be wise to set down your intention in writing – in, say, a signed letter to the recipient – to safeguard against the gift being mistakenly treated as a *donatio mortis causa* (and thus being treated as part of your estate if you survive).

A further point to watch out for is that a gift which is made by cheque is not made until the cheque has been *cleared* against the giver's account. If death takes place before then, the gift would become invalid.

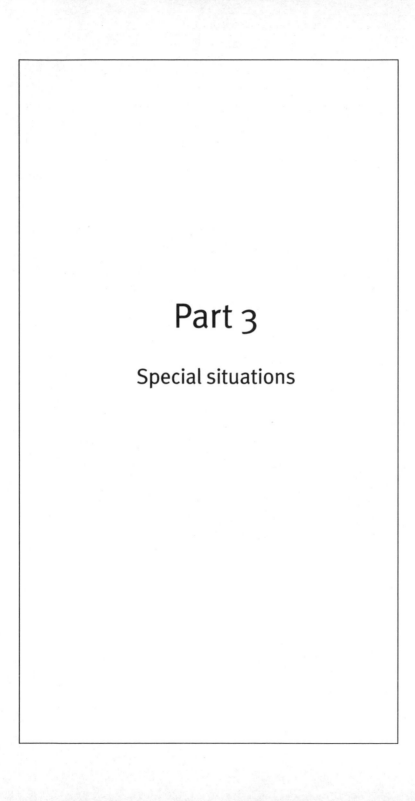

Part 3

Special situations

Chapter 14

Your home as a gift

A ROOF OVER YOUR HEAD

'If we gave the house to you now, Becky, it would mean a lot less tax to pay at the end of the day,' explained Joan. 'But where would you and Dad live? You surely wouldn't want to stay here with all our children around you?' quizzed Becky, trying hard to take in the whole idea. 'Good grief, no!' laughed Joan. 'That might not achieve the tax savings we had in mind anyway. No, Dad and I were planning on moving to the cottage. After all, we don't need to be in town these days. Well, what do you think?'

In essence, your home is no different from any other asset which you own. It can form part of your estate and can be the subject of a gift in much the same way as any other possession you own. As such, the bulk of this book applies to your home as much as to any other asset. However, because your home is likely to be your most valuable possession, it is worth drawing together here some of the points which should be borne in mind if you are contemplating making a gift of your home either as a lifetime gift or at the time of death.

Who owns what?

If you own your home jointly with someone else, it is important to think about how you own it. As discussed in Chapter 6, there are two forms of joint ownership (in England and Wales): joint tenancy and tenants in common.

If you own your own home as a joint tenant with someone else, you each have equal shares in the home and have identical rights to enjoy the whole home. On death, the share of the owner who dies passes automatically to the remaining co-owner(s). This is very simple and convenient and can be the best arrangement for married couples and other partners in stable relationships, especially if the value of their estates taken together is no more than the tax-free slice for inheritance tax (i.e. £275,000 in 2005–6).

However, owning the home as tenants in common gives you greater flexibility and better scope for tax planning. Tenants in common still have the right to enjoy the whole home but you each have distinct shares in the home which need not be equal and do not pass automatically to the other owner(s) on death. Instead, the share of the home is passed on in accordance with your will or, if you had not made a will, the rules of intestacy.

We have already seen in Example 13.1 how failing to use the tax-free slice when the first partner of a married couple dies can result in an unnecessarily large tax bill when the second spouse dies. With ownership of the home arranged as tenants in common, it becomes possible for each spouse to arrange to use their tax-free slice by, for example, passing their share of the home on to their children instead of to their wife or husband. This can save inheritance tax (IHT) overall but is worth doing only if you can be sure that the surviving spouse will continue to have a secure home – for example, by giving him or her the protection of a formal tenancy agreement.

The importance of a will

Chapter 10 described the problems which can arise if you die intestate – i.e. without having made a will. These can be especially acute if your home is the main asset in your estate.

If you die without a will and you are survived by children or other relatives, your husband, wife or civil partner inherits outright only a certain part of your estate. He or she does have the right to opt to take his or her share of your estate in the form of the home rather than other assets. But what if that share of your estate is worth less than the home? The husband, wife or civil partner may well find that part of the home has to be put into trust for the benefit of young children, say, or that older offspring or more distant relatives insist on the sale of the home in order to release their own inheritance as cash.

The position of an unmarried partner is even worse. He or she may have no automatic right to share in your estate. However, if he or she has been your partner throughout the two years up to death or has been financially dependent on you, he or she can apply to the courts under the Inheritance (Provision for Family and Dependants) Act 1975 (see page 195).

Therefore, if the home is jointly held as tenants in common, it is essential that you make a will specifying how your share of the home is to be passed on.

Your home as a lifetime gift

If you expect your estate at death to exceed the tax-free slice, it would be very convenient if you could give away your home now in your lifetime. Making a gift of your home to your children, say, would count as a potentially exempt transfer (PET). There would be no IHT to pay at the time you made the gift and, provided you survived seven years, no IHT at all. There is, however, a small snag: if you give away your home, where do you intend to live? If you mean to stay in the home, the gift will not work for IHT purposes, because it will count as a gift with reservation (see page 74).

There are a couple of ways around this problem, though neither is very satisfactory. First, you could share the home with the people to whom you give it. Provided you all live together and share the running costs of the home, the gift should not count as one with reservation. But, if the recipients subsequently move out, the gift will become a gift with reservation – so make sure you do not fall out!

The second solution relies on the caveat that a gift is not a gift with reservation if you give full consideration in money or money's worth for the use you continue to make of the gift. For example, you could give away your house but pay the full market rent to live there under a tenancy agreement or licence. Or you could buy a lease at the full market rate which lets you live in it for some specified period – for example, long enough to cover your expected remaining years, plus a few extra years to be on the safe side. Alternatively, you might offer your services as, for example, a housekeeper or gardener, provided the value of your work was equivalent to the market rent for the property you continue to occupy.

Other promising ideas tend to fall foul of the rules governing associated operations (see page 79) or fail to save tax by unwittingly creating an interest in possession so that the home continues to be treated as owned by the beneficiary rather than transferred to, say, a discretionary trust (see Chapter 7). Tax experts, from time to time, come up with other complicated schemes. But their legal status is often unclear and the HMRC is quick to lay a challenge. And, since 6 April 2005 onwards, there is a strong risk that a scheme that escapes the gift with reservation rules will instead trigger the pre-owned assets tax (see Chapter 5). If you want to explore this area further, get professional advice from an accountant* or other tax adviser.*

Benefits which should not trigger the gift with reservation rules

The IHT legislation says that a gift with reservation occurs if the recipient of a gift does not enjoy the gifted assets 'virtually to the entire exclusion of the donor and of any benefit to him'. These words are not defined but the HMRC has provided some guidance on benefits you might still enjoy without triggering the reservation rules. In relation to a home you have given away, they include:

- you stay in the home in the absence of the recipient for no more than two weeks a year
- you go to stay in the home with the recipient but for no more than a month a year
- you are invited to make social visits that do not include overnight stays, provided you visit the recipient no more often than you would have done if the gift had not been made
- you stay temporarily with the recipient for a special reason, such as while you or the recipient is convalescing or your home is being redecorated
- you visit the home in order to babysit or for some other domestic reason.

Change of plan

The only satisfactory way of giving your home as a lifetime gift is if you genuinely do have somewhere else to live – for example, a retirement cottage or moving in with friends or relatives. But suppose your circumstances change and you move back into the home you had previously given away? This could trigger the gift with reservation rules. However, if you become unable to maintain yourself because of old age, infirmity or some other reason and your moving back into your old home is a reasonable way for the recipient of the gift – who would have to be your relation or spouse – to provide care for you, the gift with reservation rule will not apply.

Equity release schemes

As described in Chapter 13, using an equity release scheme can be a way of reducing the value of your estate for inheritance tax purposes without either moving home or triggering the gift with reservation rules. Normally you take out such a scheme with a commercial company. However, you could enter into a private arrangement with a relative or friend but privately arranged schemes taken out since 7 March 2005 could trigger a pre-owned assets tax charge (see Chapter 5).

Watch out for CGT

Giving away your home does not normally trigger a capital gains tax (CGT) bill, because any gain on your only or main home is generally exempt. In some situations, however, there will be a CGT bill. These arise where:

- you have lived away from home for a time
- you have let out all or part of the home
- part of the home has been used exclusively for your work
- the garden was greater than the normal size for a home of that type (usually taken to be greater than half a hectare).

Keep your options open

Do not be in too much of a hurry to give away your home. People are tending to live longer but increasingly need some degree of professional care in their later years. This is very expensive and many people are surprised to find that the state foots the bill only if their income and assets are very low – see page 213. Taking out long-term care insurance, as described on page 213, might be a solution. If not, the home which you had expected to pass on to your children might in the end be needed to fund nursing or residential home costs. Your home can also be a valuable source of additional income if your resources become tight in later old age. Taking out an equity release scheme is not just a way of reducing inheritance tax. The main use of such schemes is to provide yourself with extra income or capital if your finances are tight.

Chapter 15

Giving to children

A NICE LITTLE NEST-EGG

'She is just beautiful', crooned Yuen, falling instantly in love with his first grandchild. 'Now, Mum, I want to invest a little nest-egg for young Lily here. It will help her when she goes to university.' Lily's Mum smiled: 'Yuen, she is far too small for us to worry about that sort of thing now.' 'No, my mind is made up – whatever I invest now could be worth three or four times that amount by the time she reaches 18.'

There are many reasons for wanting to make a gift to a child. You might want to build up a nest-egg that the child can draw on when, say, he or she goes to university or buys his or her first home. Alternatively, you might want the money to be available sooner to help with education costs or as a tool to help the child learn how to handle money.

There are two main concerns when considering gifts to children:

- the tax-avoidance rules that may affect gifts from a parent to a child
- how to arrange the gift, given that the child may be too young to hold an investment or to use the gift wisely. One option in the case of children born on or after 1 September 2002 is the child trust fund (see pages 234, 235 and 237), but other arrangements may be more suitable.

Gifts from parents

Every person, however young, is within the tax system and so benefits from the basic tax allowances, in particular the personal allowance for income tax (£4,895 in 2005–6) and yearly tax-free slice for capital gains tax (£8,500 in 2005–6). In theory, families could save tax by spreading their income and assets across all family members including the children. But in the case of income tax, the anti-avoidance 'settlement' rules prevent this.

If a parent makes a gift to a child who is under the age of 18 and unmarried, and the gift produces more than £100 a year income, the whole of the income (not just the excess over £100) is taxed as that of the parent who made the gift. The £100 limit applies to each parent and each child, so two parents could jointly make gifts to each child, which would produce up to £200 a year income without triggering the anti-avoidance rule.

EXAMPLE 16.1

Andy and Rebekah have jointly invested £5,000 for each of their two daughters in building society accounts. At present, each account earns 3.5 per cent a year interest and produces £175 a year in income. This is less than the limit of 2 × £100 = £200 (a double limit applies here because the gift is from both parents) at which the anti-avoidance rules kick in. Therefore, the income each daughter gets is treated as that of the child and is tax-free because it is covered by each daughter's personal allowance.

However, Andy and Rebekah should keep an eye on their daughters' investments. If interest rates rise the income each daughter gets could quickly exceed the £200 limit, in which case all of the income would be taxed as that of the parents. Because it was a joint gift, half would be taxed as Andy's income and half as that of Rebekah.

The anti-avoidance rules do not, at the time of writing, apply to capital gains produced by a gift from a parent, nor do they apply to some types of tax-free income. So by choosing the investments carefully you can still make some tax-efficient gifts to your child – see below.

However, the government has proposed that the anti-avoidance settlement rules should be extended to apply equally to capital gains from a future date (possibly 6 April 2006 onwards).

The rules apply in only a limited way to accumulation-and-maintenance trusts (see page 114), so these can be a good way of tax-efficiently building up a nest-egg for your child if you have a reasonably large sum to invest. (The costs of setting up and running a trust make it uneconomic for small sums.) But you will run into the anti-avoidance rules if you want to draw the income out of the trust either to give direct to the child or to use for his or her benefit (for example, by paying school fees). See Chapters 7 and 8 for more information.

Investing for a tax-free income

If you invest a gift you have made to your own child and it produces tax-free income, in most cases the anti-avoidance rules do not apply so it will not matter if the gift produces more than £100 income. The exception here is mini cash individual savings accounts (ISAs).

Mini cash ISAs are not an option for most children because you have to be aged at least 16 to be eligible (and 18 for stocks and shares ISAs). There is no tax on income from an ISA so you might think there would be no problem if parental gifts to a teenager were invested in cash ISAs. But, unusually for tax-free income, the anti-avoidance rules specifically apply to cash ISAs so, if the income from the parental gifts exceeded £100 it would be taxed as that of the parent.

The main investments that parents can make for their children without being taxed on the income are National Savings & Investments (NS&I) children's bonus bonds, friendly society tax-efficient savings plans, stakeholder pensions and the child trust fund. See 'Investments for children' on page 230 for details.

Investing for gains instead of income

For as long as the anti-avoidance rules apply only to income from parental gifts, you can get around them by giving your child investments that are expected to produce capital gains instead. Suitable gifts might be growth-oriented unit trusts and open-ended investment companies (OEICs), and capital shares in split-capital investment trusts – see 'Investments for children' on page 230 for details. You could also consider collectors' items such as paintings and antiques.

At the time of writing, the government had indicated its intention to extend the anti-avoidance rules to capital gains produced by parental gifts, but no details had been announced of how this would work in practice. Presumably, gains in excess of an annual limit would be taxed as gains of the parent. But it is not clear whether the limit would be £100 as it is for income, whether the limit would apply to combined income and gains, nor whether the new rules would apply to gifts already made or only gifts made after a certain date.

Gifts from other people

The anti-avoidance rules apply only to parental gifts. They do not affect gifts from grandparents, uncles, aunts, friends of the family or anyone else. To avoid confusion with the HMRC you should be able to distinguish these gifts from any parental gifts. It would be sensible to invest the two types of gifts separately – for example, you could put small parental gifts in a building society account and gifts from other people in another account. It is also a good idea to ask people who give money to your child to accompany it with a brief note stating the amount of the gift and who it is from. Keep such notes and letters in a safe place in case the HMRC needs to see them.

Where a child is young, money is often given to the parents to invest or use on the child's behalf rather than being given directly to the child. This may in effect create a trust with the parent as the trustee who is obligated to use the money as instructed by the person who made the gift. Even though the parent may then open an investment in the child's name, the gift should not count as a parental gift and so should not be caught by the anti-avoidance rules.

Deciding how to arrange your gift

Before deciding which investments to choose for a child, you first need to decide how to arrange your gift.

You could invest money now in your own name and later on give the proceeds to the child. This has the advantage of flexibility because you choose the precise timing of the gift and in the meantime you have the freedom to change your mind, for example, if you run short of money or the child turns out to be a spendthrift. If you are not already making full use of your yearly ISA allowance, you could use this to invest for a tax-free return. The main drawback of this approach is the failure to make use of the child's own tax allowances. In addition, the investment remains part of your estate until the gift is finally made. So if you die before handing over the gift, there could be inheritance tax (IHT) to pay.

It is usually more tax-efficient to make an immediate gift to the child. Often this means asking the child's parents (if you are not yourself the parent) to manage the investment on his or her behalf, but children can operate their own bank and building society accounts and NS&I investment accounts. They can also hold tax-efficient friendly society plans in their own names.

Instead of making a gift direct to a child, you could put it in trust. The simplest option is a bare trust (see page 111). If you hold something on bare trust for, say, your grandchild, the child is treated as the owner of the asset for tax purposes, but he or she can also take possession as soon as he or she reaches age 18 (or marries if younger). This is also a drawback with the child trust fund, where the child can use the money from the fund in any way they like once they reach age 18.

Another possibility that gives you more control over the gift is an accumulation-and-maintenance trust (see page 114). This will be appropriate only if you are giving a relatively large sum (say, £50,000 or more). A big advantage of this type of trust is flexibility – for example, you could set one up to benefit all your grandchildren, even those who are not yet born, and you can delay the point at which the investments pass to a child until age 25. In the meantime, the income from the trust can be used for the child's or children's maintenance, education or other benefit.

Investment-type insurance policies (such as endowment policies or investment bonds) can be written in trust so that any benefits payable on surrender, maturity or your death are paid direct to a child (or children). However, the insurance company pays tax on income and gains from investments held through an insurance policy. This tax can't be reclaimed by the policyholder, so insurance-based investments tend to be suitable only for higher-rate taxpayers or if you are involved in complicated IHT planning (see Chapter 13).

EXAMPLE 15.2

Yuen has just become a grandparent and wants to invest a lump sum of £3,000 for his granddaughter, Lily, to build up a nest egg to help her when she reaches adulthood. The gift falls within Yuen's yearly tax-free allowance for inheritance tax. He decides to put the money into a unit trust. Yuen is the legal owner of the units but the account is designated as 'Yuen Chan a/c Lily Chan'. This effectively creates a bare trust with Yuen holding the units as nominee for Lily. For tax purposes, Lily is the recipient of any income and gains from the units, and can set her allowances against them. To make doubly sure the bare trust is recognised, Yuen could write to his tax office saying that he has made this investment on behalf of Lily.

Investments for children

The investments you choose to give a child depend largely on the purpose of the investment, the amount involved and whether you want to invest on a regular basis or as a single lump sum, how long you want to invest, the amount of risk you are comfortable taking, and how the investment is taxed. Table 15.1 suggests some suitable investments depending on the purpose you have in mind.

Table 16.1 Investments for children

Aim of the gift	Suitable investments
Teach the child money management skills	Bank or building society account Cash ISA (if child is age 16 or over)
Encourage the child to learn how to save	Bank or building society account NS&I investment account Cash ISA (if child is aged 16 or over)
Build up a nest-egg	Child trust fund NS&I children's bonus bonds NS&I premium bonds Friendly society tax-efficient plan Unit trusts and OEICs Investment trusts
Build up a pension	Stakeholder pension

To encourage money-management skills, cash gifts direct to the child are likely to be best. These can be paid into a bank or building society account. Many providers offer accounts specifically for children with free gifts, regular magazines and so on. It is important that the child has ready access to the account, so check out banks and building societies that have branches near the child's home.

If your main aim is to build up a nest-egg over the medium to long term (five to ten years or more), share-based investments are likely to be more suitable. In the past, share-based investments have tended to produce higher returns than bank and building society accounts. But share-based investments involve capital risk. If you are not comfortable with this risk, stick to the safer investments such as cash-based child trust funds, savings accounts or NS&I children's bonus bonds.

A middling-risk option would be a stakeholder child trust fund. Another medium-risk option would be a friendly society tax-efficient plan (sometimes marketed as 'baby bonds') invested on a with-profits basis. However, government rules limit the maximum investment in these plans to £25 per month or £270 per year per person. With such a small amount, any flat-rate charges can eat heavily into the investment, so check the impact of charges carefully before you invest.

This leaves a share-based child trust fund or unit and investment trusts as the main choices for long-term growth. A child can't hold unit and investment trusts direct, however you can make the investment in your name but 'designated' for the child. This is normally enough to ensure that a bare trust is created, though to be sure you could write to your tax office stating your intention that the investment be treated as belonging to the child.

Finally, if you are thinking very long term indeed, you can pay up to £2,808 a year into a stakeholder pension scheme for a child. This limit applies per recipient, so if you want to make gifts to several children you could pay in up to £2,808 a year for each of them. The child will not usually be able to take any proceeds from the scheme until he or she has reached at least age 55.

If you are not sure which investments to choose, get advice from an independent financial adviser (IFA).*

The investments in detail

Bank and building society children's accounts

Description/suitable for Accounts especially for children, usually offering introductory gifts, magazines and so on. Useful as a way of teaching children how to manage money and getting them into the savings habit.

Return and charges Interest, usually variable, on the amount invested. No explicit charges.

Risk No capital risk (see box opposite).

How long you invest Usually these are instant access accounts.

Minimum investment Usually £1.

Maximum investment Usually none.

Tax Interest usually paid with income tax at the savings rate already deducted. Higher-rate taxpayers have extra to pay. Starting-rate taxpayers can reclaim some tax. Non-taxpayers should either reclaim the tax or arrange to be paid gross interest. Usually the interest counts as the child's income (but see 'Gifts from parents' on page 225) and the child is likely to be a non-taxpayer.

How to invest Contact relevant bank or building society.

Mini cash ISAs

Description/suitable for Savings account that pays tax-free interest. Many are instant access accounts. Must be aged at least 16.

Return and charges Interest on the amount invested. This is often variable, but occasionally fixed. Interest rates may be tiered with higher rates paid on larger balances. No explicit charges.

Risk No capital risk (but see box below).

How long you invest For instant access accounts there is no set period. For other types of accounts, check the conditions.

Minimum investment Often £1.

Maximum investment £3,000 a year – this is the limit set in the tax rules.

Tax Tax-free interest.

How to invest Contact provider which may be a bank, building society or NS&I.* You cannot hold an ISA on behalf of someone else (such as a child).

Capital risk

In this section, unless specifically mentioned, we have assumed that the risk of your losing capital because the provider goes out of business is minimal. In the event that this does happen, you might be eligible for compensation from the Financial Services Compensation Scheme.* The compensation limits are shown in Table 15.2.

Table 15.2 Financial Services Compensation Scheme limits on compensation

Type of savings or investment	Level of cover	Maximum pay-out
Deposits (e.g. bank and building society accounts)	100% of the first £2,000 90% of next £33,000 0% of anything more	£31,700
Non-insurance investments (e.g. unit trusts and OEICs) and bad investment advice	100% of first £30,000 90% of next £20,000 0% of anything more	£48,000
Insurance-based investments (e.g. insurance bonds, personal pensions)	100% of first £2,000 Up to 90% of remainder	Unlimited

NS&I children's bonus bonds

Description/suitable for Bonds that can be bought by anyone aged 16 and over for someone aged 16 or less. Useful as a way of giving a small nest-egg to a child.

Return and charges Fixed return made up of interest and bonus added at end of term. No explicit charges.

Risk No capital risk. NS&I issues investments on behalf of the government which is very unlikely to default. Locking into a fixed return means the child would miss out if competing interest rates rose.

How long you invest Five-year term. The child can have the money back early, but then loses interest. At the end of five years, you can reinvest for a new fixed return over five years, provided the child is still under age 16. Bonds must be cashed by age 21.

Minimum investment £25.

Maximum investment £3,000 per issue per child.

Tax Interest is tax-free, even if the child becomes a taxpayer. Treated as child's income even if the bond is a gift from a parent (see page 225).

How to invest NS&I* or through post offices.

NS&I premium bonds

Description/suitable for Bonds that give you the chance to win prizes by, in effect, gambling with the interest you would otherwise have earned.

Return and charges Prizes ranging from £50 up to £1 million. Random prize draw is held every month. Each £1 invested counts as a separate bond and has a chance to win. In June 2005, the yearly prize fund as a percentage of the total invested was 3.2 per cent. No explicit charges.

Risk No capital risk. NS&I issues investments on behalf of the government which is very unlikely to default. In June 2005, the chance of winning any prize with a single bond was 1 in 24,000. If winnings are not reinvested, or winnings are small, your capital is vulnerable to inflation risk.

How long you invest No set period.

Minimum investment £100.

Maximum investment £30,000 plus reinvested prizes.

Tax Prizes are tax-free.

How to invest NS&I* or through post offices. Bonds can be bought on behalf of children by parents and grandparents.

Cash child trust fund (CTF)

Description/suitable for Scheme for children born on or after 1 September 2002. The government provides vouchers (£250 at birth topped up to £500 for children in low-income families and similar amounts expected at age seven and possibly on entering secondary school). These are invested in the child trust fund and must be left untouched until the child reaches 18. Parents, friends and anyone else can add to the fund. At 18, the young person can use the fund in any way they choose. Parents choose how to invest the fund by opting for the cash version described here, a stakeholder CTF (see opposite) or a share-based CTF (see page 237). If parents fail to open a CTF within a year of receiving the vouchers, the HMRC selects a stakeholder CTF for the child. The child can have only one CTF at a time but can switch from one CTF to another (either with the same or a different provider) at any time.

Return and charges Interest is added. Usually variable. Lump sum paid out at age 18. No explicit charges. May be charges or loss of bonus on switching.

Risk No capital risk (but see box on page 233). Cash CTFs are the lowest risk type of CTF and suitable where parents do not wish to take any risk, but this is not necessarily the most suitable choice for such a long-term investment.

How long you invest for Until age 18.

Minimum investment The government vouchers.

Maximum investment The government vouchers plus up to £1,200 a year from anyone else.

Tax Interest is tax free. Treated as the child's income even if money in the fund includes gifts from parents.

How to invest Contact the provider which may be a bank or building society. For a full list of providers, see the HMRC* child trust fund website.

Stakeholder child trust fund (CTF)

Description/suitable for Scheme generally as for cash CTFs (see above). To use the name 'stakeholder' this type of CTF must meet various conditions, concerning, for example, the way it is invested and charges.

Return and charges Pays out a lump sum at age 18. Charges must come to no more than 1.5 per cent a year of the value of investments in the fund. There must be no charge for switching into or out of a stakeholder CTF.

Risk Medium risk. Many stakeholder CTFs work basically like unit trusts (see page 237). The price of units can fall as well as rise so you are exposed to capital risk. A stakeholder CTF must be invested in a range of assets including stock-market investments. The aim is to balance a reasonable chance of long-term growth with a controlled level of capital risk. The fund must also be 'lifestyled' which means that, from age 13 onwards, the fund shifts out of stock market investments and into safer deposits in order to lock in gains and protect against the effects of any sharp fall in the stock market as the child approaches age 18.

How long you invest for Until age 18.

Minimum investment As for cash CTFs (see page 235). If you want to add extra to the fund on top of the government vouchers, a stakeholder CTF must accept amounts as low as £10 (whether as a one-off sum or regular investment). Some accept lower amounts.

Maximum investment As for cash CTFs (see page 235).

Tax There is no tax for the investor to pay. Investments in the underlying fund build up largely tax free but dividends from shares and similar income has had tax at 10 per cent deducted and this cannot be reclaimed.

How to invest Through direct contact with providers who are mainly banks, friendly societies and fund managers or through an IFA★. However, all CTF providers must offer the option of a stakeholder CTF, so banks and building societies offering cash CTFs will also offer access to a stakeholder CTF sometimes from another provider. For a full list of providers, see the HMRC★ child trust fund website.

Friendly society tax-efficientplans

Description/suitable for Friendly societies are similar to insurance companies and generally offer similar types of product. But friendly societies are able to offer small savings plans that give you a largely tax-free return (in contrast to most insurance policies where the insurance company has already paid tax on the return from the underlying investments). Useful as a way of building up a small nest-egg. Some of these plans are specifically marketed as investments for children.

Return and charges The plan usually pays out a lump sum after a set number of years, for example ten years. Usually, there is an administration fee when you invest. If the plan is invested on a unit-linked basis (similar to a unit trust), there is usually an initial charge (up to, say, 5 per cent) and an annual management charge (for example, 1.5 per cent a year of the value of the investment fund) with other costs charged direct to the fund. If the plan is invested on a with-profits basis (see box overleaf), charges influence the level of bonuses.

Risk Capital risk varies depending on the underlying investments.

How long you invest Usually you must invest for at least ten years. If you cash in your investment early, surrender charges reduce the amount you get back – perhaps to even less than you had invested.

Minimum investment Varies from one society to another.

Maximum investment £25 a month or £270 a year.

Tax There is no tax for the investor to pay and the investments in the underlying fund build up largely tax-free, but dividends from shares and similar income has had tax at 10 per cent deducted and this cannot be reclaimed. Treated as child's income even if plan is a gift from a parent (see page 225).

How to invest Through direct contact with friendly societies or via an IFA.★

Share-based child trust fund

Description/suitable for As for cash CTFs (see page 234).

Return and charges Pays out a lump sum at age 18. Usually an up-front charge (up to 5 per cent or so of the amount invested) and an annual management charge (generally from 0.5 up to 1.5 per cent a year of the value of the fund). Other charges are deducted direct from the fund. Often charges for switching between funds.

Risk Medium to high risk. Many work basically like unit trusts (see below). The price of units can fall as well as rise, so you are exposed to capital risk. You can often choose from a wide range of funds.

How long you invest for Until age 18.

Minimum investment As for cash CTFs (see page 235). For investments on top of the government vouchers, minimum varies from one provider to another, for example, £10 to £100 for regular sums and £10 to £500 as one-off amounts.

Maximum investment As for cash CTFs (see page 235).

Tax There is no tax for the investor to pay. Investments in the underlying fund build up largely tax free but dividends from shares and similar income has had tax at 10 per cent deducted and this cannot be reclaimed.

How to invest Through direct contact with providers who are mainly friendly societies, fund managers and stockbrokers or through an IFA★. For a full list of providers, see the HMRC★ child trust fund website.

Share-based unit trusts and oeics

Description/suitable for You buy 'units' in a unit trust (or shares in an OEIC) which give you a stake in an investment fund. The fund is a ready-made portfolio of many different shares. You can choose funds that aim to produce income and/or growth.

Return and charges The return takes the form of income distributions usually paid/credited every six months and/or, if you sell your units for more than you paid, a capital gain. You can choose growth funds that pay low or no distributions. There is usually an up-front charge (up to 5 per cent or so of the amount you invest) and an annual management charge (usually around 1 to 1.5 per cent a year of the value of your investment). Other charges are deducted direct from the investment fund.

With-profits investments

Your savings grow through the addition of yearly bonuses which, once added, can't usually be taken back. The size of bonuses depends largely on the growth of an underlying investment fund which is typically invested in shares, gilts, corporate bonds, property and cash, but also on the overall profitability of the provider's business. Bonuses are smoothed by keeping back in reserve some growth from good years to top up your return in poor years. An extra 'terminal' bonus is also added when the policy matures.

The broad spread of investments in the investment fund and the fact that bonuses once added cannot normally be taken away reduces capital risk, making the with-profits basis a medium-risk approach to investing. However, you are not totally protected from stock market swings. If you cash in your policy early and investment returns have been poor, the provider can levy a 'market value reduction' (MVR) on top of any surrender charges and this effectively claws back some of the bonuses that had already been credited to your policy. Note that the level of future bonuses is not normally guaranteed. A company which is financially strong – for example, with a high level of reserves – is generally more likely to maintain its bonuses in future.

Risk The price of your units can fall as well as rise, so you are exposed to capital risk. However, investing in a broad spread of different shares reduces risk by reducing your exposure to the misfortunes of any one company. Over the long term, share-based investments have tended to rise at least in line with inflation and in line with the growth of the economy as a whole.

How long you invest No set period but because the value of the investment fund can fall as well as rise you should normally aim to invest for the long term (more than five years).

Minimum investment Varies from, say, £500 or more as a lump sum and £50 per month for regular savings.

Maximum investment None.

Tax Distributions are paid with tax at 10 per cent already deducted. Non-taxpayers cannot reclaim this tax. There is no further tax to pay for starting-rate and basic-rate taxpayers. Higher-rate taxpayers must pay extra. Capital gains are taxable, however if you have unused allowance there may be no tax to pay.

How to invest You can go to the provider direct, but you'll often pay less in charges if you go to a discount broker★ or fund supermarket.★ You can also invest through most IFAs★ and many stockbrokers.★

Investment trusts

Description/suitable for These give you a stake in an investment fund and so are an alternative to investing in unit trusts or OEICs, however they work in a different way. An investment trust is a company whose business is running an investment fund. The fund might specialise in shares, gilts, bonds, property and so on. You invest indirectly in the fund by buying the shares of the investment trust company. The share price is heavily influenced by the value of the investments in the trust but is also affected by other factors, such as whether the company has large borrowings and the balance of supply and demand for the company's shares.

Return and charges In a conventional investment trust, your return is in the form of dividends, usually paid out twice a year and, if you sell the shares for more than you paid, a capital gain. A 'split capital trust' is different. It has a set date on which the company will be wound up. There are two main types of shares: 'capital shares' which receive no income but get most of the proceeds of selling the investment fund at wind up; and 'income shares' which receive all the income from the fund in the form of dividends and only a small share of the fund at wind up. You incur dealing costs when you buy and sell investment trust shares, and there is stamp duty to pay on purchases. In addition, the trust company levies an explicit annual management charge, often in the region of 1 per cent of the value of the fund. Other charges are deducted from the fund.

Risk The price of your shares can fall as well as rise, so you are exposed to capital risk. However, the broad spread of different shares in the investment fund reduces your exposure to the misfortunes of any one company. Over the long term, share-based investments have tended to rise at least in line with inflation and in line with the growth of the economy as a whole. The potential returns and also the risks increase if the trust borrows money to invest (a process called 'gearing'). Some, but not all, investment trusts have invested in each other's shares. This practice also increases risk because if one investment trust performs badly this also affects the performance of the other trusts that have bought its shares. It is important to check the extent of borrowing and cross-holdings before you invest.

How long you invest No set period but, because the value of the investment fund can fall as well as rise, you should normally aim to invest for the long term (more than five years).

Minimum investment Most investment trusts run their own savings schemes through which you can invest, say, £500 or more as a lump sum or £50 or more a month as regular savings. If instead you buy shares through a broker, dealing costs make transactions below, say, £1,000 to £1,500 uneconomic.

Maximum investment None.

Tax Dividends are paid with tax at 10 per cent already deducted. Non-taxpayers cannot reclaim this tax. There is no further tax to pay for starting-rate and basic-rate taxpayers. Higher-rate taxpayers must pay extra. Capital gains are taxable, however if you have unused allowance there may be no tax to pay.

How to invest Through the trust company's own savings scheme or a stockbroker.* Some fund supermarkets* offer investment trusts which can be relatively cheap way to invest.

Stakeholder pension schemes

Description/suitable for A way of saving for retirement. Anyone – even a child – can have a scheme. Other people can invest in your scheme on your behalf. Money invested early in life has a long time to grow so makes a particularly valuable contribution towards retirement savings.

Return and charges Your money can be invested either on a unit-linked basis (similar to unit trusts) or a with-profits basis (see box on page 238).

Risk Capital risk varies depending on the underlying investments.

How long you invest Until at least age 55.

Minimum investment £20 whether this is a regular contribution or a lump sum.

Maximum investment £2,808 a year (unless the child has earnings in which case more can be invested).

Tax The government adds basic-rate tax relief to the contributions (even if you are not a taxpayer). Gains and most of the income from investing the contributions are tax-free. But income from shares and similar investments has had tax at 10 per cent deducted and this cannot be reclaimed. You can take part of the proceeds as a tax-free lump sum; the rest must be taken as taxable pension.

How to invest Through direct contact with pension providers or via an IFA.★

Chapter 16

Giving to charity

GIVE MORE, PAY THE SAME
'Looks like a Save the Children appeal,' said Philip, bending to pick up a small envelope from the mat and passing it to his wife, Mary. 'We must give something,' she said. 'Oh, did you see this form printed on the back … "Add nearly 30 per cent to the value of your gift just by filling in your name and address"… ? That sounds like a good deal if ever there was one. I wonder how it works?'

Tax benefits for charities

A great advantage to organisations of having charitable status is that they become eligible for a variety of tax benefits. As long as they meet certain conditions, charities currently enjoy complete freedom from income tax, capital gains tax (CGT) and corporation tax on their income and profits from most sources. In addition, when they receive donations, charities may be able to claim back income tax which has been paid by the giver through the gift aid scheme.

Advantages for donors
Gift aid

You can get tax relief at your highest rate on money you give to charity or a community amateur sports club through the gift aid scheme. You can make gifts of any amount this way.

The amount you give is treated as having had tax relief at the basic rate (22 per cent in 2005–6) already deducted. The charity then claims the tax relief from the HMRC and adds it to your gift. In this way, every £10 you give in 2005–6 is worth £10 / (100% – 22%) = £12.82 to the charity. Put another way: for every £10 you want the charity to receive, you pay only £7.80 – the government pays the rest.

If you are a higher-rate taxpayer, you can claim extra tax relief equal to the difference between relief at the higher rate (40 per cent in 2005–6) and the basic-rate relief you have already deducted from the gift. Higher-rate relief is either given through an adjustment to your pay-as-you-earn (PAYE) code or through the self-assessment system.

To use the gift aid scheme you simply need to make a declaration (see example opposite) that includes:

- the name of the charity
- a description of the gift
- your name
- your address including your postcode.

The declaration should normally be in writing but does not have to be on any special form and can be made in any way, including fax or Internet. Alternatively, if you are making a donation by phone, you can give the details orally and the charity must send you a written record of your declaration – you then have 30 days in which to change your mind about making the gift.

The declaration can cover a single gift or series of gifts if you are making regular donations.

EXAMPLE 16.1

In August 2005, Philip and Mary decide to respond to a Save the Children appeal. They put £5 in the collecting envelope and fill in the form on the back. Save the Children will be able to claim tax relief from the Inland Revenue of £5 × 22% / (100% – 22%) = £1.41, bringing the total gift to £6.41. Mary is a basic rate taxpayer but Philip is a higher-rate taxpayer, so it is more tax efficient if the gift is in his name, since he can claim extra relief. Tax relief at 40 per cent on the gross gift of £6.41 would be £2.56 but Philip has already had basic-rate relief by deducting it from his donation. Therefore, Philip claims extra relief of £2.56 – £1.41 = £1.15. In this way, Save the Children receives £6.41 at a cost to Philip of just £5 – £1.15 = £3.85.

Example of a gift aid declaration

 I am a UK taxpayer and want Save the Children to claim back the tax on my gift. My tax bill this year will be more than this gift.

Name *Philip Brown*

Address *10 New Street*

Newtown

Somerset

Postcode *AB1 CD2*

It would help us if you say how much you have given.

Amount *£5*

EXAMPLE 16.2

Following the death of a close friend from cancer, Philip gives £78 to the UK Cancer Research in 2005–6. He makes the donation by phone. The charity asks him for his name and address and to confirm that he is a taxpayer. A few days later, Philip gets a copy of these details. The charity is able to claim back basic-rate tax relief of £78 × 22% / (100% – 22%) = £22, bringing the total it receives to £100. Through his self-assessment tax return, Philip claims higher-rate relief which comes to 40% x £100 – £22 = £18. The charity has received £100 at a cost to Philip of just £78 – £18 = £60.

EXAMPLE 16.3

Mary is not a regular churchgoer but likes to go to a service from time to time. Last Sunday, she noticed a pile of envelopes as she entered the church with 'Gift Aid' printed across the top. The steward explained that, provided she was a taxpayer, instead of just putting cash direct on the collection plate, she could first put her offering in one of these envelopes, filling in the form on the front. That way the church could claim back tax relief on whatever she gave. Mary put £3 in the envelope. The church can claim back £3 × 22% / (100% – 22%) = 85p, bringing the total offering to £3.85 at a cost to Mary of just £3.

Gift aid and age allowance

If you're aged 65 or over, you qualify for a higher age-related personal allowance – see Table 16.1. And, if you are a married man and you or

Table 16.1 Age allowances and income limits1 at which they are lost in 2005–6

Age you reach during the tax year	If you are married, age your wife reaches during the tax year	Maximum personal allowance	Maximum married couple's allowance	Income limit at which extra age-related allowance(s) lost
Single person or married woman[2]				
Under 65	Not applicable	£4,895	Not applicable	Not applicable
65–74	Not applicable	£7,090[3]	Not applicable	£23,890
75 or over	Not applicable	£7,220[3]	Not applicable	£24,150
Married man[2]				
Under 65	Under 71	£4,895	Not applicable	Not applicable
	71–74	£4,895	£5,905[4]	£26,750
	75 or over	£4,895	£5,975[4]	£26,890
65–70	Under 71	£7,090[3]	Not applicable	£23,890
	71–74	£7,090[3]	£5,905[4]	£31,140
	75 or over	£7,090[3]	£5,975[4]	£31,280
71–74	Under 75	£7,090[3]	£5,905[4]	£31,140
	75 or over	£7,090[3]	£5,975[4]	£31,280
75 or over	Any age	£7,220[3]	£5,975[4]	£31,540

Notes: [1]You start to lose £1 of age-related allowance for every £2 by which your 'total income' exceeds £19,500 in 2005–6.
[2]In 2003–4, you can elect for either £2,280 or £1,140 of the married couple's allowance to be transferred to the wife (not shown in this table) but the age-related addition always stays with the husband and any reduction is based on his income.
[3]The personal allowance is never reduced below a basic amount – £4,895 in 2005–6.
[4]The married couple's allowance is never reduced below a basic amount – £2,280 in 2005–6.

your wife were born before 6 April 1935, you can qualify for married couple's allowance which includes an age-related addition. However, if your 'total income' exceeds a given limit (£19,500 in 2005–6), your age-related allowances are reduced until they reach a basic amount. The rate of reduction is £1 for every £2 by which total income exceeds the limit.

'Total income' is basically your income from most sources (excluding tax-free income, for example from a cash ISA or National Savings & Investments Certificates) less certain expenses that qualify for tax relief. Gift aid donations are one such expense.

If you are in the income bracket where you are losing (or have just lost) age allowance, making donations by gift aid is especially tax-efficient. In addition to the charity claiming back relief on your gift, you will get an increase in your allowance that will reduce your tax bill.

EXAMPLE 16.4

Mary's dad, Stan, is 76 and a widower. In 2005–6, Stan has an income of £24,200 from his state and private pensions. This is too high for him to qualify for any age-related personal allowance, so he gets just the basic personal allowance of £4,895. His tax bill for the year is £3,996.30.

But then Stan decides to give £156 to the Royal Naval Benevolent Trust. The charity is able to claim back £156 × 22% / (100% − 22%) = £44, so the 'grossed-up' donation is £156 + £44 = £200. This reduces Stan's 'total income' to £24,200 − £200 = £24,000. This is £24,000 − £19,500 = £4,500 more than the age allowance income limit and means the maximum age allowance for someone of his age of £7,220 is reduced by £4,500 / 2 = £2,250 to £4,970 – slightly more than the basic allowance. As a result his tax bill falls to £3,979.80. Stan saves £16.50 in tax. In other words, the charity gets £200 at a total cost to Stan of £139.50.

Gift aid and tax credits

Working tax credit and child tax credit are state benefits which are integrated with the tax system in the sense that the amount of credit you can get depends broadly on your income for tax purposes. If you are a couple, credits are based on your joint income. Gift aid donations are deducted from income in assessing how much you can get in tax credits.

Working tax credit is designed to help people who work but have only a low income. Households with no children would be unlikely to qualify if their income exceeds around £11,300 (single person) or £15,600 (couple) in 2005–6. However, households with children can qualify for either both credits, or just child tax credit, up to much higher levels of income. In 2005–6 you can get at least some child tax credit if your income is up to £58,175 (or £66,350 if you have a child under one year old).

In particular, a basic family element of child tax credit equal to £525 in 2005–6 (or £1,050 if you have a child under one year old) is paid until your household income reaches £50,000. The family element is reduced by £1 for every £15 above that limit. Therefore, if your income is above £50,000, a gift aid donation can be very tax-efficient if it also increases the child tax credit you get.

EXAMPLE 16.5

Andrea and Bob have one child and an income of £53,000 in 2005–6. The full tax credit is £525 but this is reduced by (£53,000 – £50,000) / £15 = £200 to £325. If Bob gives £500 to charity through gift aid, the charity receives £500 / (100% – 22%) = £641.03. Bob is a higher-rate taxpayer and so also gets higher-rate tax relief of (40% – 22%) × £641.03 = £115.39. But the couple's income for child tax credit is also reduced by the gross gift aid donation (rounded up to the nearest £1) to £53,000 – £642 = £52,358. Their child tax credit is now reduced by only (£52,358 – £50,000) / £15 = £157.20 to £367.80. In total, tax relief and extra credit come to £299.21 which is 46.7 per cent of the gross gift aid donation. Looked at another way, the charity gets £641.03 at a cost to Bob and Andrea of just £341.82.

Carrying back gift aid donations

For gift aid donations made on or after 6 April 2003, you can elect to have the gift treated for tax purposes as if it had been paid in the previous tax year.

Your election must be made to the HMRC in writing on or before the date on which you deliver your tax return for the year to which the donation is being carried back. There is space on the tax return to make this election.

For example, suppose you make a donation during 2005–6 which you want to carry back to the 2004–5 tax year. Your tax return for 2005–6 must be filed no later than 31 January 2007. This means you have until 31 January 2007 to both pay the donation and file your return. You cannot carry back the donation if you make it after 31 January 2007. Moreover, if you file your return early – say, by 30 September 2006 – you cannot carry back a donation made after that date.

To use the carry back election, you must have either income or capital gains in the earlier year on which you have paid tax.

Using the election affects only the tax relief you get and not the amount that can be reclaimed by the charity or sports club. It still claims back relief based on the basic tax rate for the year in which the donation was actually paid.

Carrying back a donation might save you tax in the following situations:

- you are a non-taxpayer or starting-rate taxpayer this tax year (see overleaf) but paid tax at the basic or higher rate last year
- you are a basic-rate taxpayer this year but paid tax at the higher rate last year
- your income last tax year was in the range where you were losing age allowance.

Note that carrying back a gift aid donation does not affect a claim for tax credits because for this purpose the donation continues to be deductible for the year the donation was paid, not the year to which it was carried back.

Donating a tax rebate to charity

You can also use your tax return to elect that all or up to a set amount of any tax rebate is donated to a single charity of your choice. The HMRC will then automatically pass the rebate to the charity you have selected.

You can opt for the donation to be made using Gift Aid by ticking the appropriate box on the tax return. The charity will then be able to claim back basic rate tax relief when it receives the donation. If you are a higher rate taxpayer, you claim higher-rate tax relief on the donation through the next year's tax return. For example, if you are completing your tax return for 2005–6 and opt to donate a rebate of tax paid in 2005–6, you claim higher-rate relief through your 2006–7 tax return (which you will normally receive in April 2006 and must send back by 31 January 2007).

Gift aid if you pay little or no tax

Do not use gift aid if you are a non-taxpayer or will have only a very low income tax and/or capital gains tax bill for the year in which you pay the donation (or the year to which you elect to carry it back).

If you are a non-taxpayer, the charity will still claim the relief from the HMRC. But the HMRC will then ask you for tax equal to the relief given.

Similarly, if your tax bill for the year is less than the amount of tax relief that you are treated as having deducted from your donation, the charity will still claim full tax relief on the donation, but the HMRC will ask you for tax equal to the excess relief given.

In working out how much tax you have paid, some reliefs are ignored – for example, tax credits on dividends, and allowances like married couple's allowance given as a reduction in your tax bill.

EXAMPLE 16.6

Lucy, is 68. She has an income of £7,200 a year from her state pension, a small widow's pension and a small amount of savings. Tax on her income is expected to be £11 in 2005–6. In September 2005, Lucy decides to give £200 to The Friends of Verrington Hospital, a local charity supporting the hospital where her late sister was nursed through her final illness. If Lucy makes the donation through gift aid, she will be treated as having deducted tax relief from the gift of £200 × 22% / (100% – 22%) = £56.41. This is £56.41 – £11.00 = £45.41 more than her expected tax bill for the year, so she can expect her tax office to adjust her bill to collect the extra £45.41. To avoid this, Lucy makes the gift without using the gift aid scheme.

Other points to note about gift aid

You can't combine gift aid with any other tax-efficient advantageous way of giving to charity. For example, you can't claim gift aid relief for donations made through a payroll giving scheme (see page 252).

Your gift will not qualify for gift aid if you (or someone connected with you, such as a family member or close business associate) in return gets some benefit as a result of the gift and the benefit exceeds the limits shown in Table 16.2. However, there is a special exception that means you don't count the following benefits:

- the right to free or reduced-price entry to properties preserved for the public benefit, where maintaining such properties is the main or sole purpose of the charity and the opportunity to benefit is publicly available
- the right to free or reduced-price entry to observe wildlife, where the conservation of such wildlife is the sole or main purpose of the charity and the opportunity to benefit is publicly available.

To take advantage of gift aid some charities started to ask visitors to make a donation under the scheme instead of paying the normal daily fee for

Table 16.2 Maximum benefit allowed as a result of a gift if it is to qualify for gift aid

Size of your gift	Maximum benefit allowed	Example
up to £100	25% of the value of the gift	You give £50; any benefit must be worth no more than £50 × 25% = £12.50
over £100 up to £1,000	£25	You give £500; the maximum benefit is £25
over £1,000	2.5% of the value of the gift	You give £1,500; any benefit must be worth no more than £1,500 × 2.5% = £37.50
AND		
All gifts to the same charity during the same tax year	£250	You make 20 gifts of £100 to the same charity. In line with the rule above, 25% of each gift would give a total potential benefit of 20 × £25 = £500, but this rule caps that benefit at £250.

admission to their properties or premises. From 6 April 2006 onwards, the government is tightening the rules so that such donations qualify for gift aid only if the donation gives you admission to the charity's premises without any special restrictions for at least a year or the amount you give is at least 10 per cent more than the normal admission price.

Covenants

A covenant is a legally binding promise to give something to someone (or to do or refrain from doing something). In the past, it has been a common way of agreeing to make regular donations to a charity and, providing certain conditions were met, the donations qualified for tax relief under rules that applied specifically to covenants.

From 6 April 2000 onwards, the special rules no longer apply. Instead, covenanted donations come under the normal rules for gift aid (see above). You can still make gifts by deed of covenant if you want to, but there is no tax reason for doing so.

Payroll giving schemes

Payroll giving (also called 'Payroll deduction') is a method of making regular gifts to charity out of your pay-packet. It is open only to employees and only to those whose employer operates a payroll giving scheme. From 6 April 2000 onwards, you can give any amount using this scheme.

The scheme works like this. Your employer sets up an arrangement with an agency approved by the HMRC (in fact, a few employers have set up their own agencies). You then tell your employer how much you want to give each payday and to which charity or charities. The employer deducts the specified amount from your pay and hands it over to the agency, which arranges for the money to be transferred to the charities you picked. (The agency may make a charge – for example, 5 per cent of the donations it handles – to cover its own running costs, but sometimes there is no charge or your employer might separately cover any administration costs.) Your donation is deducted from your pay before tax (but not National Insurance), so you automatically get full income tax relief. Payroll giving is popular with charities because they receive the whole (gross) donation direct from you, avoiding any paperwork and delay involved in claiming tax relief from the HMRC.

One of the largest agencies running payroll giving schemes is the Charities Aid Foundation (CAF),* which operates a scheme called Give As You Earn (GAYE). It offers three different options:

- **Direct donation** Each employee chooses the charities to receive his or her donation each month
- **CAF Charity Account** Donations are paid into a special account from which you can make donations of any size to any charities. See page 50 for more details
- **Staff charity fund** Employees pool their individual donations to form a single account from which donations of any size can be made to any charities.

EXAMPLE 16.7

Mary earns £810 a month, before tax, working in the local supermarket. The supermarket operates a payroll giving scheme through which Mary gives £10 a month each to Help the Aged and Barnardo's. Normally, Mary would pay £67.56 a month in income tax (during the 2005–6 tax year) but after deducting the payroll giving from her pay, the tax bill is reduced to £63.16 a month. In other words, she gets tax relief of £4.40 a month, which reduces the cost to her of the £20 she gives to charity to just £15.60.

If your employer operates a payroll giving scheme, he or she can provide you with details and an application form.

You do not have to keep up your donations for any minimum period of time. You stop making them whenever you like simply by informing your employer of your wishes.

Payroll giving cannot be used in combination with any of the other tax-advantaged ways of giving to charity. So, for example, you cannot claim gift aid relief on donations made through a payroll giving scheme. HMRC rules do not allow payroll giving to be used to pay subscriptions entitling you, for example, to membership benefits from a charity.

Giving things rather than cash

You do not have to give just cash as a charitable donation. You could instead give something you own: for example, land, premises, a car, furniture or investments such as shares. Normally you might have to pay capital gains tax (CGT) and even inheritance tax (IHT) when you give something away. But gifts to charities and, from 6 April 2002, community amateur sports clubs, are generally completely free of these taxes.

For the exemption from IHT to apply, you must relinquish all your rights to whatever it is that you are giving. For example, there might well be a tax bill if you gave the freehold of your home to a charity but continued to live there. For more details about the way CGT and IHT work, see Chapters 2–4.

In addition to the CGT and IHT reliefs described above, gifts of some types of assets to charities – but not community amateur sports clubs – can also qualify for income tax relief. Since 6 April 2000, this applies to gifts of shares and similar investments and, from 6 April 2002 onwards, it also applies to gifts of land or buildings.

Gifts of shares or similar investments

You can claim income tax relief when you give any of these investments to a charity:

- shares or securities listed on a recognised stock exchange
- unlisted shares or securities dealt in on a recognised stock exchange (including the Alternative Investment Market)
- units in an authorised unit trust
- shares in an open-ended investment company (oeic)
- an interest in an offshore investment fund.

You can claim the market value of the shares or units you give (plus any costs of disposal you incur) as a deduction from your income. This means you get income tax relief up to your top rate. If you receive anything for the shares or units – either cash or a benefit in kind – this is deducted from the amount you can claim.

This relief is available not only for gifts to charities but also to the National Heritage Memorial Fund, the Historic Buildings and Monuments Commission for England, the British Museum and the Natural History Museum.

Giving shares or units direct to charity, rather than selling them first and giving cash, can be very tax-efficient where you would stand to make a gain on the shares or units if they were sold. If the shares or units are standing at a loss, it can be more efficient to sell them first and give cash.

Note that you can only claim this income tax relief against your income and not against any capital gains you make on other sales or gifts. This means giving shares or units will not be tax-efficient if you do not have enough income against which to set the relief.

EXAMPLE 16.8

Harry, who is a higher-rate taxpayer, wants to make a substantial donation to the Arthritis Research Campaign (ARC). He is considering funding his donation by selling some HBOS plc shares.

Harry could sell the shares for £2,500, of which £1,000 would be taxable. He has already used up his CGT allowance for the year (see page 49), so he would have to pay tax of 40% × £1,000 = £400. This would leave £2,500 – £400 = £2,100 to give to ARC. The gift would qualify for gift aid (see page 00), so ARC would claim back basic-rate tax relief on the £2,100 and Harry would get higher-rate relief on the gift. This would mean ARC received £2,692 in total at an overall cost to Harry of £2,100 + £400 – £485 = £2,015.

Instead, Harry could give the shares direct to ARC. There is no CGT to pay on gifts to charity. And Harry can claim income tax relief on the market value of the gift which is £2,500. This means Harry gets income tax relief of 40% × £2,500 = £1,000. The charity sells the shares to realise the full £2,500. In this way the charity gets £2,500 at a cost to Harry of £2,500 – £1,000 = £1,500. Therefore, giving the shares direct is the better option.

EXAMPLE 16.9

Melanie, a higher-rate taxpayer, is considering giving some shares to the Woodland Trust. The market value of the shares is £1,000 but if Melanie sold them she would make a loss of £200. She could set this loss against gains on other assets, which would save her up to 40% × £200 = £80 in capital gains tax (less if she could claim taper relief – see page 50). If she gives the £1,000 proceeds from the sale to the Woodland Trust, the gift would qualify for gift aid (see page 243). The Trust could claim back basic-rate relief, bringing the total value of the gift to £1,282. Melanie could claim higher-rate relief of £231, reducing the total cost to her to £1,000 – £80 – £231 = £689. Put another way, the charity receives £1.86 for every £1 it costs Melanie.

Instead, Melanie could just give the shares direct to the Woodland Trust. There is no capital gain or loss on gifts to charities. However, Melanie could claim income tax relief on the market value of the shares, which comes to 40% × £1,000 = £400. The Trust sells the shares to realise £1,000. In this way, the charity gets £1,000 at a cost to Melanie of £1,000 – £400 = £600. Put another way, the charity receives £1.67 for every £1 it costs Melanie, so selling the shares and donating the cash raised would be more tax-efficient.

Gifts of land or buildings

Income tax relief is available on a gift of land or buildings to charity – but not community amateur sports clubs – made on or after 6 April 2002. Giving land or buildings works in much the same way as giving shares (see above). So you can claim the market value of the property plus any disposal costs less anything you receive in exchange.

The property must be in the UK but can be either freehold or leasehold. You must completely give up your ownership rights and, if you own the property jointly with other people, you must surrender your rights to the charity.

In general, relief is withdrawn if, within five years of 31 January following the tax year in which you give the property away, you acquire any interest or right in the property. There are two exceptions: first, if you acquire the interest through the death of someone; and second, if you pay the full going rate for the interest or right – for example, if you live in the property but pay the full market rent.

To claim the relief, you must have a certificate from the charity concerned describing the property, the date it was given and stating that the charity has accepted the gift.

As with a gift of shares, giving land or buildings direct to a charity will generally be tax-efficient if you would otherwise make a taxable gain on selling the property. But, if selling it would realise a loss, it will be more tax-efficient to sell the land or buildings first and then donate the proceeds to charity using gift aid.

Other ways of giving to charity

Charitable bequests

If you leave money or assets to charity in your will, your estate pays no IHT on the gift. (Your estate is all your possessions less any debts at the time of death.)

A bequest to charity can also save IHT in a second way, because the value of your estate is reduced by the amount of your gift to charity. This can mean less IHT on the estate as a whole. Bear in mind, though, that making a bequest to charity cuts down the amount of the estate left for your survivors to inherit, so you should not use this as a tax-saving method unless you intend to make philanthropic gifts anyway.

All gifts from your estate when you die – whether to charity or to other organisations or to people – are free of CGT.

A solicitor* can help you to insert an appropriate clause in your will to leave a bequest to charity. Some charities offer you help in making your will – for example, paying the cost – in the hope that you will leave something to the charity. For the will to be legally watertight, it is essential that there can be no question of the charity having brought undue influence to bear on you. If it was thought that a charity had pressurised you into leaving it a bequest, your will could be challenged by other beneficiaries and, in the end, your gift to the charity might not be made after all. To avoid any problems of this sort, you should ensure that:

- you have written details of the arrangement by which the charity is helping you to make your will and the procedures to be followed
- you do not proceed if the charity's help is conditional on your making it a bequest

- the solicitor takes instructions from you alone and not the charity
- no details of your will are disclosed to the charity without your consent
- you do not proceed if you feel in any way pressurised to include the charity in your will.

CAF Charity Account

The Charities Aid Foundation (CAF)★ is a charity whose aim is to promote charities generally and give them support and assistance. One of the services it runs is the CAF Charity Account. This is like a bank account with the sole purpose of making gifts to charity. The advantages of the Charity Account are that the money you give is increased by tax relief and you have a convenient, flexible way of giving to a wide range of charities. CAF makes a charge for running the account. It works as follows.

You pay money into your Charity Account using the tax-efficient means already discussed: gift aid (see page 243), payroll giving (see page 252) or gifts of shares and similar investments (see page 254). Because CAF is itself a charity, it is able to claim tax relief on the money you pay in using gift aid and it adds this to your account. With payroll giving you qualify for tax relief directly as normal. With gifts of shares, your gift is free of CGT and you can claim income tax relief. CAF sells the shares and then credits the proceeds to your account.

CAF sets minimum limits on the amount you can pay into the account of either £100 as a lump sum or £10 a month if you pay in regularly. In 2005, CAF's charges for running the account were 4 per cent of sums up to £14,500 and 1 per cent of any excess up to £80,000, and a part of the amount you pay in is donated to the National Council for Voluntary Organisations (NCVO).★ The money in the account does not earn interest.

When you want to make a donation to charity from your account, you can do this in several ways:

- online transfer, where you access your account over the Internet and carry out a variety of transactions including making donations
- phone transfer
- by post using a Charity Account chequebook
- by standing order, if you want to make regular donations to a particular charity.

You can make donations to any charity, whether registered or not.

Note that you do not get any further tax relief when you make the donation, because it has already had the benefit of tax relief when you first paid the money into the Charity Account.

The normal rules which apply to gift aid and payroll giving apply when you are paying into the CAF Charity Account. For example, the CAF Charity Account is not suitable if you pay little or no tax and would receive a bill from the HMRC for the tax relief paid over to CAF by gift aid (see page 250).

Gifts from trusts

A trust is a special legal arrangement where money, shares or other property are held for the benefit of others (see Chapter 7). Trustees have the duty of seeing that the property in the trust and any income and gains from it (which together make up the 'trust fund') are used as set out in the trust deed and rules. With a 'discretionary trust', the trustees are given the power to decide how the trust fund is used (within any constraints imposed by the trust rules).

Special tax rules apply to trusts (see Chapter 8) but gifts to charity from a discretionary trust can be very tax-efficient. The charity will be able to reclaim all the income tax – usually at 40 per cent (in 2005–6) rather than just the basic rate – that the trust has paid on the income it gives. If the trust makes a gift to charity of capital, there will be no CGT or IHT to pay.

Setting up your own charitable trust can be even more tax efficient (see page 115).

Community investment tax relief

Although not a way of giving to charity as such, this scheme, which started in January 2003, is another way of helping disadvantaged communities. The scheme lets you claim tax relief on loans you make to, or shares you buy in, a community development finance institution (CDFI).

CDFIs are bodies accredited by the government and set up to provide finance for small businesses and social enterprise projects.

You do not invest directly in the businesses and projects yourself. Instead you lend to, or invest in, the CDFI and claim income tax relief of up to 5 per cent a year of the amount involved for a maximum of five years. (Relief is restricted to the amount needed to reduce your tax bill for the year to zero, so could come to less than the full 5 per cent.) To claim the tax relief, you must have a certificate from the institution. An HMRC booklet, *Community investment tax relief (CITR) scheme: A brief guide for investors* (no reference number), is available from tax offices★ and the HMRC★ website.

The scheme has so far not attracted a great deal of interest from private investors, but the tax relief means that on a loan or investment of, say, £1,000 you would be able to claim a tax reduction of 5% × £1,000 = £50 a year. This is equivalent to earning interest at 6.4 per cent if you are a basic-rate taxpayer or 8.3 per cent if you pay tax at the higher rate. On top of that some schemes also pay a modest rate of interest on the amount you lend.

CDFIs include a wide range of bodies from major banks to small credit unions and, with many, there is no certainty that you will get all your money back so, if you are interested, you need to check carefully the level of risk involved. Under the tax rules, you will not be able to get any of your money back during the first two years and you will have to wait five years to get the full amount back.

For a list of CDFIs, see the Community Development Finance Association's★ website.

Donation cards (affinity cards)

A number of charities and credit card companies have joined forces to issue donation cards (aslo called 'affinity cards'). These are normal credit cards but the card issuer promises to make donations to charity (or sometimes non-charitable groups, like football clubs) when you first take out the card and each time you use it. The donations are fairly small, for example, £10 when you take out the card and 5p each time you buy something using the card.

If you use a credit card anyway, a donation card is a way in which indirectly you can give to charity, but check that the card terms and conditions are competitive. If not, you would probably do better taking out a card which offers a better deal and using the money you save in interest or earn in cashback to make your own donations direct to charity using one of the tax-efficient schemes outlined in this chapter.

If you do not normally use a credit card, be wary of taking out a donation card. Do not risk putting yourself in a situation where you run up debts you cannot afford.

Addresses

Accountant – to find one

Association of Chartered Certified Accountants
29 Lincoln's Inn Fields
London WC2A 3EE.
Tel: 020 7396 7000.
Website: www.acca.co.uk

Institute of Chartered Accountants in England and Wales
PO Box 433
Chartered Accountants' Hall
Moorgate Place
London EC2P 2BJ
Tel: 020 7920 8100
Website: www.icaew.co.uk

Institute of Chartered Accountants in Ireland
CA House
83 Pembroke Road
Dublin 4
Republic of Ireland
Tel: (00 353) 1 637 7200
Website: www.icai.ie

Institute of Chartered Accountants of Scotland
CA House
21 Haymarket Yards
Edinburgh EH12 5BH
Tel: 0131 347 0100
Website: www.icas.org.uk

Capital Taxes Office (HM Revenue & Customs)

England and Wales
Ferrers House
Castle Meadow Road
Nottingham NG2 1BB

Northern Ireland
Level 3
Dorchester House
52–58 Great Victoria Street
Belfast BT2 7QL

Scotland
Meldrum House
15 Drumsheugh Gardens
Edinburgh EH3 7UG

Tel: 0845 234 1000 (for forms and leaflets)

IHT200 Orderline:
0845 234 1020
Probate & IHT Helpline:
0845 30 20 900
Website: www.hmrc.gov.uk/cto

Charities Aid Foundation
25 Kings Hill Avenue
Kings Hill
West Malling
Kent ME19 4TA
Tel: 01732 520000
Website: www.cafonline.org.uk
CAF Charity Account:
Website: www.allaboutgiving.org

Charity Commission

London
Harmsworth
13–15 Bouverie Street
London EC4Y 8DP
(Central Register open
9am–5pm)

Liverpool
12 Princes Dock
Princes Parade
Liverpool L3 1DE
(Central register open
9am–4.30pm)

Taunton
Woodfield House
Tangier
Taunton
Somerset TA1 4BL
(Central Register open
9.30am–4pm)

Tel: 0870 333 0123
Website:
www.charitycommission.gov.uk

**Community Development
Finance Association**
Room 101
Hatton Square Business Centre
16/16a Baldwins Gardens
London EC1N 7RJ
Tel: 020 7430 02222
Website: www.cdfa.org.uk

**Discount broker – some
examples**

*Chase de Vere Financial
Solutions plc*
Cambridge House
Henry Street
Bath BA1 1JS
Tel: 0845 6000 900
Website: www.chasedevere.co.uk

Hargreaves Lansdown
Kendal House
4 Brighton Mews
Clifton
Bristol BS8 2NX
Tel: 0845 345 0800
Website: www.h-l.co.uk

**Financial Ombudsman
Service**
South Quay Plaza
183 Marsh Wall
London E14 9SR
Tel: 0845 080 1800
Website: www.
financial_ombudsman.org.uk

Fund supermarket – some examples

www.adviceonline.co.uk/
investdecisiontree.html
www.fidelity.co.uk
(Funds Network)
www.h-l.co.uk
www.tqonline.co.uk

HM Revenue & Customs (HMRC)

The HMRC was formed from April 2005 onwards through the merger of the Inland Revenue and HM Customs & Excise

- For local tax enquiry centres look in The Phone Book under 'HM Revenue & Customs' or 'Inland Revenue'.
- For your local tax office, check your tax return, other tax correspondence or check with your employer
- See also Capital Taxes Office above
- HMRC Orderline (IHT): 0845 234 1000
- HMRC Orderline (self assessment): 0845 9000 404
- HMRC Orderline (taxback for non-taxpayers): 0845 9000 444
- Website: www.hmrc.gov.uk
- Child trust fund website: www.childtrustfund.gov.uk

Independent Financial Adviser – to find one

IFA Promotion

For a list of IFAs in your area, contact the telephone number below.
Tel: 0800 085 3250
Website: www.unbiased.co.uk

The Institute of Financial Planning

Whitefriars Centre
Lewins Mead
Bristol BS1 2NT
Tel: 0117 9345 2470
Website:
www.financialplanning.org.uk

My LocalAdviser

Website:
www.mylocaladviser.co.uk

Personal Finance Society (PFS)

Formed by the merger of the Society of Financial Advisers (SOFA) and the Life Insurance Association (LIA)
For a list of independent financial advisers who all have more than just the basic qualifications, contact:
20 Aldermanbury
London EC2V 7HY
Tel: 020 8530 0852
Website: www.thepfs.org

Institute of Professional Will Writers
Trinity Point
New Road
Halesowen
West Midlands B63 3HY
Tel: 08456 44 20 42
Website: www.ipw.org.uk

Insurance broker – to find one

British Insurance Brokers Association (BIBA)
For a list of brokers in your area, contact BIBA at:
14 Bevis Marks
London EC3A 7NT
Tel: 0870 950 1790
Website: www.biba.org.uk

MyLocalAdviser
Website:
www.mylocaladviser.co.uk

Law Societies

The Law Society (England and Wales)
113 Chancery Lane
London WC2A 1PL
Tel: 0870 606 6575
Website: www.lawsociety.co.uk

The Law Society of Northern Ireland
Law Society House
98 Victoria Street
Belfast BT1 3JZ
Tel: 028 90 2316 14
Website: www.lawsoc-ni.org

The Law Society of Scotland
26 Drumsheugh Gardens
Edinburgh EH3 7YR
Tel: 0131 226 7411
Client Relations Office
(complaints): 0845 113 0018
Website: www.lawscot.org.uk

Law Society Consumer Complaints Service (England & Wales)
Victoria Court
8 Dormer Place
Leamington Spa
Warwickshire CV32 5AE
Helpline: 0845 608 6565
Minicom: 0845 601 1682
Website: www.lawsociety.org.uk

National Council for Voluntary Organisations (NCVO)
Regent's Wharf
8 All Saints Street
London N1 9RL
Tel: 020 7713 6161
Website: www.ncvo-vol.org.uk

National Savings & Investments (NS&I)

Children's bonus bonds, investment account
Glasgow G58 1SB

Premium Bonds
Blackpool FY3 9YP

Cash mini ISA
Durham DH99 1NS

Tel: 0845 964 5000
Minicom: 0800 056 0585
Website: www.nsandi.com

Probate Registry (England & Wales)
To obtain probate forms, leaflets and information
- Your local Probate Registry. See Phone Book under 'Probate Registry'
- Probate & IHT Helpline: 0845 30 20 900
- Website: www.hmcourts-service.gov.uk/cms/wills.htm

Probate and Matrimonial Office (Northern Ireland)
Royal Courts of Justice (Northern Ireland)
Chichester Street
Belfast BT1 3JF
Tel: 028 9023 5111
Website: www.courtsni.gov.uk

Sheriff's Court (Scotland)
To obtain confirmation forms, leaflets and information
- Your local Sheriff Clerk. See Phone Book under 'Sheriff's Court'
- Operations & Policy Unit, Scottish Court Service Headquarters, Hayweight House, 23 Lauriston Street, Edinburgh EH3 9DQ Tel: 0131 229 9200
- Website: www.scotcourts. gov.uk/sheriff/index.asp

Society of Will Writers
Eagle House
Exchange Road
Lincoln
Lincoln LN6 3JZ
Tel: 01522 687888
Website: www. thesocietyofwillwriters.co.uk

Solicitor – to find one
Contact the Law Societies above or Society of Trust and Estate Practitioners below for a list of members

Society of Trust and Estate Practitioners (STEP)
26 Grosvenor Gardens
London SW1W)gt
Tel: 020 7838 4890
Answerphone for list of members: 020 7838 4885
Website: www.step.org

Stockbroker – to find one

Association of Private Client Investment Managers and Stockbrokers (APCIMS)
114 Middlesex Street
London E1 7JH
Tel: 020 7247 7080
Website: www.apcims.co.uk

London Stock Exchange
10 Paternoster Square
London EC4M 7LS
Tel: 020 7797 1000
Website: www.londonstockexchange.com

Tax adviser – to find one

The Chartered Institute of Taxation
12 Upper Belgrave Street
London SW1X 8BB
Tel: 020 7235 9381
Website: www.tax.org.uk

Tax Enquiry centre
See HM Revenue & Customs above

Tax office
See HM Revenue & Customs above

Trading Standards Office
This is a department of your local council. Look in The Phone Book under 'Councils' or the relevant council's name. Website: www.tradingstandards.gov.uk

Which? Books
Littlehampton Book Services
Faraday Close
Durrington
Worthing
West Sussex BN13 3RB
Tel: 01903 828557
Website: www.which.co.uk

Index

Wills and Probate

If you die without making a will your wealth could go to the very person you least want to have it and your loved ones could lose out, perhaps to the Inland Revenue.

The practical, easy-to-follow advice contained in *Wills and Probate* has already helped thousands of people to make their wills. Whether you are single, married, divorced or co-habiting, it will show you how to write your will in such a way that your wishes can be carried out without any complications.

The second part of the book covers probate: the administration of the estate of someone who has died. The book will enable you to decide whether you can make your own will or administer an estate confidently by yourself or whether you should call on professional help.

Covering the law and procedure in England and Wales, and outlining the main differences which apply in Scotland and Northern Ireland, this revised edition contains sample forms and also describes what happens if there is no will.

ISBN 1 84490 018 5   256 pages   £11.99

Available from all good bookshops. Alternatively, contact Which? direct on 01903 828557 or www.which.co.uk to place an order. Postage and packing are free.

Money in Retirement

A striking feature of modern life is that people are living longer. On average, retirement now accounts for a third of adult life. To enjoy these years to the full, you need to keep your finances in good shape. The work-out starts on the day you decide to draw a pension and continues throughout retirement. This practical guide will help you make the most of your money. It covers:

- **Pensions** The choices you make at the point of retirement could determine your financial well-being for the rest of your life.
- **Savings and investments** In retirement, your goals and risks are usually different from those of earlier life. This guide takes you step-by-step through building an appropriate plan and selecting suitable investments.
- **Boosting your income** Other ways to finance retirement are considered, such as equity release schemes, carrying on working, and claiming all the state benefits to which you are entitled.
- **Tax** Dealing with tax returns and self-assessment can seem daunting, especially if you have spent a lifetime being taxed through PAYE. This guide shows you how to get on top of the system.
- **Inheritance** With a bit of forward planning you can pass on your wealth to your heirs, rather than the Inland Revenue.

ISBN 1 84490 013 4   288 pages   £11.99

Available from all good bookshops. Alternatively, contact Which? direct on 01903 828557 or www.which.co.uk to place an order. Postage and packing are free.

Planning your Pension

From 2006, planning your pension should become much easier as the government sweeps away most of the complicated rules that have restricted the amount and ways you can save. This new edition of *Planning Your Pension* explains how the new regime will work and how to make the most of the savings opportunities available between now and 2006.

Using straightforward language, this guide takes you through all the key issues, such as:

- how much you should save
- what the state will provide
- how to get the best from an employer's scheme
- stakeholder schemes
- personal pensions and whether to switch from one to a stakeholder pension
- how to boost your pension
- pension choices when you change jobs
- pension planning if you're facing redundancy or divorce, or caring for children or an older person
- how to trace old pensions
- how to claim your pension once you retire
- how retirement savings and pensions are treated for tax

Armed with *Planning Your Pension*, you will no longer feel daunted or confused about retirement planning. Clear explanations, charts and numerous examples unravel the mysteries of pensions to put you firmly in control of your future.

| ISBN 0 85202 998 5 | 352 pages | £11.99 |

Available from all good bookshops. Alternatively, contact Which? direct on 01903 828557 or www.which.co.uk to place an order. Postage and packing are free.

What To Do When Someone Dies

For many people, the first experience of making the sorts of arrangements that are necessary following a death comes only when they have been bereaved and least feel like finding out what needs to be done. *What To Do When Someone Dies* guides readers through the process practically, sympathetically and informatively. The book covers:

- how to register a death
- the role of the coroner
- choosing between burial and cremation
- how to claim any state benefits that may be due
- arranging a funeral without a funeral director
- humanist and other non-Christian funerals
- organ donation
- arranging your own funeral if you want to plan ahead.

The book covers the law and practice in England and Wales and highlights in separate sections the important differences which apply in Scotland. A list of useful addresses is also included.

ISBN 1 84490 014 2   192 pages   £11.99

Available from all good bookshops. Alternatively, contact Which? direct on 01903 828557 or www.which.co.uk to place an order. Postage and packing are free.

Be Your Own Financial Adviser

From education to dental care, retirement to home ownership, increasingly you are expected to take a more active role to ensure the financial wellbeing of you and your family.

Whether you want to manage your money yourself or simply be in the driving seat when you get advice, this guide will equip you with the knowledge and techniques you need.

In simple language, with numerous case studies, tips and flow charts, *Be Your Own Financial Adviser* shows you how to identify your financial goals and create a plan to meet them without falling into the traps of unsuitable products, high charges and hidden risks. It will help you:

- Save for emergencies.
- Protect your family.
- Protect your income.
- Insure against illness and dental bills.
- Buy a home.
- Help your children.
- Save and invest for growth or income.
- Build up retirement income.
- Pass on your money tax efficiently.

ISBN 1 84490 012 6   368 pages   £11.99

Available from all good bookshops. Alternatively, contact Which? direct on 01903 828557 or www.which.co.uk to place an order. Postage and packing are free.